Pathways in
Christian Music Communication

American Society of Missiology Monograph Series

THE ASM MONOGRAPH SERIES provides a forum for publishing quality dissertations and studies in the field of missiology. Collaborating with Pickwick Publications—a division of Wipf and Stock Publishers of Eugene, Oregon—the American Society of Missiology selects high quality dissertations and other monographic studies that offer research materials in mission studies for scholars, mission and church leaders, and the academic community at large. The ASM seeks scholarly work for publication in the Series that throws light on issues confronting Christian world mission in its cultural, social, historical, biblical, and theological dimensions.

Missiology is an academic field that brings together scholars whose professional training ranges from doctoral-level preparation in areas such as scripture, history and sociology of religions, anthropology, theology, international relations, interreligious interchange, mission history, inculturation, and church law. The American Society of Missiology, which sponsors this series, is an ecumenical body drawing members from Independent and Ecumenical Protestant, Catholic, Orthodox, and other traditions. Members of the ASM are united by their commitment to reflect on and do scholarly work relating to both mission history and the present-day mission of the church. The ASM Monograph Series aims to publish works of exceptional merit on specialized topics, with particular attention given to work by younger scholars, the dissemination and publication of which is difficult under the economic pressures of standard publishing models.

Persons seeking information about the ASM or the guidelines for having their dissertations considered for publication in the ASM Monograph Series should consult the Society's website—www.asmweb.org.

Members of the ASM Monograph Committee who approved this book are:

Paul Kollman
University of Notre Dame

Michael A. Rynkiewich
Asbury Theological Seminary

Wilbur Stone
Bethel Seminary

Pathways in Christian Music Communication

The Case of the Senufo of Côte d'Ivoire

ROBERTA R. KING

American Society of Missiology
Monograph Series

3

☙PICKWICK *Publications* • Eugene, Oregon

PATHWAYS IN CHRISTIAN MUSIC COMMNICATION
The Case of the Senufo of Côte d'Ivoire

American Society of Missiology Monograph Series 3

Copyright © 2009 Roberta R. King. All rights reserved. No part of this publication may be reproduced or transmitted in any form, electronic or mechanical, or stored on any information storage and retrieval system without prior permission in writing from the publishers. For permissions write to Wipf & Stock Publishers, 199 W. 8th Avenue, Suite 3, Eugene OR 97401.

Pickwick Publications
A Division of Wipf and Stock Publishers
199 W. 8th Ave., Suite 3
Eugene, OR 97401

www.wipfandstock.com

ISBN: 978-1-55635-927-9

Cataloguing-In-Publication data:

King, Roberta R.

    Pathways in Christian music communication : the case of the Senufo of Côte d'Ivoire

    xx + 288 p. ; 23 cm. Includes bibliographical references and index.

    American Society of Missiology Monograph Series 3

    ISBN: 978-1-55635-927-9

    1. Music—Religious aspects. 2. Church music—Africa. 3. Communication—Religious aspects—Christianity—Case studies. 4. Ethnomusicology. 5. Senufo (African people)—Social life and customs. I. Title. II. Series.

ML3797 K55 2009

Manufactured in the United States of America

Books published in the American Society of Missiology Scholarly monograph series are chosen on the basis of their academic quality as responsible contributions to debate and dialogue about issues in mission studies. The opinions expressed in the book are those of the authors and are not represented to be those of the American Society of Missiology or its members.

To my parents,
Robert Seevers and Gwendolyn Rose King,
who modeled a sincere love for the Lord Jesus Christ,
a compelling enthusiasm for doing mission,
and a contagious delight in music.

Contents

List of Tables / ix

List of Figures / x

List of Maps / xii

List of Photographs / xiii

Preface / xvii

Acknowledgments / xix

PART ONE: Foundations for Music Communication

    1   My Personal Path / 3

    2   Pathways to Music Communication Research / 12

    3   Toward a Theory of Christian Music Commuincation / 27

PART TWO: Background to the Case Study

    4   The Senufo and Their Life-Paths / 51

    5   Stepping Stones toward Senufo Christian Songs / 63

PART THREE: A Musical Analysis

    6   Musical Paths to Christian Communication / 81

    7   The Music Channel on the Path / 102

PART FOUR: A Study of Song Texts

    8   Song Texts: A Path to Worldview Discovery / 123

    9   Song Texts: Pathway to a Developing Theology / 138

Contents

PART FIVE: Music as Communication

10   The Pathway of a Song / 165

11   Moving Further along the Pathway of a Song / 176

12   Reaching the Path's Destination / 193

   Appendix A: Song Texts / 205

   Appendix B: Senufo Song Survey—1987 / 224

   Appendix C: Focus Group Question Guide and Interview Samples / 229

   Appendix D: Storytelling Song: The Man from Torogo / 243

   Appendix E: Senofu Song Transcriptions / 256

   Appendix F: A Model for Initiating Grassroots Theologizing / 260

   Glossary / 267

   Bibliography / 271

   Discography / 277

   Index / 279

Tables

Table 1	Activities that Christians Abandon	132
Table 2	Names of God	142
Table 3	Characteristics of God	145
Table 4	What God Has Done	148
Table 5	What God Does	150
Table 6	The Believer's Position Before God/Jesus	152
Table 7	The Believer's Interaction with God	153
Table 8	Positive Activities for Christians	160

Figures

Figure 1   Research in the Korhogo Region of Côte d'Ivoire / 17

Figure 2   Model for Doing Christian Music Communication Research / 25

Figure 3   Ingredients in Communication / 36

Figure 4   Engel's Interpersonal Communication Model (1979:39) / 37

Figure 5   McCroskey's Rhetorical-Communication Process / 38

Figure 6   Transaction Music Communication / 40

Figure 7   The Converging Paths Within Missiology / 43

Figure 8   Association of Evangelical Baptist Churches of Côte d'Ivoire: Baptized Members / 61

Figure 9   Multi-Channel Music Communication / 88

Figure 10   Elements in the Linguistic Channel / 91

Figure 11   Elements in the Music Channel / 93

Figure 12   Elements in the Performance Channel / 100

Figure 13   Senufo Christian Song Form #1 / 104

Figure 14   Senufo Christian Song Form #2 / 105

Figuer 15   Interlocking and Pendular Melodic Intervals / 107

Figure 16   The Relation of Clapping to the Melodic Structure / 111

Figure 17   Jegele (Balafon) Performance Patterns / 117

Figure 18   The Dense Texture of a Senufo Christian Song / 118

Figures

Figure 19   The Three Dimensions in the Song Pathway / 166

Figure 20   Believers' Attitudes Toward the Songs / 171

Figure 21   Non-believers' Attitudes Toward the Songs / 173

Figure 22   Songs Are Like the Word of God / 184

Figure 23   The Cognitive Dimension / 186

Figure 24   The Behavioral Dimension / 190

Figure 25   The Pathway of a Song / 192

Figure 26   Model for Doing Christian Music Communication Research / 194

Maps

Map 1   The Senufo Peoples and Their Languages / xiv

Map 2   Senufo Research Area / 22

Photographs

Photo 1   Senufo musicians on their way to a funeral / xvi

Photo 2   Believers from the Fɔrɔ Church / 12

Photo 3   Senufo Family from the Village of Zanakaʔa / 15

Photo 4   A Senufo Village / 20

Photo 5   Senufo Graineries / 53

Photo 6   Boloye Dancers Emerging from the Sacred Forest / 55

Photo 7   Dancing the *Boloye* / 56

Photo 8   Dancing the Christian Faith / 82

Photo 9   Senufo Composers / 98

Photo 10   Singer with *Caliw* / 112

Photo 11   *Kaanrigi*, Senufo Metal Scraper / 113

Photo 12   Believers Playing Senufo Christian *Balafons* / 114

Photo 13   Singing with Clapping / 167

Photo 14   Contextualized Music in Worship / 181

Photo 15   Senufo Believers Singing Their Faith / 196

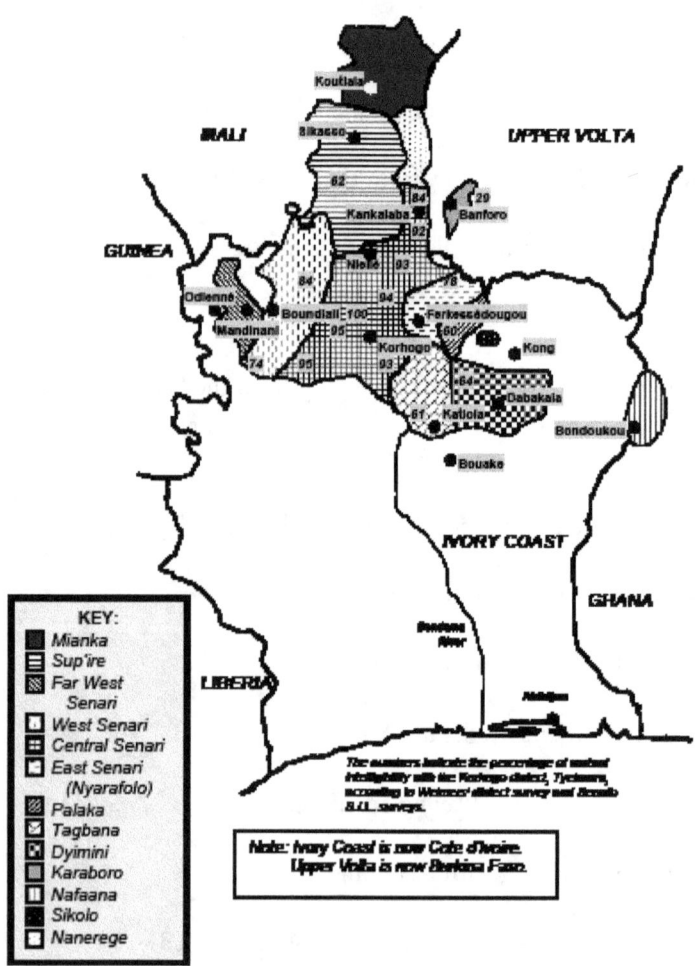

Map 1
The Senufo Peoples and their Languages
(adapted from Mills 1984:xiv)

Photo 1: Following the *kologo* (path), Senufo musicians on their way to a funeral

Preface

LIFE IS A PILGRIMAGE. For the Senufo of Côte d'Ivoire life consists of following the *kologo*, the path, the road, the way. *Kologo* is a key Senufo word that speaks of the directions they choose to follow in life.

The meaning of *kologo* carries a significance in the life and language of the Senufo not unlike the word *hodos* in the language of classical Greece or during the time of the first century Christians. In all three instances, the "road" or "path" denotes a chosen life direction and routing, "the way" is the way one lives, the "path" one follows, the spirit and pattern of life in which one walks.[1]

The majority of Senufo today continue to choose the "path of *Poro*," a "primary structure of religious and socio-political order in the villages."[2] Although there is a burgeoning of believers who are choosing to walk the "Jesus road," many have yet to understand the eternally significant option of following that path.

In my own pilgrimage, I have chosen to follow certain paths, especially as God has led me into the important task of "declaring His glory among the nations" and "proclaiming his salvation day after day" (Ps 96:2, 3 NIV). Following this path led me to the continent of Africa where I became involved in presenting another life-path to the Senufo via culturally appropriate music. It is significant that we choose the right path. That concern composes the topic of this dissertation: presenting the "Jesus road" to the Senufo people through another path, the path of Christian music communication.

---

1. Glaze, "Abstract," 1.
2. Ibid.

Acknowledgements

WHEN AN INVESTIGATION SUCH as this one has taken place over a period of several years (1984–1989), it is difficult to adequately recognize all those who have prayed, supported, encouraged, and advised along the way. I am grateful to the many people who have helped along my journey. It was my purpose to grapple with the relationship between ethnomusicology and Christian communication in the African context. For his never tiring encouragement, challenges, and insights as I pursued this task, I am deeply grateful and indebted to my mentor Charles H. Kraft. Thanks to all of the faculty in Fuller Theological Seminary's School of Intercultural Studies professors,[3] and most particularly to Paul G. Hiebert and Dean S. Gilliland who served on my doctoral committee.

I feel especially honored to have had Professor J. H. Kwabena Nketia serve on my doctoral committee. His deep understanding, guidance, and expertise in ethnomusicology and African music have made an immeasurable contribution to this study and to my own personal development. For his kind and supportive counsel, I am profoundly grateful.

I want to also recognize Mary K. Oyer for her delightful introduction to African music and Joyce Scott for her part in instilling in me an enthusiastic love and spiritual concern for the peoples and musics of Africa. I am also appreciative of Daystar University's understanding role in allowing me to be away from my faculty responsibilities in Nairobi, Kenya while pursuing research among the Senufo peoples.[4]

I am immensely grateful to the board of WorldVenture for its innovative and supportive appointment of an ethnomusicologist,[5] to Warren Webster who took up the cause, and to Rev. Richard Jacobs who oversaw my work during those years of research. Naturally, I am most grateful to the Côte d'Ivoire field of WorldVenture at the time of this research—especially Rev. Merrill and Helen Skinner, Rev. Harold and Dorothy van den Berg, Rev. Richard and Elizabeth Mills, and Ruth Casey.

---

3. At the time of the research, the current School of Intercultural Studies was called School of World Mission.
4. At the time of the research, Daystar University was Daystar University College.
5. WorldVenture was formerly known as Conservative Baptist Foreign Mission Society and CBInternational.

Acknowledgements

I am particularly appreciative of the Association of Evangelical Baptist Churches of Côte d'Ivoire and its leaders for their willingness to work with me. An indebtedness and deep gratitude is especially owed to Ouattara, Dossongomon, who served as my advocate to the Senufo Baptist church and to Soro Ngana Joseph who served faithfully as translator, informant, and friend.

Finally, I am especially pleased to have worked with Nɔnyimɛ, Jɛniba, Flaca, Sandɛɛn, and Sɛnyɛnɛgatɛnɛ, Christian Senufo composers who have been my tutors in Christian music communication within the African context.

More recently, as this work moves into publication I want to gratefully recognize the fine work of Georgia Grimes Shaw who helped to convert and edit the manuscript from its early form to the present and to Jeff Simons who redesigned the figures and tables.

PART ONE

Foundations for Music Communication

I

My Personal Path

WHEN I FIRST ARRIVED in Nairobi, Kenya in 1978 I was not quite sure how I would fit into the task of doing mission in a cross-cultural setting. As a musician, I had plenty of training and experience behind me. A bachelor's degree in piano performance and my new Masters of Music in music education added to 14 years as a church organist and even more years of playing French horn in orchestras, bands, and traveling Christian music ministry teams indicated that I was well-equipped to help in some way. Yet, I was not sure what role a musician who was also a woman might play in the planting of the Christian church in Africa. I had come to Africa to discover just that.

You can imagine my excitement as I attended my first Sunday morning church service. Naively, I expected African music to be a dynamic force within the church service. Certainly, there would be drums. To my surprise, our first hymn was "A Mighty Fortress is our God" sung at half-tempo and accompanied by piano and a Hammond organ. I began to question why I had come to Africa to sing the same hymns that we had at home. This great hymn of the Reformation has always been a favorite of mine, but, having studied in Germany for two years, I was well aware of what German fortresses looked like and represented. The only fortress that I knew of in Kenya was down in the port-town of Mombasa, and that had been built by the Portuguese.

During these first weeks in Kenya, I started visiting various church services always looking to see how they worship and if, by chance, someone might be using African[a] style songs of praise. During this period, the dynamics of a Sunday evening service really made an impression on me. The song service began with a hymn, "What a Friend We Have in Jesus," and was followed by a chorus, "Heaven Came Down and Glory Filled My Soul." Then, amazingly, a guitar and drums were brought out and a song was sung in Kiswahili, rather than English. The atmosphere in the church changed drastically. There was refreshment, vitality, excitement, and joy. I looked at my neighbor standing next to me. He was a visiting Kenyan pastor from another church and had been very staid during the first two songs. Now he came to life: a new reality shone through his eyes as his whole body moved to the rhythm of the song. There was something happening here that I did not understand, but I knew I needed to explore it further.

Meanwhile, as an intern with Daystar Communications, I was being trained for cross-cultural work in their annual International Institute for Christian Communications. I was learning communication principles that made such claims as "Communication is Involvement."[1] I was also learning that communication takes place within a context, and/or a people's culture. In other words, anthropological insights are crucial to effective communication cross-culturally. As a musician, I kept relating these new principles to music and began concluding that music is a very powerful medium of communication.

I had heard of ethnomusicology while working on my Masters degree at the University of Oregon. Now I began to wonder if maybe I should not have looked into it more seriously. Fortunately, the Africa Inland Church had just requested that Joyce Scott begin a program to encourage the development of indigenous hymns for the church. I became one of the early teachers in seminars she initiated now called the AIC School of Music. Our intensive courses throughout the country of Kenya allowed me to dip into ethnomusicology on the field. At the same time, I also began to study African music and ethnomusicology on a more formal basis. I was beginning to realize that there is much more to music than meets the ear. Music is an important and effective means of communication and has a major role to play in the planting and growth of the church worldwide. Thus began my quest to research and develop more appropriate ways for presenting the Gospel through the vehicle of a people's music. This quest has led to the problem before us in this dissertation.

Background to the Problem

My focus for this study will be the church in Africa. The statement of the problem and research questions revolve around "how and why" culturally appropriate songs might make a significant difference in the effective communication of the Gospel and arise out of two major historical factors in the planting of the Christian church in Africa. These factors continue to remain a very real and contemporary issue for national leaders, missionaries, and overall church growth strategies today.

---

1. Smith, *Make Haste Slowly*, 40.

First, for the most part, missiological study observes that most of the music in the African church has come from foreign communicators. Along with the expansion of Christianity into Africa came much of the cultural baggage of the missionary. The early missionary, whose highest goal was to preach the Word of God to the "heathen," was not originally trained to be sensitive to the communication channels inherent in the receptor culture. There was little or no attempt to understand customs that were foreign. Indeed, it was usually assumed that most African customs were foreign, pagan, and highly distasteful. Typical of such attitudes is the description of the initial missionary attitudes among the Kikuyu of Kenya:

> Almost all the Protestant missionaries to Kenya viewed all native customs and traditions with abhorrence. They saw nothing good in African dances, music or in such important African traditions as circumcision and initiation ceremonies. They lumped them together as heathen and immoral without trying to understand them, what they were for and what significance they had in the life of the people to whom they had come to teach Christianity. No African, according to the Missionaries, could become Christian before giving up his old, treasured customs.[2]

This lack of understanding and abhorrence for such cultural practices as indigenous music led missionaries to use and introduce the music that was familiar, understood, and treasured by themselves. They were ignorant of the communication principle that points out "the receiver is the most important link in the communication process."[3] Rather than taking the receptors' impressions and perceptions into mind, they introduced, in all sincerity, music that was assumed to be correct, of the best quality, and even 'sacred'. Most probably, missionaries were inundated with so many new problems that the music that was convenient and "good enough for mother" was assumed to be God's music and therefore good enough for the new converts. Second, foreign tunes with foreign rhythms were introduced into the Church. Along with other aspects of his new faith, the African convert was forced to accept a new musical language—one that was often not understood in the way that it was intended. The expression of the African convert's worship and adoration of his new Lord was not allowed to be a genuine or meaningful expression of his relationship with God. Rather, he was extracted out of his own cultural milieu and presumed upon to lift his voice to God in some unknown musical tongue. This probably was accepted by the African with the thought that perhaps

---

2. Temu, *British Protestant Missions*, 155.
3. Berlo, *The Process of Communication*, 2.

the music had some type of magical element to it (or at least greater power than his or her music) and therefore was not intended to be understood.

Thus we see that in terms of missiological theory, the foreign music of the missionary in all its incomprehensibility on the part of the African was inappropriate for the African's direct communion with God and genuine expression of worship. The music did not communicate clearly or accurately. Instead of music contributing to, enhancing, and clarifying the message, meaningful communication and expression of that message was blocked.

Current Dilemma

There is, then, a preponderance of western hymns in use in the African church today. With western hymns used in such an overwhelmingly standardized way, one often questions if there is indeed a genuine need to deal any further with contextualization of Christianity through music. For example, western hymns are sung fairly enthusiastically in large urban churches in both Kenya and Ghana. Some of the finest western hymn singing I've heard in Africa has been in the Baptist churches of the rural Kivu province in eastern Zaire. Western hymns seem to have found a home in both urban and rural settings and apparently have not created any major detriment to the growth of the African church in these areas.

At the same time, however, African Christian song-styles are beginning to emerge on a regular basis. In the city of Accra, Ghana, churches are adopting African Christian songs that have come from the more traditionally rural areas because they did not want to miss out on such good and meaningful songs. In the same Baptist churches in Zaire, where western hymns are sung so well, only one or two hymns are allowed to be sung by the congregation during the whole service. This is because the church services are so overwhelmed with new Christian songs that there is very little time left for congregational singing of western hymns. These new songs are coming from choirs and vocal ensembles that each requires presenting a minimum of two songs in a service. It is not uncommon to find anywhere from five to nine such vocal groups in any one church. There are choirs for such groups as the mother's union, the youth, the children, and the men's association. By the time that each of these choirs has sung their limit of two songs plus the one they sang while seated, just about every member of the congregation has participated in singing songs that are much more grounded in their own African styles. There is no need or time to sing much as a congregation since everyone has participated musically with their particular vocal group. African Christian songs are beginning to find their place within the African church.

Another aspect that stands in contrast to the western hymns used within most African churches is the question of effectively communicating to those people groups that are virtually untouched by the Christian Gospel. The Digo of the Kenyan coast fit within this category. Although a westernization process is taking place all around them, they are choosing to maintain their customs and traditions, including their own musical styles which are integrally interwoven with their culture. Western Christian hymns appear to be far from their own worldview perspectives and musical needs. What are the implications for effective evangelism through the use of culturally appropriate music that will speak within their world of cultural patterns?

The dilemma becomes, then, to determine and define the nature of culturally appropriate songs. What is a culturally appropriate song? How does one know when it is appropriate? In Africa, we may classify music into three general styles: western styles, traditional styles and the musics that are hybrids of western and traditional styles. There are African peoples who are very far along the path moving towards westernizing. There are also those people who choose to remain close to their traditional life-style, while yet other people are more in transition between the two alternatives, selecting what is important to them from each. Each of these types of people has their corresponding musical preferences.

We must ask the question: is it right to impose upon one group of people what is appropriate for a different group? Should, for example, traditional people be forced to use song styles that are more appropriate for westernizing people? Must the peoples in transition between the traditional and westernizing worlds be compelled to choose between purely western or purely traditional song styles? Are westernizing peoples only interested in western music? When is music (song) appropriate for people and what is its relationship to Christian communication?

Determining and defining culturally appropriate songs in light of their influence within the African church can lead to the development of more effective Christian communication. In order to grasp the potential for the use of culturally appropriate songs in the Christian communication process, then, it is necessary to investigate if and how their use makes a difference in effectively communicating the Gospel in Africa. Thus our problem statement is as follows.

Statement of the Problem

The problem to be addressed in this study is whether the use of culturally appropriate songs makes a significant difference in effective communication of the Gospel and, if so, "how and why." Accompanying research questions include:

(1) What are the operational links involved in bringing about the creation of culturally appropriate songs for Christian communication?

(2) How does musical sound and musical behavior contribute to the overall communication process?

(3) How do the texts of culturally appropriate Christian songs reveal and influence the cognitive understandings of the participants?

(4) How do culturally appropriate Christian songs work in the lives of participants affectively, cognitively, and behaviorally?

This problem statement and accompanying research questions required locating a contemporary situation where the development and use of culturally appropriate songs has occurred in a fairly spontaneous way. I discovered such a situation in the Conservative Baptist Foreign Mission Society's work in the north of Côte d'Ivoire among the Senufo, the ethnic group that will serve as the main focus of this study.

Rationale for the Study among the Senufo

When I first arrived in Korhogo, Côte d'Ivoire in West Africa towards the latter half of April, 1985, as the Conservative Baptist Foreign Mission Society's first ethnomusicologist, I did not expect to hear the music that greeted me in the Evangelical Baptist Churches among the Senufo. Missiological literature on music in the church speaks only of the need for indigenous music.[4] My three years of teaching music in Kenya validated such literature since the singing of western hymns is the predominant mode of singing praises to God there. Besides, I had just visited CBFMS work in Senegal and found not even a hint of African music being used in the church. I viewed myself as functioning in the field of public relations aimed at advocating contextualized music and providing convincing theories that it would make a difference in church growth.

To my great surprise, I discovered what the Senufo church and mission leaders already knew. Senufo believers were singing their faith in their own Senufo style. In the process of collecting songs, obtaining transla-

---

4. Chenoweth, "Spare Them Western Music!," 30–35.

tions of song texts, recording various worship services, participating in the games and songs at the girls' school camp, and spending a special musical evening with Senufo believers sharing their songs with me, I was amazed and delighted to see God at work using the people's music.

Here was a unique case. There was no need to try to convince people that they could use their own music to praise God. They were already doing it. There was no need to formulate anthropological arguments concerning form and function as it relates to music, no need to question whether secular musical forms and instruments could be employed in a Christian setting. It was already happening. Questions that always arise in missiological theory and in churches where indigenous forms have not been used up to the present were being dealt with in a real-life context—that of the Senufo. Here was an opportunity to go beyond the mere call for contextualization of music. It provided an occasion to deal with issues from the inside out rather than theorizing from the outside hoping to work toward the inside of a people's music communication system.

Thus it is that I chose to confine my research to the Senufo. I felt that research among them would make a significant contribution to missiological literature and research for three reasons. First, it would provide relevant data in relation to the development and use of culturally appropriate songs as tools for communicating Christ. I would not have to ask the question: Can it be done? Rather, I could move on and ask "how" and "why" does the use of culturally appropriate songs make a difference in Christian communication. Second, it would serve as a unique case study since indigenous music is already occurring, allowing me to extend and expand theoretical questions. Third, it would serve as a critical case in testing a well-formulated theory, that contextualized music, the use of culturally appropriate songs, makes a difference in church growth, by confirming, challenging, or extending that particular theory. The conditions for testing this theory were already present in the Senufo church.

Goal and Objectives

The goal of this study, therefore, is to create a model for investigating the dynamics and processes at work in Christian music communication. This will provide for us a juncture between missiology and ethnomusicology, the bringing together of two paths. For our purposes here, the term Christian music communication will refer to music that carries the Christian message with the primary intent of effectively communicating that message.

This approach is based on three major assumptions. First, music is an effective means of communication that stimulates human beings in a powerful and influential way. Second, the impact of music communication is high because it employs a multiplicity of communication codes, most particularly sound code(s), linguistic code(s), kinesic code(s), and presentation code(s). When each of these codes is appropriate to the context and correctly wedded, the impact on the receptor is greater than the use of a single code. Finally, this new approach to music as Christian communication will foster positive church growth patterns, both qualitatively and quantitatively.

Included within the parameters of this study are two major objectives. The first objective seeks to delineate the main elements and considerations in the development of culturally appropriate songs. Since societies are not static but rather dynamic in their willingness to adopt from other societies, they cannot be protected from the influences embedded in the barrage of music coming from other peoples. Composers may choose to incorporate new stylistic elements into their musical style. What, then, constitutes a culturally appropriate song for effective Christian communication?

The second objective seeks to generalize and expand theories about the use of culturally appropriate songs in Christian music communication and the part they play in the greater expansion of the Kingdom of God.

Need and Purpose

Within this study, I am indirectly addressing one of the most significant features of our era of missions: the call for the contextualization of Christianity. Kraft exhorts us to pursue the development of a "dynamically equivalent church"—one that employs indigenous forms familiar and meaningful to the receiving society.[5] Tippett likewise points out that one of the main features of an indigenous church is that they practice "worshipping in patterns they understand."[6] African ethnomusicologists agree with these missiological statements. Nketia underscores this when he comments:

> If churches in Africa are to grow as African churches and not as extensions of parishes and bishoprics as some of them are now, then they must be allowed to take root in the soil of the African culture in which they are planted, so that they may grow in stature as institutions of our own.[7]

---

5. C. Kraft, *Christianity in Culture*, 100.
6. Ibid., 85.
7. Nketia, "The Contribution of African Culture to Christian Worship," 268.

When such observations are made, music is usually singled out as one of the first areas where contextualization needs to take place. On the African continent today, songs drawing from the roots of various cultural heritages are sweeping through the African church. National church leaders and missionaries alike are recognizing the increasing phenomenon of new song forms rooted in a people's cultural heritage. It is generally recognized that the use of such culturally appropriate songs is playing an important role in the growth and development of relevant Christian practices in Africa.

There is a growing intuitive consensus about the importance of music, its communicational qualities, and its effectiveness in influencing the cause of Christ's mission. Yet research in the area of musical communication, though recognized as important, usually remains isolated from missiological study. Statements concerning the importance of appropriate music continue to be made but are left without research and in-depth investigation. Many have come to believe that ethnomusicology, the study of music in culture, has a contribution to make to the field of missiology, but they are not quite sure how and in what way. The purpose of this study is to speak to such assumptions and to delineate the ways in which ethnomusicology and missiology may join forces. It is based on the intention of fostering effective Christian communication within a given society through music.

Systematic inquiry into the dynamics and processes involved in music communication required the development of a methodology that would meet the demands of research. A number of methodologies were considered. The key requirement was to define a methodology that would allow for the study of a phenomenon within its current situation that did not require the restraints of a control group. We now turn our attention to that issue.

2

Pathways to Music Communication Research

It had been a long road getting to this point. The small mud-and-thatch home could hardly hold the nine of us but there was a gentle and accepting rapport between us as we sat on the wood benches from the church. The wooden door swung on its hinges, allowing the bright sunlight to provide some light in the room. One woman, her hair-do shaped by a plain white scarf, was explaining how songs had helped her in her walk with Jesus. Suddenly, she lifts her voice and sings one of the songs. The rest of the group sings the response. I'm amazed, all eight Senufo believers are totally involved in this group interview. She cuts the song short and explains about the song, "When my heart is troubled and I sing, then I find joy once again. It's the same joy as if one was preaching words from the Bible. Songs really help me!"

Photo 2: Believers from the Fɔrɔ Church who participated in the focus group

Pathways To Music Communication Research

I reach down to make sure the tape recorder is still working. We're almost at the end of the second 90 minute tape! They don't seem to want to stop. What a contrast to last year when people would hardly talk at all. Now Kazye, the group leader, continues the testimonies about songs: "All the songs help me but the one that says to 'Stay with Jesus' is the one I like the most . . . Since I know the path of Jesus and that he also loved me and chose me, I want to be with him in heaven."[1]

Finally, after more than three hours of discussion, we, the leaders, brought the meeting to a close. Yes, it had been a long road to finding ways to encourage discussion about Senufo Christian songs in the believers' lives. A new path to research had been discovered. I noted that I must remember to take this path again.

The Many Alternatives within Research

Researching Christian music communication is a complex task. Several methodologies (paths) formed an ensemble of possible approaches to particular aspects of music communication. Among them was a one-time experiment, a survey, participant observation, learning to sing the songs, and to perform on the musical instruments. Each of these approaches has its own strengths and weaknesses. For example, the one-time experiment is capable of dealing with research questions of "how and why," focusing on a contemporary event such as the influence of new songs. It requires, though, a control over the behavioral events. It is also limited to a study within a very short period of time and is not capable of adequately tracing over a longer period of time the overall influence of music or songs in the receptors' lives. The survey, on the other hand, is capable of telling who had heard the songs, where they had been heard, and what the opinions of the songs were. It is limited, however, in making significant comments about the music, itself.

Each method was helpful at a certain point. However, as I continued further into my research, I felt that none of them was individually capable of dealing sufficiently with the multiple facets of music communication. I began searching for a more appropriate methodology.

The Case Study as Major Methodology

In order to deal with the needs and requirements of researching Christian music communication in light of the problem statement and its accompanying major research questions, I selected a methodology that would allow

---

1. King, Focus Group Interviews, Foro.

for simultaneous investigation in several areas. This was necessary due to the highly complex nature of music events and their inter-relationships with and influence on society. The case study was selected as the major methodology. The method allows the investigator to scrutinize a phenomenon from several different angles. Thus, it is conducive to studying the complex components of music events. Indeed, the case study's "unique strength is its ability to deal with a full variety of evidence-documents, artifacts, interviews, and observations."[2] It allows the researcher to investigate the multiple aspects of the music event in a comprehensive and multi-dimensional way.

However, the overriding consideration in selecting the case study methodology is its distinct advantage in dealing with a contemporary phenomenon or set of events over which the researcher has little or no control. If Christian ethnomusicologists as missiologists are going to develop strategies that effectively penetrate contextual church planting situations, then they must not deal with the music event as a phenomenon within a vacuum. Rather, they must deal with it as one found within a real situation. It is my experience that when one is working with such an attractive medium of communication as music and especially new songs, maintaining control either over the dispersion of the music or over the human subjects is next to impossible. For this reason, the one-time experiment is inappropriate.

Thus, I selected the case study, technically defined by Yin, as my major methodology:

> A case study is an empirical inquiry that: *investigates a contemporary phenomenon within its real-life context; when *the boundaries between phenomenon and context are not clearly evident; and in which *multiple sources of evidence are used.[3]

This is reflective of the situation as I began to study the Christian songs among the Senufo in 1985. The emergence and use of new Christian Senufo songs was very much a contemporary phenomenon that was occurring in the overwhelming majority of churches. This use of songs was taking place within a real-life context where it was difficult to distinguish between the phenomenon and the context. In order to begin to grasp the various aspects of this phenomenon, the use of multiple sources of evidence and approaches to research was required in an attempt to unravel the complexity and pervasiveness of music's influence among the Senufo.

---

2. Yin, *Case Study Research*, 19.
3. Ibid, 23.

The research design of this case-study is an embedded single-case study carried out among the Evangelical Baptist churches of the Senufo people of northern Côte d'Ivoire. My approach meant that I employed a number of methodologies within the design of the case study. Each level of analysis of music communication required different data collection techniques ranging from historical investigation to the implementation of focus group interviews. I did this in an effort to create triangulation in the research where the object of study is approached from many angles in order to verify the validity of the investigation.[4]

Collection of the Data

The collection of data was conducted over a period of four years from 1985 through 1988 within the Korhogo region of Côte d'Ivoire. The case study is, therefore, diachronic. I conducted the study in three main stages, drawing upon several methodologies embedded within the context of a case study.

Photo 3: Gbowele and his family who hosted the researcher, Roberta King, in the village of Zanaka?a

---

4. See Wimmer and Dominick, *Mass Media Research*.

The first stage, conducted in 1985, of research was investigatory. It consisted of basic observations of music events in the Baptist churches of Côte d'Ivoire and of an informal survey based on interviews, with both national pastors and missionaries, concerning the needs of the church with regard to music. Since a Senufo Christian song style had already been developed, the musical needs of the church became content and appropriate songs for various occasions. The majority of the songs spoke of the people's conversion experience, stating, for example, that they had "joined the Jesus road" and thus no longer needed to do what Satan had formerly demanded of them. The song text would then list the various sins of their former life. This would become the main content of the song with its description of the demands of Satan. Church leaders were concerned that the people learn more about God and grow in their spiritual formation. I was invited to return and try to encourage them to develop songs that would speak to this need.

The second stage of research was based primarily on participant-observation—a methodology employed throughout the whole investigation. It was, however, intensified and became a main focus, beginning with my 1986 visit. As an ethnomusicologist, I am intensely concerned with becoming bi-musical in an attempt to understand the music from an emic perspective by seeking to avoid relating to the music merely as an outsider. This second stage of research ran throughout the three final visits that I made to Côte d'Ivoire between 1986 and 1988. Each visit lasted from two to three months. This stage included a 7-week period of language and culture learning by living in the village of Zanaka?a in 1986 as well as constant participation, recording of the songs and observation at church worship services and major events such as the annual women's conferences, weddings, and youth fetes.

However, the event where intense participant-observation occurred took the form of workshops for the creation of new songs based on scripture with the goal of spiritual formation for the Senufo Christians. The first workshop was held for three weeks in 1986, followed in 1987 by a 10-day workshop and a 7-day workshop in 1988. Senufo Christian composers were selected to attend the workshops based on their abilities to compose songs that people would readily sing and that would impact their Christian life-style. The decision was made by national leaders but included suggestions by missionary leadership. Based on interviews with national leaders, gaps in the people's Biblical understandings and Christian lifestyle were determined. Relevant scriptures were located and then suggested for the composing of new songs to aid in the maturing of the believers. The workshop format included Bible study, discussion of the songs needed, assigning of the scripture texts to be used, and sufficient time given for the creation of the song usually in the afternoon and evening. Presentation and recording of the newly created songs took place the following day and included discussion of the content and appropriateness of the new songs. A final recording session of all songs created at the workshop was made for distribution to the church. The new songs were then presented at the women's conferences as a means of disseminating them and observing responses to them.

Since the New Song Workshops functioned as a continual undergirding for doing participant-observation, this led to the third stage of research. Secondary methodologies were employed and included a survey, content analysis of the song texts, the conducting of focus group interviews, and *balafon* lessons.

An overview of the research schedule can be visualized as follows. It shows the way in which each methodology builds into additional approaches to doing research in music communication.

Figure 1
Research in the Korhogo Region of Cote d'Ivoire

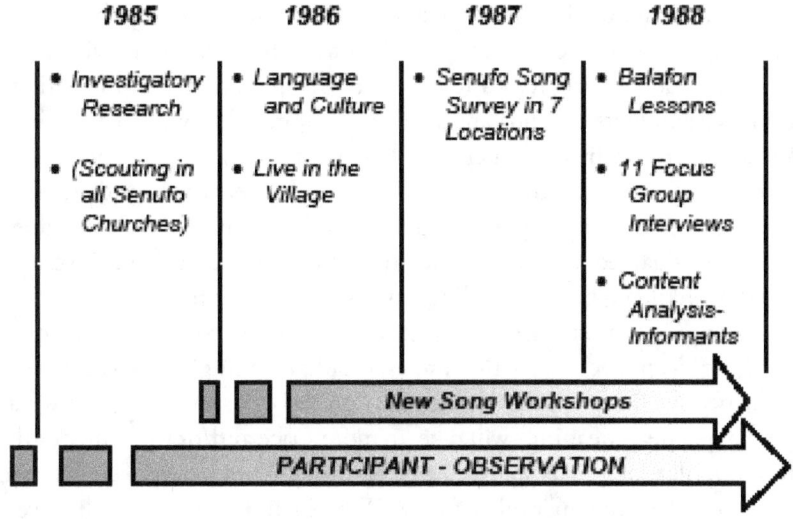

Secondary Methodologies Employed

Three secondary methodologies were employed within the context of a case study. Among them were a survey, content analysis of the song texts, and focus group interviews. The Senufo Song Survey was conducted in 1987 from February 17 to March 27. It consisted of an interview schedule made up of questions focusing on the new songs that had been composed in the 1986 New Song Workshop plus the introduction of one of the 1987 new songs. Eighty-nine Senufo Christian believers were interviewed in seven different locations concerning these songs and their influence in the believers' lives. Four trained, national Christians administered the survey orally. This included the playing of recorded songs from which to pose the questions. Each interview lasted on the average of 45 minutes.

Major objectives of the survey included determining:

(1) Senufo conceptions about music

(2) if the new songs from 1986 were being sung

(3) the villages to which the songs had spread

(4) which songs have made an impact in people's lives

(5) the way in which the songs had spread

(6) elements that make a song singable and popular

(7) comprehension and retention of a song text

Sizable difficulties were encountered in administering the survey, including the major difficulty of finding available translators with sufficient educational background to complete the questionnaire in its written form. Respondents did not appear to feel comfortable with the method. Apparently, the individual interview along with the use of paper and pencil in their presence seems to have posed a sort of barrier that kept them from answering the questions spontaneously and fully. In spite of the difficulties, information gained was valuable for triggering further in-depth investigation that would go beyond the limits of a survey, see Appendix B.

Content analysis of the song texts was conducted as a means to researching deep-level issues that are especially meaningful and important to the people. Based on the communication theory assumption that whatever has greater "meaning" will take up more space and/or time, fifty of the most popular song texts were selected for study. These songs were selected from three different periods of time. They include; (1) songs that were known and sung before the 1986 New Song Workshop, (2) songs that were most popular with the respondents to the Senufo Song Survey of 1987 (which I refer to as "the Current Senufo Repertoire"), and (3) most commonly sung songs created in the 1987 New Song Workshop. Going beyond quantitative analysis, a qualitative analysis was done in an attempt to determine major cultural issues and worldview perspectives and how they meshed with the Christian message. Consultation with two national informants who specialize in translation, as well as verification of the text transcriptions by mission translators, was sought in a systematic way in an attempt to gain "emic" perceptions of words and phrases.

Finally, questions and new issues that were brought to light as a result of the above survey led to further research about the people's response to songs that was best investigated by means of focus group interviews. The Focus Group Interview method serves as a means of doing qualitative research allowing for opportunities to probe deeper into specific issues.[5] Basically, the Focus Group Interview is a controlled discussion led by a moderator with a homogeneous group of people. The group size may range anywhere from 6–12 people. One of its advantages is an easy interaction between the participants, leading to the free flow of ideas and opinions.

Our Focus Group interviews took place in Senufo villages where there was an active Baptist church. Once we arrived in a village and had greeted the appropriate people, my two national informants would announce that we had come to do the discussions we had requested two days earlier. The people who had been selected to participate usually chose to conduct the group discussions either inside the small church building or within a Senufo home and not out in their open courtyards. The benches were arranged in a large circle or square.

---

5. Ibid., 48(5).

Photo 4: A Senufo village

Crucial to Focus Group Interviews are the moderators selected to generate and control the discussion. The success of these interactions rests on their ability to relate well with the participants and to ask the questions well. Two moderators were selected. One, Nangaluru, was an informant for Bible translation and was considered a mature leader in the Senufo church. The other moderator, Ngana Soro, was my regular informant, a leader among the youth planning to attend Bible school. Interestingly, each moderator developed his own particular style that matched the age group he worked with. Nangaluru, for example, conducted Focus Group Interviews with the adults and was very methodical in eliciting answers to the questions. He would ask the question to each person individually and allow him/her to respond. Then, he would turn to the next person, ask the very same question and give the new person an opportunity to answer. Ngana Soro, on the other hand, dealt with the youth who have had more schooling. They were more open to the volleying of ideas between themselves. However, Ngana made sure that each person had an opportunity to make a statement.

Careful planning was also needed in order to run the Focus Group Interviews. In addition to selecting and training the moderators in the objectives of the discussions, a Question Guide was developed. Both Nangaluru and Ngana Soro played an important role in actually drawing up the question guide since they were the experts in knowing how to ask questions. I used this time of drawing up the question guide as a means of training them by discussing the major areas of interest to me and the purpose for conducting the discussions. We decided to begin the discussions by playing a tape recording of a well-known Senufo Christian song and to use that as a springboard for launching into the discussion as a whole.

The Question Guide for the Focus Group Interviews was composed of questions in three main areas (see Appendix C for the full question guide):

(1) Believers' thoughts about the Christian songs.

    (a) How have songs helped them in their walk with Jesus?

    (b) Is it true that songs can minister to them like the Word of God, as we were told the year before in the survey?

(2) Nonbelievers' thoughts about Christian songs.

    (a) Do nonbelievers like the Christian songs?

    (b) Have Christian songs helped people in the salvation process?

    (c) Do nonbelievers sing the Christian songs?

(3) Believers' thoughts about the new songs and their musical styles looking for clues to the basic requirements for culturally appropriate songs among the Senufo.

    (a) Do they prefer long or short songs?

    (b) When do they clap?

    (c) What should the texts of the songs speak about?

Eleven focus group interviews were conducted. It was felt that the young people might not feel free to express themselves if they were questioned at the same time as the adults. Thus, six sessions were conducted with the youth (15–25 years old) and five sessions were conducted with the adults (26 years old and above) in six different locations (see Map 2). The total number of people interviewed was 78: 40 adults and 38 young people. All participants were active in the Senufo Baptist churches. While it appeared difficult for the people to respond to the survey, they were more than responsive to the Focus Group interviews. One group was so responsive that after more than three hours of discussion, it was difficult to get them to stop sharing.

The major difficulty encountered was finding a suitable time for the interviews due to conflicting schedules between those who work in their fields and the moderators who wanted to hold the sessions during the daylight hours. This determined to some extent the selection of participants.

All sessions were recorded and later transcribed. Where the use of paper and pen appeared to be something of a block in the survey, the tape recorder was not offensive to the people. It is an item with which they are familiar and use to listen to their own songs. The groups were so responsive to the discussions, that they and others who heard about the sessions requested copies of the tapes so that they could listen again.

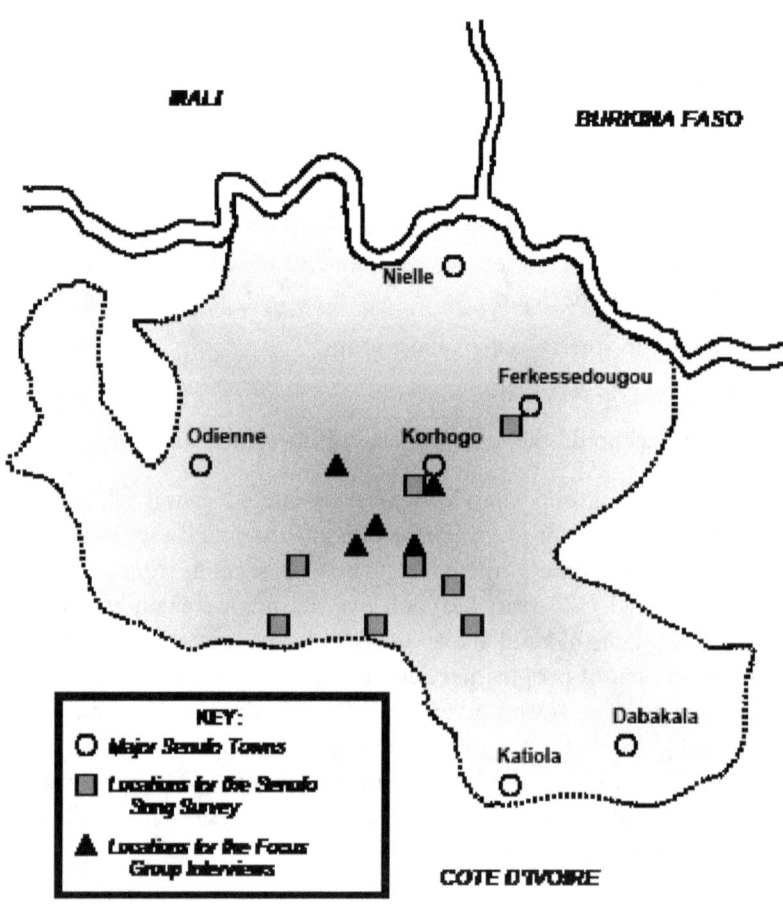

Map 2
Senufo Research Area

The bringing together of the data collected throughout the case study required developing a systematic approach to reporting the findings and presenting summatory observations within an appropriate context. Analysis of materials includes a research corpus of:

(1) 50 song texts out of 172 texts collected,

(2) 39 audio-cassette tapes of recorded Christian songs,

(3) 1 audio-cassette tape of traditional funeral music,

(4) 105 pages of single-spaced transcriptions from the focus group interviews,

(5) 20 tables based on the survey data, and

(6) field notebooks and individual interviews.

The collection and analysis of data led to the development of a model for doing music communication research and will provide the basic structure of my presentation.

Model for Doing Christian Music Communication Research

Due to the complex nature of any music event within a given society and in order to meet the requirements of the problem statement/question, I have developed a guiding model for initiating Christian music communication research around which a series of research questions may be posed.

The model (see Figure 2) may be divided into two main areas of study; that is (1) background to the particular case in point, and (2) major research domains that focus on the unique contributions of a people's music in the overall Christian communication process.

The main research questions that form the background of a particular case include investigations in the areas of: (1) a general ethnography of a people group, (2) a study of the historical dynamics of church growth in a particular area, and (3) an ethnohistorical study of the development of Christian music among a particular social or ethnic group.

The main questions for the major research domains concerning music in the communication process include the:

(1) study of music as communication in terms of its influence in the receptors' lives,

(2) study of specific musical dimensions/aspects contributing to the overall music communication process,

(3) general study of music's role in culture in the form of an ethnomusicological study of a people's music culture,

(4) study of song texts in terms of content analysis, and

(5) study of applied ethnomusicology where investigations and projects draw on what is already at work within the culture of a people in order to make a positive contribution to communication of a given message.

Scope of this Study

One, of course, could do extensive research in each of the areas. Our major goal is, however, to investigate music as it plays a role in the overall Christian communication process. Therefore, we will focus our attention on four main questions on the Christian music communication model as exemplified for us among the Senufo people of northern Côte d'Ivoire.

First, in the ethnohistorical unit I will investigate the various stages and processes that serve as operational links needing to be traced over time in the development of Senufo Christian songs and leading into the contemporary Senufo church life as it is today. Second, in the musical analysis unit I will research and analyze how musical sound and behavior contribute to the overall communication process for the Senufo. What are the communication dynamics at work within the actual production of music? Third, I will analyze the song texts in terms of their ability to reflect the integration of the people's worldview with the Christian message in response to the question of how the songs influence Senufo cognitive understandings of the Christian message. Fourth, in the music as communication unit, I will investigate the role of Senufo Christian songs in the lives of the receptors in terms of response to the Christian message affectively (attitudinally), cognitively, and behaviorally.

**Figure 2
Model for Doing
Christian Music Communication Research**

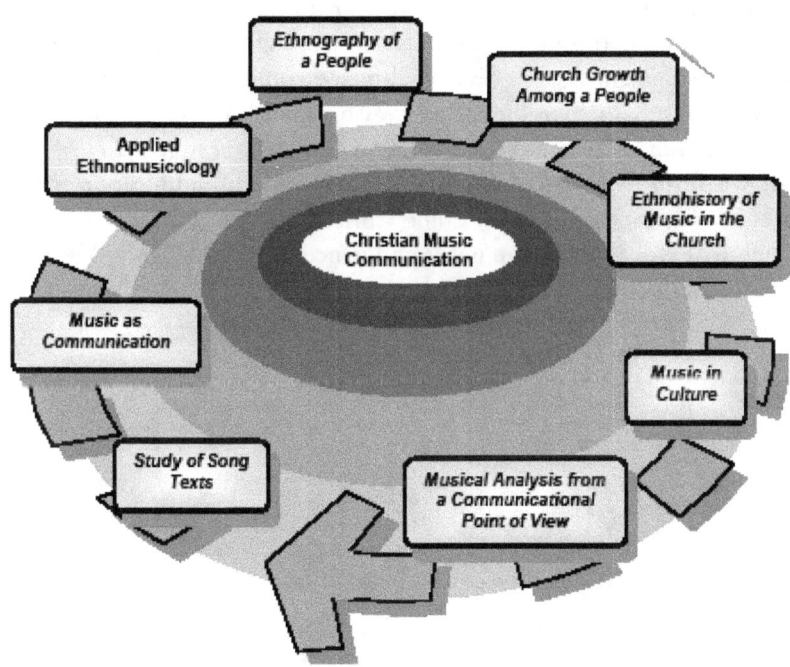

Limitations

There is not sufficient latitude within this study to develop a full ethnomusicological study of the Senufo in general, although the need for it is recognized and imperative[6] I am restricting myself here to the study of Christian Senufo songs that have developed among the Association of Evangelical Baptist Churches of Côte d'Ivoire as a part of the work of the Conservative Baptist Foreign Mission Society.

Likewise, I will only make a cursory study of the ethnography of the people and the history of church growth among the Senufo as they relate to and are relevant to setting the scene for our in-depth study of music communication.

---

6. An ethnomusicological study is currently in process by a researcher from Tours, France.

Finally, the applied ethnomusicology unit of research shown in the model has been used as a means for eliciting information in the other domains and will not, therefore, be handled as a unit to be analyzed. Rather, it has served as a methodological springboard for research. In addition to this, it simultaneously contributes source information to the various domains and leads to the ultimate goal of this study in Christian music communication. This ultimate goal is that we might develop culturally appropriate songs/music for effective Christian communication in the areas of evangelism, Christian formation, worship, and leadership training.

What, then, becomes the theoretical basis for our inquiry? How have I drawn from the areas of ethnomusicology and communication theory in order to create a model for doing Christian music communication research that will speak to the needs and concerns of missiology? We focus next on that particular question.

3

Toward a Theory of Christian Music Communication

Ethnomusicologists assert that music functions in many ways. One of the most readily recognized functions of music is its ability to function "on a number of levels as a means of emotional expression."[1] Songs, more specifically, may serve as either individual or collective expressions of ideas and emotions that are not revealed in ordinary discourse.[2] The range of emotions expressed is wide and varied from love songs to social protest songs. The study of the expressive function of music is one of the more accessible areas of ethnomusicological research. Yet, the expressive function of music is only one of ten functions that have been recognized by Merriam.[3] Among these ten functions inherent in music is that of communication.

Although music throughout the history of humanity has most often been closely associated with religion, its role in relation to a particular religion and its communicative attributes have been largely neglected in terms of critical and evaluative study. That music communicates has been assumed rather than addressed. Thus, the study of Christian communication through the use of culturally appropriate music is an unspecified or new field of study. It represents the merging together of several disciplinary paths in an attempt to provide access to understanding the processes involved in the creation and performance of music within a Christian communication situation. The major path or foundation within this domain of study draws from the field of ethnomusicology. The parallel path of communication provides an approach to ethnomusicology. Finally, all of these paths converge to make a contribution to the field of missiology.

---

1. Merriam, "The Anthropology of Music," 219–23.
2. Ibid.
3. See ibid., 219–27 for a full discussion of the ten functions of music.

Two Major Paths in Ethnomusicology

When you first look on the map of academia, ethnomusicology appears as a small path, perhaps somewhat esoteric in its orientation. Certainly, in comparison to the study of Christian theology, which has its origins dating back to the first century, ethnomusicology is a young discipline barely rooted in the last century[4] and further back where simple and non-academic "descriptions of Asian, African, and Latin American native musics by missionaries, travelers, and civil and military officials" were first contributed.[5] The term "ethnomusicology," however, was not coined until 1959 by Jaap Kunst.

When you begin to study the ethnomusicology path, you discover that it is a broad double-lane road. Its dual nature is a distinctive feature of the discipline[6] and has at times caused "schisms" between those scholars who call themselves ethnomusicologists.[7] For, while one group of scholars focuses attention on the "music sound," another emphasizes the study of "music behavior." Rather than allowing either aspect to rise to prominence, the great debate has dealt with the question of how to bring about an effective fusion of the musicological and the anthropological paths found within ethnomusicology.[8]

Although most ethnomusicologists will acknowledge and pay lip service to the dilemma of bringing together the two fields, they very often end up emphasizing one field over the other. The proponents of studying "musical sound" correctly advocate direct involvement with and focus of study on the music itself in the scientific search for knowledge about music.[9] This is particularly evident in Mantle Hood's definition of ethnomusicology as stated in the "Harvard Dictionary of Music," where he says: "Ethnomusicology is an approach to the study of any music, not only in terms of itself but also in relation to its cultural context."[10]

Although Hood includes studying music within its cultural context as well as in terms of itself, his definition of cultural context appears to be limited to the items related to music within the immediate context of studying a particular musical genre or instrument.[11] For example, he gives examples of cultural context questions for the Japanese *koto* that concen-

---

4. Ellis, "On the Musical Scales of Various Nations."
5. Nettl, "Ethnomusicology," 2.
6. Merriam, "The Anthropology of Music," 1.
7. Stone, *Let the Inside Be Sweet*, 11.
8. Merriam, "The Anthropology of Music," 17.
9. Hood, *The Ethnomusicologist*, 3, 6–7.
10. Hood, "Ethnomusicology," 298.
11. Stone, *Let the Inside Be Sweet*, 15.

trate on researching the several different types of *koto*, the distinctive style periods of musical literature for the instrument, the influence of other musical genres and instruments, and the history of Japan as it relates to music, dance, poetry, and theatre.[12]

When such an approach to cultural context is taken, there are no direct considerations of the role and influence of music within the broader aspects of society. The problem develops, then, that the anthropological areas of study, as well as any other subject that may touch upon music, may then be considered relevant and interesting, but they serve more as appendages to the discipline or as a separate area of study.

Crucial to the development and path of ethnomusicology was the new emphasis on the study of music "in" culture and music "as" culture first suggested by Merriam in 1964. It went beyond the simple ethnographic statements that looked at the overt uses of song or music within a tribal group from the earlier period of comparative musicology. Now music became an object of study in terms of its role, use, and function within a society. This approach was taken up in an effort to determine the significant and meaningful relationships between music and culture. Ethnomusicology, for Merriam, became the study of music as a human phenomenon as opposed to the study of music as a mere sound phenomenon. For others, the goal was expressed as the study of "humanly organized sound" and "soundly organized humanity."[13] The result was, that drawing from the social sciences and anthropology, it became a discipline based more on "how" you went about the study than "what" you studied: anthropological methods and formal analysis of music techniques were employed.

These two major paths in Ethnomusicology have not remained totally separate from each other nor have they remained uninformed by other disciplines. For example, the field of linguistics has offered certain models for studying music,[14] while folklore studies have offered approaches to studying song texts. Ethnomusicology is interdisciplinary[15] and as such has had difficulty in formulating its own unique and distinctive paradigm.[16] Yet, perhaps this is its strength in that music reflects and restructures culture at multiple levels and must therefore be informed by various disciplines.

---

12. Hood, *The Ethnomusicologist*, 31–32.
13. Blacking, *How Musical is Man?*
14. Feld, "Linguistics and Ethnomusicology,"197–127; Bright, "Language and Music," 26–32.
15. Nettl, *Theory and Method in Ethnomusicology*, 15–16.
16. Stone, *Let the Inside Be Sweet*, 13.

However, the main thrust of ethnomusicology correctly continues to search after a blending of studies in "music sound." In relation to studies in "music behavior." The justified concern is that "music sound" not be divorced from its cultural context or that the study of "music behavior" not lead away from the study of the actual musical sound. Several options have been offered. Among them, a juncture of the social and musical spheres has been suggested by Nketia, who stipulates that cultural analysis does not take one away from music when focusing on the cultural patterns that develop around a musical event. Thus, the ethnomusicologist studies today what has come to be designated as "music cultures." The study and analysis of a "music culture" itself would then inform the theoretical ways in which the "music culture" is reflective of, and influential in, society as a whole. This approach to ethnomusicology is important to our study in that music as communication must be studied not only for its overt influence within a society in general but also for the way in which it is organized as a mode of communication relative to its musical structures, textual guidelines, performance requirements, and function within the context of a particular musical event.

Concepts about Music

Within the search to fuse the two major paths of ethnomusicology arises the need to deal with concepts about music. The boundaries for a clear definition of music vary from culture to culture. From my point of view, music as a concept is much broader than a mere combination of tones that may be analyzed formally. Rather, drawing from the anthropological path, music must be studied within its context of being a product of human activity. Nettl allows for this when he defines music as "human sound communication outside the scope of spoken language."[17] The emphasis, here, focuses on human beings creating musical sounds. Such a definition presupposes the differences in defining music that occur between cultures. The dynamic and ever-changing quality of music is recognized, then, in the fact that "Music is a product of the behavior of human groups, whether formal or informal: it is humanly organized sound."[18] Music is not an entity in itself, but rather is the result of human interaction. Its main intention is communication.

Thus, the dictates of musical sound, its production, and the involvement of human beings may vary from society to society. For example, the term "music in Africa" refers to something much broader than what

17. Nettl, *The Study of Ethnomusicology*, 24.
18. Blacking, *How Musical is Man?*, 7.

is perceived as music in Western societies. Among the Kpelle of Liberia, "music sound is conceived as part of an integrally related cluster of dance, speech, and kinesic-proximity behavior . . . occurring in particular time-space dimensions."[19] It is more than just the mere organization of sounds since it extends beyond sound alone into the use of movement, language, and spatial dimensions. In another part of Africa, among the Nsenge of Zambia, one of the requirements of music is that it possesses "the power to bring people together in brotherhood."[20] Thus it is that for the Nsenge a song with a simpler musical construction would be perceived as more musical since it allows large groups of people to participate in the music-making event.

Such concepts about music are taken into consideration throughout our study among the Senufo. We recognize that music is made up not only of musical sounds that have been organized by humans, but it may include varying concepts of a particular society as well as other forms such as dance, poetry, and drama. Such an aggregate of individual forms allows them to serve simultaneously as expressive channels utilized by human beings as they interact with one another. Therefore, the differing concepts of music within various societies necessitate the broadening of the ethnomusicologist's study of music to include the relationship of music to and within these various forms.

The focus, then, may also be adjusted to studying the intention of the music-making process-communication. Blacking specifies this further for us when he explains that music as humanly organized sound is "intended for other human ears and possibly enjoyed by the composer's friends, and thus concerned with communication and relationships between people."[21]

Music as Communication

Music as communication drawing from the "music as behavior" side of ethnomusicology is recognized as a major function of music.[22] It has remained, however, somewhat enigmatic to address and research. In his discussion of music as a function of communication, Merriam highlights its ungraspable nature:

> . . . the major problem is that while we know music communicates something, we are not clear as to what, how, or to whom. Music is not a universal language, but rather is shaped in terms

---

19. Stone, *Let the Inside Be Sweet*, 1.
20. Blacking, *How Musical is Man?*, 12.
21. Ibid.
22. Merriam, "The Anthropology of Music," 223.

of the culture of which it is a part. In the song texts it employs, it communicates direct information to those who understand the language in which it is couched. It conveys emotion, or something similar to emotion, to those who understand its idiom. The fact that music is shared as a human activity by all peoples may mean that it communicates a certain limited understanding simply by its existence. Of all the functions of music, the communication function is perhaps least known and understood.[23]

Thus the literature on music as communication per se is neither consistent nor enormous. Terence McLaughlin's writing on "Music Communication" attempts to deal with the essential nature of music, which he views as organic in its ability to express human experience.[24] His purpose is to analyze the possible ways in which music can be expressive and the physiological mechanisms that allow such transmissions of the experience. His study is limited for our purposes by the fact that he deals with music from a western perspective. He has also divorced music as communication from its cultural context. Significant for us, however, is his tenet that music communicates on multiple levels triggering reconciliation or harmonization between the levels of the mind.[25]

A broader definition of music as communication is needed, however, in order to develop a fuller understanding of music communication where both the cultural context and the musical sound are analyzed. One such definition is that of Seeger who claims that communication in music consists of "the impacts upon anyone or several senses of an individual receiver or group of receivers."[26] Yet, he does not provide specific development and applications to his definition. To what kind of "impacts" is he referring? How does this work itself out in relation to differing societies?

Providing specific applications to Seeger's definition of music as communication within Africa, Nketia contends that the "impacts" of music are created and working within three domains of a music event: "(a) the sonic materials and the structures in which they are realized; (b) the verbal texts to which sonic materials are set, and (c) the dance through which basic structures in music are articulated."[27] Rather than dealing with the problems of range, for example, as a descriptive one, he makes it a communication problem in terms of its impact on the receptors and their

---

23. Ibid.
24. McLaughlin, *Music and Communication*.
25. Ibid., 105.
26. Seeger, "Music as a Tradition," 157.
27. Nketia, "Interaction Through Music," 643.

Toward a Theory of Christian Music Communication

interpretation of musical sound. Such an approach has informed this study of music as communication among the Senufo.

But we must go a step further. The music event as a whole must become the focal point for studying the processes involved in creating meaning through the various interactions between participants and the actual production of music. As Ruth Stone has pointed out: "Studying music processually is accomplished by analyzing the transmission and reception components of the interpretive process."[28] Thus, there is a need to study the basic materials of a music event, including musical sound, song texts, and drama, that facilitate the transmission of a message. There is, however, also the need to study the reception of the "impacts" that are generated through a music event by the participants in the music event.

The term "music event" has a wide range of meanings, and the discussion of these meanings has a history within ethnomusicology. The concept "music event" has been used to range from musical "performance," studied in small units such as individual musical phrases or single musical pieces, to a much broader usage in vogue among sociologists.[29] One sociologist, Richard H. Brown, helps us understand this broader usage when he states,

> The very idea of "experience" or "having an experience" presupposes that certain phenomena have been defined as "events" and typified into a "set." A picnic, our trip to France, getting married, mother's operation *became* experiences to the extent that they are organized in the imagination into beginnings, middles, and ends, or into some other principles of form, cogency, and closure.[30]

For our purposes, when I speak of music event, I am speaking of it in this broader sense. A music event consists of a musical experience as it might be perceived by a group of people.

One must ask, then, how the participants in the music event interpret the transmission of signals? The interaction of the participants within a music event becomes the epicenter of this dissertation in that they, the participants, are the ones who create meaning. Participants within a music event are not limited to the musicians themselves. Rather,

> The participants in music events include both the individuals producing music and the people experiencing the music performance

---

28. Stone, *Let the Inside Be Sweet*, 34.
29. Ibid., 21–23.
30. Ibid., 23.

as listeners or audience, and the auditors' meanings and interpretations are just as significant as those of the performers.[31]

This definition of participant is especially important to Christian music communication, since the desire of the church is to communicate a specific message and to have it received and understood in a clear way. Participants are the interpreters of communication and thus determine the evaluation and meaning of the event, for as Blacking has commented, "Music can communicate nothing to unprepared and unreceptive minds."[32]

Thus, we note that for ethnomusicologists the study of music communication has developed so that it involves the study of the music event in terms of its musical sound and structures, its song texts, its dance, and the participants as they interact within the music event. A theory concerning music as communication, though somewhat small, is developing in which both the musical and the social are being considered. My own personal approach is to build on this in light of another path that may feed into the flow of ethnomusicology, with many of its principles already alluded to-that of communication theory.

Communication Theory: An Adjunct Path

Communication is complex and multi-faceted. It is an all-encompassing study, much the same as music, in that it deals with all of life as people attempt to express themselves and influence one another. Crucial to our considerations in this study of music communication are two categories of theoretical models as delineated by Jorgensen,[33] interaction and transaction models.

Interaction Models of Communication

Interaction models of communication emphasize that communication is a process. It is not uni-directional as in the "hypodermic needle model"[34] but defines communication as "a dynamic process whereby human behavior, both verbal and nonverbal, is perceived and responded to."[35] There is a reciprocity in communication, where the receiver indicates his/her response with what is termed as "feedback." The goal of a communication event is to bring about interaction in such a way that the understanding

---

31. Ibid., 4.
32. Blacking, *A Common Sense View*, 30.
33. Jorgensen, "Role and Function of the Media," 17–35.
34. Rogers and Shoemaker, *The Communication of Innovations*, 272.
35. Samovar and Porter, *Intercultural Communication*, 5.

of the receptor corresponds with the intent of the communicator.[36] Such communication is dependent on bringing into alignment numerous factors that influence the communication event. Models dealing with communication as interaction abound. We will restrict our attention to three of these models.

Berlo's work on "The Process of Communication" reveals the emphasis of his approach. He focuses on the dictionary definition of process as "any phenomenon which shows a continuous change in time" or "any continuous operation or treatment."[37] With such a concept of process, communication events and relationships must be viewed as dynamic, ongoing, ever-changing, and continuous. Communication is not static.

In his model (see Figure 3), Berlo deals with the four major factors in the communication process of source, message, channel, and receiver. For each of these factors, he elucidates the ingredients significant to each one. This is a strength in his model. He recognizes, for example, that both the source and the receiver will be influenced by their communication skills, attitudes, knowledge, social system, and culture as they interact in the communication process. It is such ingredients that interact within the process of communication where each one affects all the other ingredients.[38]

Berlo defines interaction as the "ideal" of communication and its goal. The purpose of this interaction is to influence people. In other words a communicator is "to become an affecting agent, to affect others, our physical environment, and ourselves, and to become a determining agent, to have a vote in how things are. In short, we communicate to influence-to affect with intent."[39]

---

36. C. Kraft, *Christianity in Culture*, 394.
37. Berlo, *The Process of Communication*, 23.
38. Ibid., 24.
39. Ibid., 58.

**Figure 3
Ingredients in Communication
(adapted from Berlo's Model – 1960:72)**

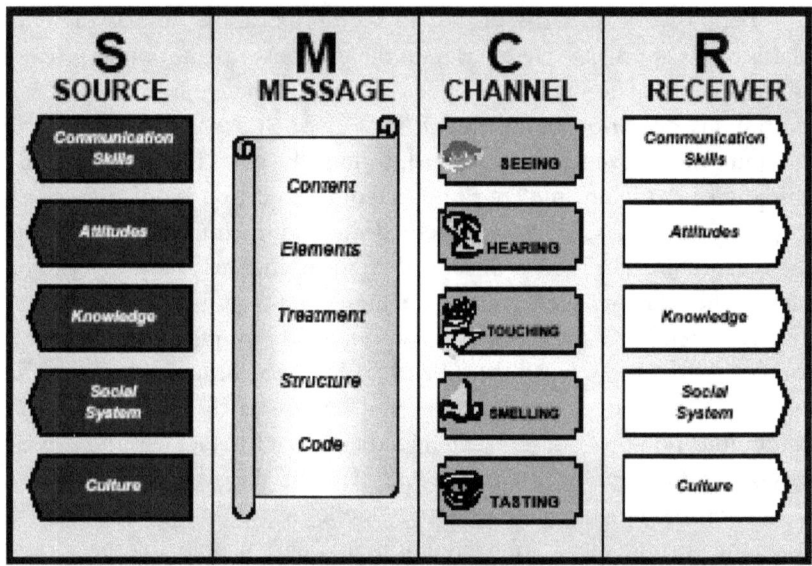

The second interaction model is Engel's interpersonal communication model. He, too, has dealt with the four basic factors in the communication process but has indicated more clearly the possible avenues through which interaction may take place.

Figure 4
Engel's Interpersonal Communication Model (1979:39)

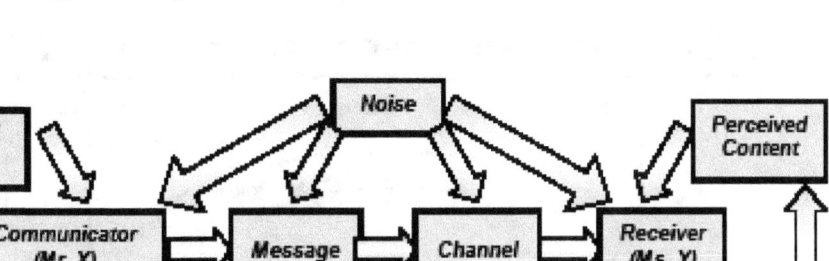

The strong features of this model are the recognition that (1) there are various possibilities for noise, (2) the communicator brings to the communication process his/her own agenda including both intended content and intended effect, and (3) the receiver perceives the content through his/her own eyes and thus is the one who determines the actual effect of the communication event. The fact that it is the receiver who decides the actual effect of the communication leads Engel to state that the receptor is "sovereign."[40]

McCroskey's model serves as our third interaction model (see Figure 5). Originating from the field of speech communication it is applicable to human communication in general. This model indicates more clearly the circular process of communication—that it is an ongoing process. Note how this is indicated through the "Feedback-Induced Adaptation" that has resulted from feedback coming via the feedback channel.

What I find particularly helpful in this model is the indication of the processing that occurs prior to and after a communication event. This shows the influence of the social and cultural context on participants involved in the communication process. In addition, McCroskey increases our understanding that noise may occur in all sections of the total communication process causing distortion of the intended message. In his model, McCroskey does not indicate the possibility of sending messages through multiple channels as is the case in music communication.

---

40. Ibid., 57.

Figure 5

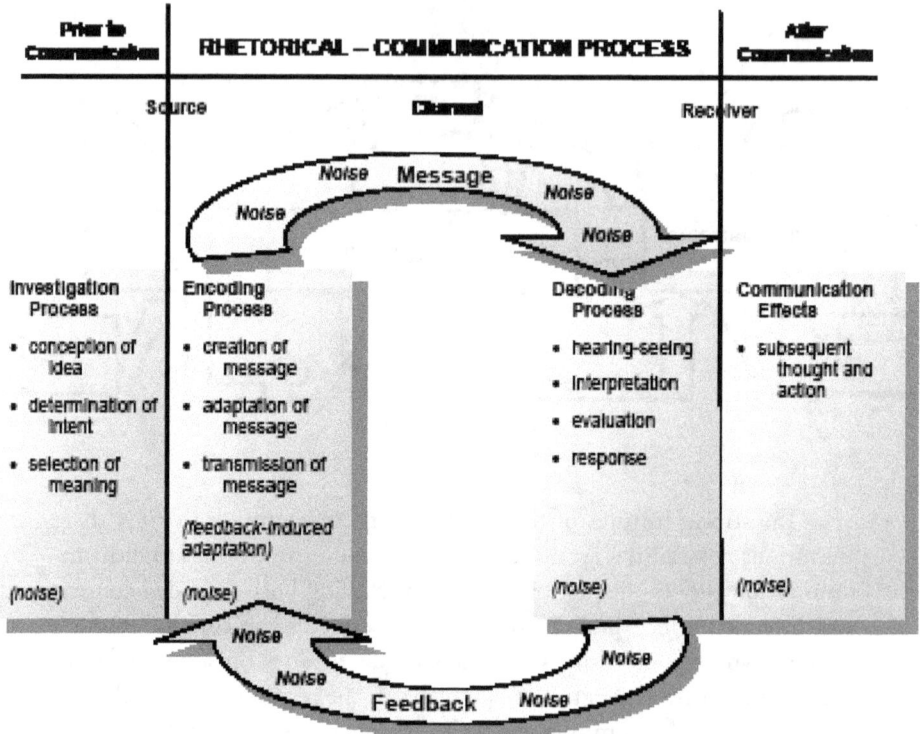

From James C. Mc Croskey *An Introduction To Rhetorical Communication: A Western Rhetorical Perspective*, 9e. Published by Allyn and Bacon, Boston, MA. Copyright © 2006 by Pearson Education. Adapted by permission of the publisher.

Transaction Models of Communication

The transaction models build on the basic components of communication as developed in the interaction models. However, they take the whole process a step further. Rather than focusing merely on the relationships between source, message, and receptor, a transactional approach sees communication as "the process of creating a meaning."[41]

Building on the concept that meanings are in the message-user,[42] Barnlund states that the aim of communication is

---

41. Jorgensen, "Role and Function of the Media," 28.
42. Berol, *The Process of Communication*, 175.

... to increase the number and consistency of meanings within the limits set by attitude and action patterns that have proven successful in the past, emerging needs and drives, and the demands of physical and social setting of the moment. It is not a reaction to something, nor an interaction with something, but a transaction in which man invents and attributes meanings to realize his purpose.[43]

Thus it is that meaning is something that is assigned or given to a communication event rather than something merely sent and received. The important aspect of communication then becomes the production of meaning rather than simply the production of messages.[44] In addition to recognizing such interaction concepts of communication as dynamic, circular, and complex, Jorgensen summarizes four new concepts suggested by Barnlund's model:

(1) Communication is continuous: it is "a continuing condition of life, a process that ebbs and flows with changes in the environment and fluctuations in our needs" (in Sereno and Mortensen 1970:89), thus focusing on the process-orientation already mentioned. (2) Communication is unrepeatable: communication is not a mechanical thing where one can expect the same message to produce the same effect over and over again. Rather we are dealing with a spontaneous system of people assigning meanings under constantly changing conditions. (3) Communication is irreversible: human communication is evolutionary, it flows forward and never backward. To think that one can erase the effects and "begin again" is an illusion. (4) Communication involves the total personality: we cannot divide body and mind, thought and action. The assigning of meaning implies also some sort of behavior involvement.[45]

The implications of both these two theoretical approaches to communication are far-reaching when applied to music communication and may be incorporated as we develop a model for music communication.

A Music Communication Model

My own approach to music communication draws from both the interactional and transactional models. Music communication is based on interaction between the participants and the channels employed in the music

---
43. Jorgensen, "Role and Function of the Media," 29.
44. Ibid.
45. Ibid., 29–30.

event. The dynamics of the total music event will, however, stimulate the meanings that are assigned via the transactions that develop.

In this model (see Figure 6), everyone involved in the music-making event is a participant. This is especially applicable to music-making within African societies (that is the Senufo) when using the call-and-response song form. Both the sources and the receptors are active participants. Due to roles of leadership, there is a designated "initiator" participant and the "interactant" participants who respond during the music-making event. They each come to the event with their own experiences, needs, and intentions.

Figure 6
(modeled after McCroskey 1972:25)

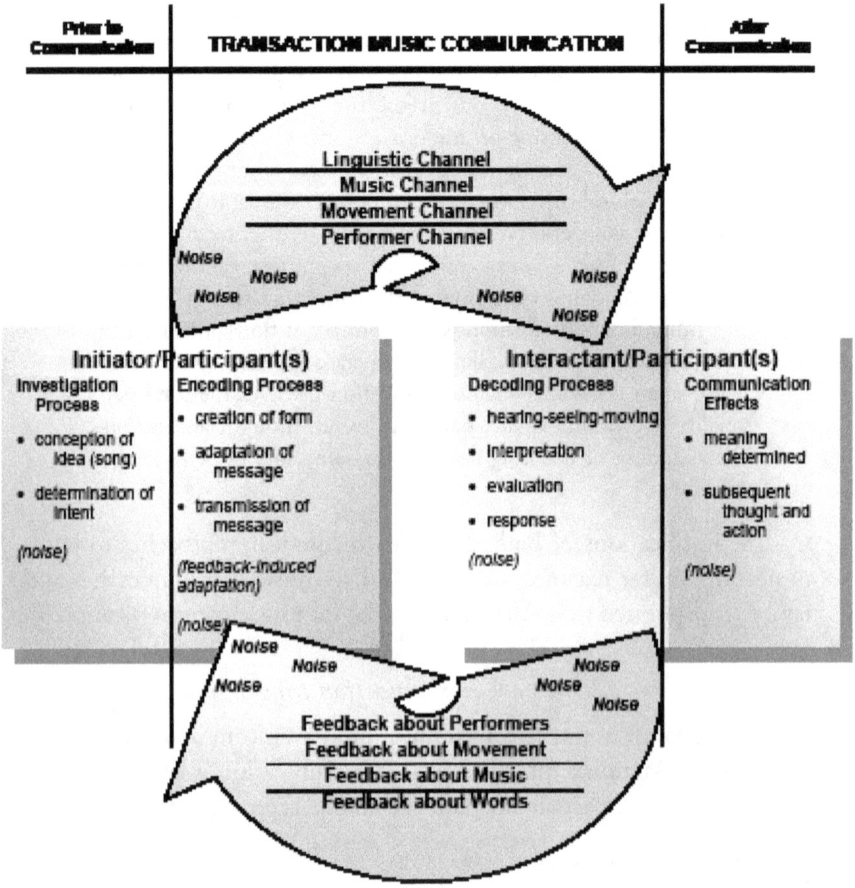

Prior to Communication	TRANSACTION MUSIC COMMUNICATION	After Communication

Linguistic Channel
Music Channel
Movement Channel
Performer Channel

Noise Noise Noise Noise Noise Noise

Initiator/Participant(s)

Investigation Process
- conception of idea (song)
- determination of intent

(noise)

Encoding Process
- creation of form
- adaptation of message
- transmission of message

(feedback-induced adaptation)

(noise)

Interactant/Participant(s)

Decoding Process
- hearing-seeing-moving
- interpretation
- evaluation
- response

(noise)

Communication Effects
- meaning determined
- subsequent thought and action

(noise)

Noise Noise Noise Noise Noise Noise

Feedback about Performers
Feedback about Movement
Feedback about Music
Feedback about Words

Toward a Theory of Christian Music Communication

Unique to the model is the viewing of what is usually seen as a single communication channel divisible into four channels. These four channels include the actual musical sound that is generated, the linguistic channel, consisting of the song texts and any other language acts involved in the music event, and the movement channel that involves dance and any other kinesic symbolism. This is parallel to Nketia's specifications for the study of music interactions as noted above. The fourth channel is the performers (participants) themselves, for they are the ones who actually facilitate the music event around which the dynamics of the communication process are generated. Opportunities for interaction and feedback between the participants abound and are necessary for such events, thus playing a significant role in the communication process.

In this model, music communication can also be seen, (1) as a continuation or extension of life processes, (2) as unrepeatable events for each music event changes according to the particular situation, (3) as irreversible in its effects, and (4) as involving the total personalities of its participants who assign meaning to the event. This is supported in Nketia's statement concerning music in African societies: "It [music] permeates all fields of social action in which interpersonal relations and roles have to be acted out, affirmed or re-defined, or occasions on which spontaneous interaction is encouraged."[46] This model, then, becomes the theoretical basis upon which our case study among the Senufo is carried out in an attempt to determine how and why the use of culturally appropriate songs make a difference in the effective communication of the Christian message.

In addition to the model, it is important to summarize and elaborate several of the basic principles concerning music communication that underlie the following study:

Principles Concerning Music Communication

(1) A Music Event is a Communication Event: Each participant who comes to the music event will derive and assign meanings to the event. Both the initiators and the interactants will either create music or listen to it with the intention of creating meaning(s) out of the event and its various components.

(2) Music Communication is a Process: It is dynamic, on-going, ever-changing and continuous.

(3) Music Communication Involves Four Main components: These components are: (1) The music initiator participants, (2) the chan-

---
46. Nketia, "Interaction Through Music," 640.

nels through which communication is facilitated and transmitted, (3) the music interactant participants, and (4) the messages that are intended to be communicated.

(4) Music Communication Employs Multiple Channels: Music communication incorporates (1) the musical sound channel, (2) the linguistic channel, (3) the movement or kinesic channel, and (4) the actual participants/performers, as channels. Each of these are effective channels of communication in themselves but when they are appropriately combined their impact is much greater than each channel individually. The whole is greater than the sum of the parts.

(5) The Meaning of a Music Communication Event is Determined by the Participants: The participants as they are interacting within the music event are deriving and assigning meaning to the multiple messages and interactions with which they are participating. Music communication is transactional.

(6) Meaning in Music Communication is Unrepeatable: Meaning deriving from a music event will change with each presentation of a particular musical item, such as a song, or a longer progression of musical items within a larger music event.

(7) Music Communication Involves the Total Person: The music event allows the person to become totally involved. There is no clear separation between the affective, cognitive, and behavioral aspects of a person. The use of multiple channels enhances the effectiveness of music communication.

(8) Meaning in Music Communication is Multi-level. The multiple contexts of the participants play a role in the assigning of meaning to an event. The interpretation of a music event is based on (1) the immediate interactions within the music event itself, (2) the social and cultural contexts of the participants as a group and (3) the personal experiences that determine to a more specific degree the meanings assigned to the music event by individual participants.

The Payoff for Missiology

We have discussed two ethnomusicological paths and the potential for merging those with a communication path. Our aim is, however, to arrive at a missiological payoff. Within the field of missiology itself are several paths that converge in pursuance of the goal of extending the Kingdom

Toward a Theory of Christian Music Communication

of God—the ultimate task of doing mission. These contributing paths of missiology include interaction between the fields of theology, church growth, cultural anthropology, and ethnohistory (see Figure 7). Likewise, the path of music communication has a contribution to make to missiology as it interacts with the other major paths it serves as an ally in conjunction with the several academic paths already developed within missiology.

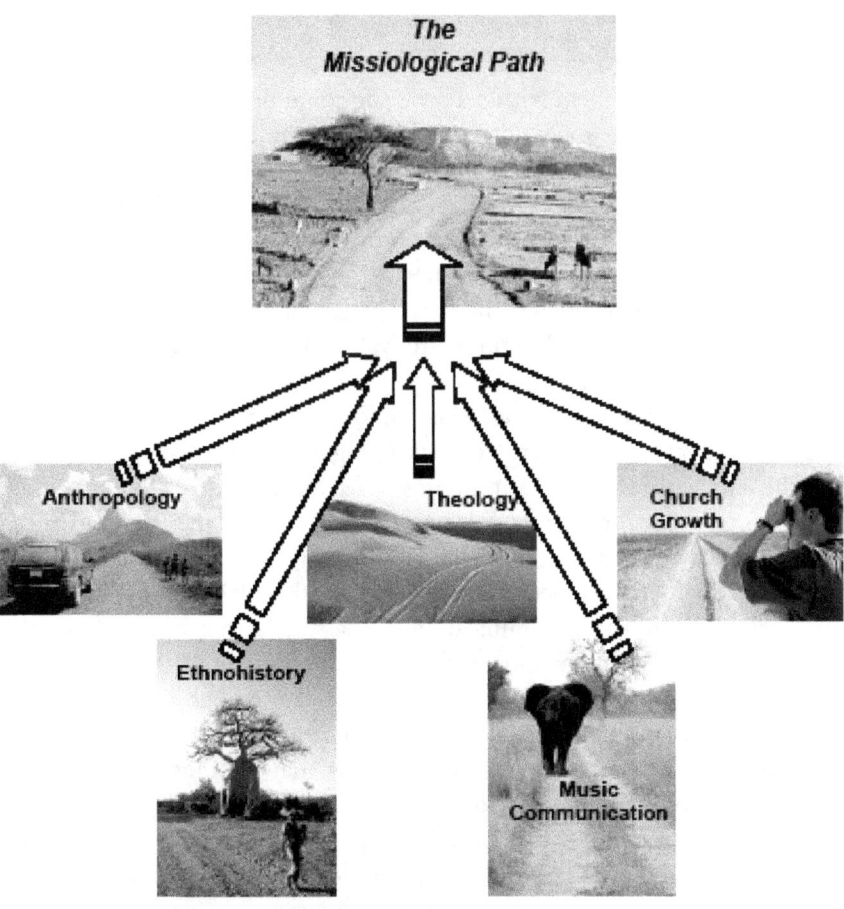

Figure 7
The Converging Paths Within Missiology

Figure 7 is intended to simply show missiology as a major path into which flows the contributing, more specific areas of study. Music communication may be seen as an essential path within the main missiological path.

In-depth investigations addressing the "how" and "why" of music communication's interaction between the various components in missiology are limited. Valid and helpful studies have, however, provided a base from which to develop a substantive field of music communication within missiology. We look now at a number of the initiatives set out by these forerunners to music communication and the potential interactions between theology, anthropology, church growth, and ethnohistory.

Music Communication and Theology

Theological development within a believing community in a cross-cultural context is one of the main concerns of missiology. This concern provides a major impetus for pursuing meaningful music communication within missions. Missiologists are interested in accurately perceived, information-based messages of Christianity. Songs provide occasions for the transmission of cognitive information and theological understandings. Hiebert affirms this in his reference to the development of a "lyric theology." In a South Indian case study. From this study, he substantiates the storing of a people's beliefs in their songs.[47]

Alan R. Tippett, on the other hand, focuses on the frequency of singing specific hymns as a means of developing a popular theological index of the laity within a given community.[48] He underscores the shaping of a people's theology through the selection of song texts for their content and the frequency of their use. Songs, then, not only serve as a storehouse of people's beliefs but also help to form a people's theological storehouse.

However, music communication goes a step further when Klem investigates oral communication techniques for communicating the scripture or Bible content.[49] His work serves as a breakthrough in overtly recognizing that music communicates with impact. His research, carried out in Nigeria, underscores the enlightening fact that the music (songs) are not merely entertainment but that they effectively transmit information. Though he focuses on communicating cognitive content and theological teachings via the use of music (song), he does not, however, investigate the unique ways in which music accomplishes its task of communication.

---

47. Hiebert, *Anthropological Insights for Missionaries*, 162.
48. Tippett, *Solomon Islands Christianity*, 186–196.
49. Klem, *Oral Communication of the Scripture*.

Thus, the study does not attempt to address "music as sound," but rather, the focus is on music as an educational tool for biblical theological training.

Music Communication and Church Growth

Another area of interaction within missiology is between music communication and church growth. For the most part, the inferences between music communication and church growth have been related more to the growth of churches in a non-technical sense. That is to say, the assumption has been composed of stipulations that correlate the relevance of music communication to the growth of churches in general outside of the technical, theoretical aspects of church growth as a discipline.

The correlation between the use of culturally appropriate music and the growth of churches in general, however, has perhaps served as the major music communication thrust within missiology. The discussion of the necessity of developing indigenous hymnody has been based on the assumption that indigenous hymns will make a major contribution to church growth. This discussion has been limited for the most part to music specialists who also happen to be missionaries. Their main focus has been on music products, indigenous hymnody, and how to go about creating them. Vida Chenoweth, an ethnomusicologist and Bible translator, has led the forefront in this discussion. Drawing from her emphasis on ethnomusicology as the study of "music as sound," her journal articles offer important guidelines in approaching the oral musical traditions of another society, list the dangers of introducing western hymns into another culture, and suggest that indigenous composers be encouraged to write hymns.[50]

Likewise, the November-December, 1962 issue of *Practical Anthropology* was devoted specifically to issues in developing indigenous hymnodies. Within its articles are discussions of such issues as the spontaneous development of local musical traditions for Christian worship and witness[51] and specific problems in uniting language and tune in West Africa.[52]

For the most part, then, music has been studied in terms of its musical sound, focusing mainly on the development of indigenous hymns.[53] It has been assumed that indigenous hymns will aid in the task of evan-

---

50. Chenoweth and Bee, "On Ethnic Music, 205–212; Chenoweth, "Spare Them Western Music!" 30–35; Chenoweth, *Melodic Perception and Analysis*.
51. L. King, "Indigenous Hymnody of the Ivory Coast', 268–270.
52. Riccitelli, "Developing Non-Western Hymnody," 241–256.
53. Friesen, "A Methodology in the Development of Indigenous Hymnody."

gelism and church growth. With this emphasis on the "music as sound" within ethnomusicology, "music as behavior" has not been fully discussed or developed. One wants to ask whether the development of indigenous hymnodies really has made a difference in the growth of churches and if so, how.

Music Communication and Anthropology

Ethnomusicology and anthropology form the locus of greatest interaction within the larger path of missiology. With ethnomusicology's strong roots in anthropology, it seems quite apparent that there is a wealth of gleanings to be obtained between the two fields. For the most part, though, early missiological literature has been concerned with simply making a plea for the value of musics that sound different to the missionary ear. It is, indeed, a very important plea for those who are working cross-culturally. The appreciation of differing musics is just one of the aspects of encouraging the learning of the value of cultures. Eugene Nida, for example, in his chapter on "Drums and Drama." In *Customs and Cultures*, effectively argues the fact that music is not a universal language (a basic tenet of the field of ethnomusicology) but he does so in non technical terms that missionaries can understand.

Although they are sparse, a few writings that speak to the "music as behavior" side of ethnomusicology have appeared. Nketia's article, "The Contribution of African Culture to Christian Worship," for example, reflects his emphasis on the need to be aware of the cultural implications, importance, and influences in the use of African cultural forms, such as music within Christian worship. However, ethnomusicological issues concerning the study of music as event and specific studies in worldview as reflected in song texts, the construction of and symbolism in musical instruments, and the actual organization of musical sound have yet to appear within missiology.

Music Communication and Ethnohistory

Related to anthropological approaches to missiology, is an area of study designated as ethnohistory. Exploring the historical context of African church music, Warnock examines "the nature of the culture contact which has taken place between Africa and the West."[54] Significantly, he shows how the period 1919–1957 experienced an appreciable softening of the church's attitude toward African music. This presented African Christians

---

54. Warnock, "Trends in African Church Music," viii.

with the "freedom to blend elements from the West (usually harmony) with materials from Africa (usually rhythm and melody)" in the most recent period of African church history, 1958–1982.[55] Although his study speaks of Africa in general terms, it raises important issues related to developing culturally appropriate songs within changing African societies. The focus is on the dynamic, ever-changing aspects of societies as reflected through their musics, an issue that confronts missiology repeatedly.

Music Communication

Finally, although the use of music in Christian communication is highly regarded within missiology, regular and systematic approaches to the study of Christian music communication have not yet developed. Music is generally viewed as one of the several alternative communicational vehicles available to the missionary who is interested in creating a "dynamically equivalent message." In the process of transculturation,[56] Kraft encourages the use of alternative communication codes over what he considers to be at times the less-effective form of monologue preaching. Thus, he helpfully acknowledges and focuses on the importance of music as a communication code within missiology.[57]

More specifically in relation to communication, two issues that speak directly to the basic tenets of my own investigation have been offered as tentative approaches to music communication within the Christian context. First, the discussion of multiple channels working within the music communication process and the need for bringing into agreement what has been designated as two channels, the musical and the linguistic, in hymnody.[58] This is helpful when looking at music as a product. The discussion takes place, however, on a purely theoretical plane and has not looked at the cultural concepts of music and what is included within a music event. Thus, the discussion lacks a treatment of other channels that may be included, such as movement, within the music event.

The second issue arises out of Goodeau's set of guidelines for developing indigenous hymnody. Of particular interest is his definition of "indigenous hymnody" that is not centered around a pure musical form such as "traditional African music," but rather it focuses on a people's response and identification with the musician keeping with communication theory and anthropological principles. This has great implications for the

---

55. Ibid., ix.
56. C. Kraft, *Christianity in Culture*, 281.
57. C. Kraft, *Communication Theory for Christian Witness*, 155–156.
58. Goodeau, "Toward an Indigenous Huymnody," 29.

development of what I designate as "culturally appropriate" songs. These two issues represent only the beginning of rich music communication interaction with missiology.

Summary

A thorough study of the dynamics of music communication events within the life of the Church is imperative. The recognition of the role of music as it interfaces with theology, church growth, anthropology, and ethnohistory in the task of missions has formed, up to this point, something of a missiological blind spot. This is quite astonishing when considering the amount of time that "music events" occupy in worship services and other church occasions. The assumptions are that music communicates and that "indigenous hymnodies" are a requirement. However, the implications of Christian music communication as it relates to Christian mission need to be developed and studied in a systematic way.

It is my contention that ethnomusicology, with its two major paths of studying "music as sound" and "music as behavior," has a major contribution to make to missiology. The discussions should not be limited to developing "indigenous hymnodies" and a few overt references to cultural contexts, however. The dynamics and impact of Christian music communication when studied in terms of musical sound, process, context, event, and social dimensions present missiology with approaches that have yet to be explored. We turn now to an initial attempt to begin that journey through our case study of Christian music communication among the Senufo of Côte d'Ivoire.

PART TWO

Background to the Case Study

4

The Senufo and Their Life-Paths

THE SENUFO-SPEAKING PEOPLE OF West Africa stretch across the north of Côte d'Ivoire (Ivory Coast), the southeast of Mali, the southwestern region of Burkina Faso, and along the Ghana-Côte d'Ivoire border. Their number exceeds one million, with more than 700,000 settled in the north of Côte d'Ivoire in addition to those who have migrated to the commercial city center of Abidjan.[1]

The Korhogo region, the focus of this study and often referred to as the capital of the Senufos, boasts the highest concentration of Senufos at more than 300,000. Eighty-four percent of the population lives in rural areas. This is shifting somewhat, however, with the influx of students coming to Korhogo town for schooling. At the time of the 1975 census, 42% of the population was under 15 years of age with only 48% of the youth attending schools. Beyond that only a small percentage of the students, approximately 30%, succeed beyond the primary school level. Thus the literacy rate is estimated at 10%.[2]

The "Senufo language" is classified as a member of the Gur or Voltaic subgroup of the Niger-Congo family. What such a classification calls a single language, however, is more accurately seen as a grouping of languages and dialects reflecting an ethnic grouping of people referred to as the Senufo.[3] Linguists have now identified thirteen distinct languages referred to generically as Senari (see Map 1). Dialects exist within each division of these distinct Senari languages.

It is important to note that no one group of people calls itself Senufo. Mills elucidates on the possible origin of the Senari-speaking peoples' reference to themselves as Senabele in relation to the more generic term Senufo:

> The people of the greater Senari area call themselves Senao (singular) and Senabele (plural). Possibly the stems *senou* of Senoufo and

---

1. E. Mills, *Senufo Phoonology*, xiii.
2. Republique de Côte d'Ivoire, "Recensement General de la Population," 44.
3. Mills, *Senufo Phoonology*, xv.

> *sena* of Senao have the same origin. The suffix *fo* of Senoufo may come from the Dyula word "speak." The idea of *sena* may be "field man" or "belonging to the field," thus coming from a combination of the stems of *seʔe* "field" and *nao* "man" or *na* "pertaining to, belonging to." This concept fits the fact that the people who call themselves Senao are traditionally farmers, and that Senoufo people of the same area who are not traditionally farmers but are artisans call themselves by the names of their artisan groups, i.e., *kpeeo* "brass worker, pottery maker," *fono* "iron worker."[4]

Each group of people, however, identifies itself according to the dialect they speak. For example, although the people who live around the Korhogo area are Senari-speakers, they speak the Cebaara dialect and the people are referred to as cebabele.

The Senufo's main occupation is farming. Since farming is pursued under extremely difficult conditions, yet necessary for existence, the identity of the Senufo is locked up in being disciplined, skilled, and productive in farming. Great prestige and respect is gained for the farmer who earns the title of "champion cultivator." Referring to these "champion cultivators," Glaze asserts, "Respected during their lifetime and paid special tribute at commemorative funerals, champion cultivators may even be said to achieve a degree of immortality since they are venerated as ancestral champions of their *katiolo*."[5] To be venerated as an ancestral champion of a *katiolo* (village) carries great distinction since the katiolo is composed of several settlements of residents, including the dominant farmer population and several of the artisan groups. The recognition of one's skill and discipline as a farmer reinforces one of the major motifs of the Senufo sense of identity.

Historically, artisan groups have migrated into the Senufo area and have become integrated into the society. They are blacksmiths, brass casters, woodcarvers, weavers, and leatherworkers. Ethnographers have discussed the relationship between the *senambele*, the farmers, and the *fijembele*, the artisans, as a possible caste system as found in other parts of West Africa. Richter points out quite convincingly, though, that it is not possible to consider the artisans a caste since this implies a hierarchical ranking.[6] Rather than being inferior groups, they are just "different," providing necessary services such as carved wood domestic and ritual items. Glaze contributes to this understanding when she claims, "These artisan

---

4. Ibid.
5. Glaze, *Art and Death*, 8.
6. Richter, "Further Considerations," 52.

groups are thoroughly Senufo in terms of language and other cultural features shared with their neighbors."⁷

Photo 5: Senufo graineries where food is tored.

A Senufo village serves as a "residential and cooperative work unit where the members share not only the same general living space but also the food harvested from communally worked land."⁸ As a matrilineal society, the women play a decisive role in village organization. Indeed, each village has its own set of male and female leadership. The male elders serve as a type of village council, while the village chief is selected from males of matrilineal descent from the village's founding family. The women, on the other hand, function as religious leaders.⁹

---

7. Glaze, *Art and Death,* 4.
8. Ibid.
9. For further ethnographical sources on the Senufo, see S. Coulibaly, *Le Paysan Senoufo*; Eid, *Paroles de Devin*; Gottschalk, *Madebele*; Holas, *L'Art Sacre Senoufo*; Keletigui, *Le Senoufo Face au Cosmos*; Kientz, *Dieu et les Genies*; Knops *Les Anciens Senufo*; Krieg and Lohse, "Kunst und Religion bei den Gbato-Senufo."

Traditional Religious Paths of the Senufo

In Senufo society, of course, there are well developed political, economic, social, and religious institutions. Our primary concern is with those cultural institutions that concern themselves predominately with the "restoration and maintenance of right relationships with the hierarchy of spiritual beings"[10] and with the worldview values that support them. Worship, prayers, and sacrifices are directed towards spiritual beings of which there are three distinct groups:

> . . . the creator deity (*kulocolo*) has priority and supreme authority. Ancestral spirits (*kuubele*, literally "the dead ones") and nature spirits (called *ndebele, madebele,* or *tugule* according to dialect) complete the three basic categories of spiritual beings believed to influence every aspect of personal and community life and requiring careful ritual attention.[11]

In addition to maintaining a hierarchy of personified spirits there is a belief in magical and impersonal sources of power that may be appropriated by an individual, based on acquired knowledge and ritual. Malignant spirits and witches are also included in the overall scheme.

At the core of these beliefs is the concept of a bipartite deity. "*Kolocɔlɔɔ*" represents the divine creator aspect of the Deity, while *kaceleeo* serves as the protective, nurturing being.[12] The female side of the deity, *kaceleeo* is often referred to as the "Ancient Mother" and works at the level of village life through the institution of the sacred forest and the Poro society. She rules over justice and punishment as murderers and thieves are brought before her sacred drum. In this way, crimes that threaten the well-being of the community as a whole are dealt with. The other aspect of this dualistic deity, *kolotyolo*, is seen as "a wholly good but relatively remote being responsible for the original Creation and for 'bringing us forth.'"[13] Since "*Kolocɔlɔɔ* is invisible and difficult to approach, two corollary spirit guises named *yirigefolo* and *nyeʔene* help make access to *Kolocɔlɔɔ* possible.[14]

---

10. Glaze, *Art and Death*, xii.
11. Glaze, "The Religious and Metaphysical," 1.
12. Glaze, *Art and Death*, 53.
13. Ibid., 54.
14. Ibid.

The Senufo and Their Life-Paths

Photo 6: *Boloye* dancers emerging from the sacred forest.

The Men's Society: Poro[15]

A level of organization at the village level integrally related to the spiritual organization of Senufo society as a whole is that of the two secret societies, one for men and one for women.[16] The *Poro* men's society provides a stabilizing and unifying force at the community level by knitting together social relationships across kinship lines and household ties. Based on a highly structured set of age grades, initiates are taught to "walk the path of *Poro*" that leads to responsibility, wisdom, authority, and power. It serves as a type of education system. Ultimately, the *Poro's* major goal is to main-

---

15. In discussing the *Poro* as a life-path among the Senufo, I am not seeking to infer endorsement of this secret society. There are many negative aspects as it relates to Christianity. Indeed, the *Poro* has served as the major confrontive source of persecution for the Senufo Christians. The major conflict between the *Poro* and Christianity has been in the area of allegiance. Senufo believers have given their allegiance to Jesus Christ, as opposed to the Satanic beings that call for allegiance found within the *Poro* society. Although I have not been able to adequately investigate the relationship between the *Poro* and Christianity, I believe there is a need to adequately understand the *Poro* in terms of cultural forms and worldview understandings.

16. For further reading about both the *Poro* and *Sande* societies of West Africa, see Bellman, *The Language of Secrecy*; Butt-Thompson *West African Secret Societies*; Gibbs, "Poro Values and Courtroom Procedures"; Harley, *Notes on the Poro in Liberia*; Monts, "Conflict, Accommodation, and Transformation."

tain right relationships with the Deity and the ancestors. Thus, every male is expected to become a member of *Poro*. A non-*Poro* member is virtually considered an outcast in the society.

Photo 7: Dancing the highly popular and acrobatic *boloye* dance at a parade in the town of Korhogo.

The Women's Society: Sandogo

The *Sandogo*, the women's counterpart to the *Poro*, functions as a divination society and provides powerful female leadership for the many extended households and kinship groups in the village. There is only one *Sandogo* society per village that includes representation from each household and matrilineal segment. The head of this society is referred to as "the Sando-Mother." Each household and matrilineal segment is represented in the society. There is a kind of "calling out" ritual when a female is selected to be consecrated into the society.

Members of *Sandogo* are responsible for both the social and religious domains of village life. Just as the *Poro* society exercises social controls and limits, the *Sandogo* work in this area by protecting and maintaining the sanctity of engagement and the marriage contract.[17] The *Sandogo* carry on a distinctive work in the religious area. According to Glaze,

---

17. Glaze, *Art and Death*, 12.

> ... each *Sando* (a member of *Sandogo*) is charged with the ritual maintenance of good relationships with beings of the supernatural world, although in practice not all Sandogo novices are able to master the demanding techniques of divination. The diviner acts as an interpreter and intermediary between the village people and their deity, the ancestors, spirits of twins, and, in particular, the bush spirits.[18]

The role of intermediary that the *Sandogo* women perform is especially strong. For example, the women have a very special part in the men's *Poro* society in the areas of ideology and ritual, where the spiritual figurehead of the men's society is a woman. The *Sandogo's* presence is absolutely necessary for the founding of a new *Poro* society and the establishment of its sacred forest sanctuary. Thus, women ultimately have more responsibility than men for seeking the goodwill and blessings of the Deity, the ancestors, and the bush spirits.

Since the *Sandogo* diviner's intermediating with the supernatural world is considered indispensable, all village decisions and performances of ritual acts are dependent on consultation with a *Sandogo* diviner. Her work is carried out in very secretive conditions. She practices divination within a small consultation chamber, where she creates an atmosphere of supernatural power through "the display of glittering yet bewildering visual forms."[19]

The Sacred Forest: Sinzanga

Another aspect of Senufo culture important to the overall religious system of the Senufo is the Sacred Forest known as *Sinzanga*. These are the sanctuaries of the *Poro* society that are found in dense groves of trees on the perimeter of the village. According to Glaze, the *Sinzanga* and its buildings are used as a "school, apolitical meeting house, a place of worship, and a kind of hidden "backstage" where the initiates prepare for ritual and theatrical performances."[20] Symbolically, each group is viewed as the family compound and village (*katiolo*) of the Ancient Mother deity. It is an intimate place where the ruling Deity may reside, work, and eat among the people. Members of the *Poro* society are considered to be her children. "This sanctuary, at an abstract level, is the nexus of divine and temporal authority in the Senufo village."[21]

---

18. Ibid.
19. Ibid, 57.
20. Ibid, 11.
21. Ibid, 53.

The Path of Islam[22]

While the traditional religious tenets of the Senufo remain at the core of their cultural institutions and worldview understandings, the external influence of Islam has added an additional level to much of Senufo religious thinking. The introduction of Islam to the Senufo is generally thought to have followed the islamization of the Mande-Jula during the 16th century near the fall of the Mali Empire when military advances brought them into Senufo territory. Jula kola traders may also have introduced Islam as they continued on their trading trails. Nevertheless, the 18th–19th century wars provided the main occasion for the expansion of Islam among the Senufo.[23]

Islam did not pose any major opposition to the fundamentals of Senufo religion. Functional substitutes within their system easily lined up with the Islamic teachings brought by the Mande-Julas. For example, the *mandebele*, bush spirits, of the Senufo correspond to the *dyna* of the Jula, while the *Sando* diviners functioned somewhat parallel to the *marabout*.[24] Further assimilation with the Jula life-style in conjunction with Islam emerges with the Senufo systematically exchanging their *fe*, family totems based on philosophical values represented by animals, for the more attractive Jula names. "The *Senoufo Soro* (leopard) became the Mande Coulibaly; *Yeo* (antelope) became Ouattara, etc. for the five basic *febele*."[25]

The effect of Islam among the Senufo has been contested. At first glance, the general perception is that it has not had such a profound effect due to its adaptability to African traditions. Yet its integration into the Senufo life-style indicates that it is not without influence. Indeed, when confronted with the Christian Gospel a common response among the Senufo for rejection of following the "path of Jesus" is that, although they find Christianity attractive, they have already chosen to follow the "path of Islam" and cannot leave it.

The Paths of Christianity

Two major options, the Catholics and the Conservative Baptists, provide opportunities for following the Christian faith among the Senufo. Although their independent works are the predominant ones among the

---

22. Again, I am discussing the path of Islam at this point merely to point out the context of the Senufo situation as confronted by the path of Christianity. It is not meant as an endorsement of the religion.
23. Willetts, *The Senoufo*, 10.
24. Ibid.
25. Ibid.

Senufo-speaking peoples of the Korhogo region, a national work drawing from the Assemblies of God tradition exists in Korhogo town. Occasionally short-term evangelistic efforts have taken place by such groups as Campus Crusade for Christ in 1986. Jehovah's Witnesses and Mormon missionaries have also been known to do short-term work in the area. It is, however, the work of the Catholics and the Baptists that has continued over a period of time.

The Catholics

In contrast to the Islamization of the Senufo, which was gradually introduced by Africans to other Africans, Christianity was first introduced into the Senufo milieu by the *Peres Blancs* (White Fathers) in Mali and Burkina Faso, while the Fathers of the African Missions of Lyon penetrated the Senufo regions of Côte d'Ivoire. After their initial contact with the Senufo in 1902, Bedel and Fer settled in Korhogo in 1904 in order to begin their work.[26]

Among the Catholics' first approaches to evangelizing the Senufo was a major attack on all cultural institutions that they considered antithetical to Christianity. They viewed Senufo society as "polytheistic, fetishistic, slavish, and immoral."[27] The majority of the priests denounced the *Poro* and forbade Senufo converts to participate in it, to undergo its series of initiations, and to be involved in the sacrifices. After 1960, with the slow rate of acceptance of Christianity, a change in opinion and policy towards the *Poro* occurred. The *Poro* was now recognized for its role in maintaining and shaping such positive values among the youth as respect for the elderly, for order, and for discipline. Senufo converts were allowed to participate in the *Poro* as long as they were not forced by the *Poro* chiefs to actively participate in the sacrifices. The priests began to see the *Poro* as "the backbone of the Senoufo society. There where the *Poro* disappeared, anarchy reigned."[28]

Growth patterns among the catholic church have changed since that time. By 1979, the year of the 75th anniversary of the diocese in Korhogo, the Catholic church claimed 12,000 Christians and 8,000 catechumens.[29] Interestingly, on the eastern outskirts of Korhogo now stands their own version of a "sacred forest."

---

26. Ibid,, 11.
27. Ibid., 14.
28. Ibid., 12.
29. Ibid.

The Baptists

The first couple with the Conservative Baptist Foreign Mission Society to penetrate Senufo territory was Rev. and Mrs. Robert Welch. They established themselves about ten miles south of Korhogo near the village of Torhogo in 1947. Just as the Catholics had experienced resistance to the Christian message during their first exploits among the Senufo, the new work by Conservative Baptists discovered that the Senufo were highly resistant to Christianity. During the first five years of work, there were no professions of faith.

Although the Senufo were a friendly and hospitable people while listening to Gospel presentations, they would not leave their fetishes. The call to destroy their fetishes and to stop sacrificing was included in the call to put one's trust in Christ. This was definitely a foreign thought to those who depended on fetishes and sacrifice in order to maintain balance between themselves and the spirits. A pattern of physical and social persecution for those who chose to abandon their dependence on the traditional system emerged and effectively hindered others from following suit.

"In 1952 seven young men were the first to be baptized. The first woman was baptized in 1953."[30] By 1958, however, a small group of Baptist Christians started to form, numbering less than 100. There were those Senufo who were ready and willing to retire from their dependence on fetishes and sacrifices. The more successful attempts at communicating the Christian message, with whole groups making a commitment to follow Christ, were those that followed structural patterns of the society. For example, while preaching in one village, one of the listeners in the group invited Rev. Merril Skinner and Rev. Harold van den Berg to come and "give God's Word" to the people in his village. The missionaries requested that the chief and his elders must come and listen to the presentation. At the end of the first presentation, the chief requested that the two missionaries return the next week. Each presentation included the need to trust in Christ along with the act of abandoning their fetishes since they were not pleasing to God. The third time that the missionaries returned with basically the same message, the chief interrogated them, saying, "But we already abandoned our fetishes last week, what do we do now?" Although the message to abandon their fetishes ran counter to their cultural practices, recognition of the chief's leadership on the part of the missionaries showed the necessary respect for their traditions and opened the way for a whole group of people to follow the Christian way. They were more interested in knowing more about this creator God, *Kolocɔlɔɔ*, who was

---
30. Conservative Baptist Foreign mission Society, *Ivory Coast Report*, 4.

perceived as being distant, than to continue on with the futility of their fetishes.

Other approaches to evangelizing the Senufo have been incorporated into the overall mission strategy. Among the more effective and helpful is that of the medical aid given at both the dispensary in Torhogo and the hospital at Ferkessedougou, treating over 100,000 people annually. Since the Senufo perceive that it takes a great power to heal, they are more open to hearing about the God of those who are practicing the healing arts on them. Conversion testimonies almost always include an attestation to the fact that God healed them through prayer and the services rendered at one of these two medical facilities.

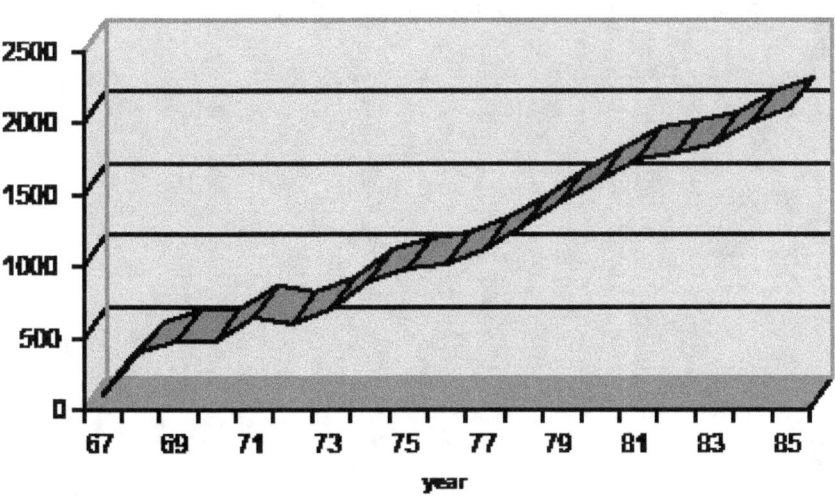

**Figure 3
Association of Evangelical Baptist Churches
of Côte d'Ivoire: Baptized Members**

Church Growth Chart
(CBFMS 1986:5)

Unfortunately, accurate statistics are not available for the early years of growth. However, with the official formation of an association of evangelical Baptist churches in 1967, more accurate statistics have been kept (see Figure 8). Church growth patterns since 1967 progress at a positive rate although somewhat slowly. From a small group of approximately 100 believers in 1967 the church has grown and claims 2400 communicants and over 5200 professing believers in 1987 (see Figure 8). Indeed, as the nationally administered Association of Evangelical Baptist Churches of Côte d'Ivoire celebrated its 20th anniversary in January 1988, they claimed 10,000 Christians, 186 churches, and 50 national pastors. The association is predominantly composed of Senufo believers but is also made up of immigrants, such as Nigerians and Jula-speakers, who have chosen to worship in the Baptist churches in the towns. The celebrations were so convincing of the church's strength among the Senufo that nonbelieving Senufos, who had formerly persecuted the church, admitted that "the Jesus road is here to stay."

One of the strikingly attractive features of the Senufo Baptist churches today is the development of its own indigenous style of praise and worship. Their songs are so attractive that they are borrowed by the Catholics and also serve as a major point of contact and involvement with nonbelievers. We turn now to a further investigation into their development and participation in the growth of the Senufo Baptist churches.

5

Stepping Stones toward Senufo Christian Songs

THE DEVELOPMENT OF A meaningful indigenous hymnody grows out of a progression of stages or stepping-stones. Each stepping stone serves simultaneously as a mark of achievement and as a launching pad. As marks of achievement, each stepping stone reflects a new joy in more genuine expressions of adoration to God. As launching pads, each stepping stone engenders further enhancement of songs towards a more vibrant expression of Christian experience and spiritual growth.

In this chapter, we investigate from an ethnohistorical perspective the stepping stones that led towards the creation of Senufo Christian songs as we know them today. Four major stepping stones or major stages in the development of a meaningful, indigenous hymnody can be identified. They are (1) early mission work, (2) new missionary gambits, (3) the first Senufo songs, and (4) developing Senufo songs. Trends, events, attitudes, and musical styles are scrutinized from both negative and positive aspects. We turn now to the first stepping-stone, focusing on initial missionary approaches to music and hymns among the Senufo.

Stepping Stone 1: Early Mission Work

The early missionaries, following in the great tradition of the Church, were concerned with adequate music for the new churches that would spring up on Senufo soil. They found themselves in the following situation.

Translated Hymns

When the first Conservative Baptist missionaries arrived in the Ivory Coast in 1947 to work among the Senufo in the town of Korhogo, there were no known Senufo Christians. Naturally, as they started preaching they wanted to also introduce the singing of Christian hymns. Not having any national believer to call upon, they resorted to the technique that has most often been used in mission work. They took the hymns that were meaningful to their own missionary community and translated them into the Senufo language.

The response to the songs during those early years was typical of the overall work. They were deadening. Just as there were no converts during the first seven years of work, there was no joy or enthusiasm in the songs. Indeed, the songs suffered from the need for interpretation in the same way that working through non-believing interpreters for a basic presentation of the Gospel created a hindrance to effective communication.

By 1958, however, there was a small fledgling group of not more than 100 believers. Their worship services were still composed of such translated hymns as "Come and Go with Me to My Father's House." The people were not at ease with the songs. They sang with great timidity, if at all, and without any motivation.[1] In fact, it is well known that the people would actually slumber or sleep while singing these translated but foreign tunes.

The missionaries were not blind to the situation. Harold van den Berg, who leads the translation team, remembers that,

> [t]he song service really was quite dead in a lot of groups and, so, by the time a person got up to preach, he really had lost his congregation . . . . Your singing, instead of being a contributing factor, was really a detraction. And so you'd almost have thought, "Well, it'd be better not to sing, just go straight into the message and afterwards, let them sing if they wanted to.[2]

What a disheartening situation. Rather than having the song service enhance the worship time, it succeeded in gagging the whole service.

Problems With Translated Hymns

Reflecting on those early hymns, Dusu Coulibaly, an early Senufo convert relates her own personal experience. Now recognized as one of the first ladies to compose Senufo songs, Dusu originally came to the dispensary at Torhogo merely looking for help with her daughter's illness. As a result of her stay there, she accepted Christ as Savior. Eventually this led to a job as the "cuisinaire" (cook) for the patients and their families. While fulfilling her work responsibilities, she was asked to learn to sing the newly translated hymns. This was painful experience for her and it became a real burden. At one point, she was totally overwhelmed. She went about the station asking other national workers if they could help her. The typical

---

1. Tuo, interview.
2. Van den Berg, interview.

response was that it was not their "work" and that she should try her best. Finally through prayer and the help of the Lord she was able to learn to sing some of the songs that she can still sing to this day if she so chooses.[3]

Dusu's story is not unusual. Singing translated hymns did not lend itself to spontaneous response in worship. What, then, are some of the elements that made such hymn singing so ineffectual for the Senufo people and hindered the growth of the Senufo church? We now consider four disrupting characteristics of those transplanted hymns.

Destroyed Meaning of the Text

African tone languages such as Senufo restrict melodic possibilities in order to maintain comprehension of a text. This means that the message of a translated hymn is most often destroyed due to the tonal relationships within a word as it relates to the melodic tonal patterns of the hymns. For example,

> When you analyzed what was being sung, it really was a wonder that anybody understood what was being said at all, because in many cases, the tones were not only wrong but sometimes the opposite of what you wanted to say.[4]

The difference of a high tone and low tone in the Senufo can be the difference between a positive and a negative sentence. For example, the phrase "we will be with Jesus." In the Senufo is *Wo lapie ne Zyezu ní* with a high tone at the end. If, however, you want to negate that and state that "we will not be with Jesus," you would say it with a low tone at the end, *Wo lapie ne Zyezu nìì*.

A second example of problems in working with a tonal language in music is that sometimes you do not have the opposite meaning but rather a totally wrong meaning altogether. Once the Christians were trying to sing a song that said, "Our Dwelling Places Are in Heaven." A tune was borrowed from the neighboring Jula people. When the verse was sung *Wo lo kpagi yaa*, with this borrowed tune, it resulted in saying "Our Houses Are Cursed Being Sick," a Senufo expression condemning a house that needs to be broken down. The song is still sung by some Christians today, who would be the only people to understand it since they have been told what the song says. Even then, there are probably Christians who do not understand what they are singing.

---

3. D. Coulibaly, interview, 1–2.
4. Van den Berg, interview.

Occasionally a translated hymn tune will just happen to somewhat match up with the tonal pattern of the language. This is what happened to the closing song that is used like a benediction, set to the tune of "One Door and Only One." The song functions as a type of creedal statement and last commitment to the Lord before going back out into the world. When the people sing it, they all reverently bow their heads with eyes closed as the final event becomes especially sacred. The text in Senufo is:

Tári ni nyɛʔɛni nínge ni, syɔɔfɔlɔw nibin,
Pe i wi yiri Zyezu, kolocɔlɔɔ Jáow.
Tári ni nyɛʔɛ ni nínge ni, syɔɔ fɔlɔw nibin,
A mii tága Zyezu Kirisi na, mii syɔɔ fɔw.

The text in English is:

Between heaven and earth there is only one savior,
They call him Jesus, God's Son.
Between heaven and earth there's only one savior,
I believe in Jesus Christ. He's my savior.

Distasteful Musical Sounds

A further problem with using foreign music is that the musical sounds themselves are often distasteful in their singing style. Van den Berg when working with his translation team on the Book of Revelation thought he would demonstrate to his national co-translators how the singing in heaven would most likely sound. He proudly played the "Hallelujah Chorus" from Handel's *Messiah*. When the selection had finished, he asked his translation team what they thought of it. The leader responded for them all by asking, "Why is all your music crying music?" Evidently, what was such a magnificent piece of praise for a westerner resembled a dirge for the Senufo translators. It would not adequately express their joy in the Lord.

An Unpleasant Atmosphere

In addition to this, the translated hymns created neither a pleasant atmosphere nor one that was contagiously filled with joy for the Senufo believers. Since they were so difficult to sing and so foreign to them, the people easily became bored. There was no room for physical movement of any kind, a situation which is alien to true Senufo music. The people often went to sleep during the singing since the hymns neither created interest nor motivated them to become involved.

Stepping Stones toward Senufo Christian Songs

Inappropriate Hymn Content

Not only were the hymns boring and unattractive but the content of the hymns did not reflect the people's spiritual level. They did not understand the concepts presented even if they could get beyond the difficulty of discovering the meaning of the text despite the destructive tune. They were at a different place in terms of their Christian experience. In selecting and sharing the songs that were close to their hearts, the missionaries had reflected their own spiritual experience rather than that of the new Senufo believers. It left the Senufo believers without anything to hang onto. Singing about "Pressing on the Upward Road" or how "Jesus is Fairer than Ten Thousand" did not grapple with the struggles of the national Christians nor did it necessarily reflect their understanding of God.

Not An African Style

Finally, the hymns were not African in style. They brought a sense of foreignness to the services. For a people who had been totally entrenched in their own musical practices and styles, the western hymns were not easy for them to learn. With their own types of pentatonic scales rather than the typical western heptatonic scale, a different sense of rhythm, the use of short tones instead of sustained tones, and the lack of movement to accompany the hymns--the total effect detracted from Christian worship.

This lack of interest in western music due to its foreignness still continues to be true among many Senufo today. During my 1986 visit when I was living in the village of Zanaka?a, I had walked down to the mission station to get some supplies. When I arrived, I found that my Senufo hostess was also there. She came and greeted me at the missionary home, where I was collecting supplies. As we talked together she noticed and asked about the piano that was sitting there. I thought I would bless her with a grandioso version of "How Great Thou Art." I started in with the big introduction and within ten seconds my Senufo friend and hostess had left the house. She was neither amazed that I could move my fingers that fast nor attracted by the style. The whole experience was out of her frame of reference since the music was not in a recognizable African style.

In comparison with this, it is interesting to note that every year when I return to worship in the Zanaka?a church, they want to know if I have brought my East African *likembe* (thumb piano) with me. They want to hear me play it. It is an African instrument that not only sounds much more African, but it possesses some tone qualities similar to the Senufo *balafon*. They do not walk away when I play the *likembe*.

Stepping Stone 2: New Missionary Gambits

The combination of these five factors in singing translated hymns began to disturb the missionaries as they realized that the music was much more of a detriment to the worship services and evangelization outreaches than it was a help. Rather than winning the attention of the audience before the sermon, the congregation was basically inattentive, bored, and even asleep. The situation was so depressing that around 1959–1960, two missionaries began attempting to encourage the people to develop their own Christian songs and to do so with great freedom.

Non-Christian Musician Hired

One of the earliest attempts to improve the musical situation came from the mission's Senufo language specialist, Richard Mills. He tried hiring a recognized non-Christian musician to create new Senufo songs for Christians. The results were dismal. As he stated, "It didn't really work."

A Challenge to Respond in Song

Another attempt to improve the Christian music came at the end of a worship service. After delivering his message for the day at the village of Nawoka[glottal]a, the missionary church planter, Harold van den Berg, turned to the people and challenged them to sing what they had just discussed. Could they not sing something about what God had done for them? He relates that,

> One of them came up with a song and we were amazed to see how immediately, since it is antiphonal singing, how when the leader had sung what he did, that the group just picked up the response immediately. It was just absolutely uncanny . . . it made your flesh creep.[5]

From this experience people started attempting, though somewhat hesitantly, to create new songs on a more regular basis.

Music Workshop as Watershed

About this same time a people movement was starting to take off. Shortly after the missionaries had challenged the people to respond to a sermon in song, a music workshop held in 1960 unknowingly became the watershed for further stimulating Senufo Christian songs. The goal of the workshop

---

5. Ibid.

was to attempt to make the hymn tunes more true to the tonal nature of the language. James Riccitelli, a Christian and Missionary Alliance missionary working in Burkina Fasso (then known as Upper Volta), came down to Korhogo in order to teach a group of American missionaries and national pastors the principles of writing songs taking cognizance of the tonal structure of the language.

What appears to have happened is that one searched for western hymn tunes that would fit the tone patterns of the language. Ricitelli began with the Senufo text first, rather than the western hymn tune, and then tried to match them up with an "appropriate" American hymn tune. The result was that you had "Come Thou Fount of Every Blessing" as a tune that could fit with words in the Senufo language. In addition to this, recognizing that the Senufo sing on a pentatonic scale, they attempted to take the tone pattern of the spoken language and work with it in their musical settings of various texts.

Difficulties with the Workshop

The immediate results of the workshop were mixed. Several songs had been created. According to missionary Dorothy van den Berg, "People sang them for a while, but they did not really last because they still were not *their* [emphasis mine] songs."[6] There were still problems of comprehension in the songs. One non-Christian Senufo woman after singing, "Come Thou Fount of Every Blessing," supposedly in her own language asked, "What language is that song in?"[7] Perhaps the tones had been followed, but the songs turned out stiff and awkward since the rhythm (intonation) of the words had not been taken into account. As long as the rhythmic aspect remained awkward, the songs were stilted even though they were closer to the people's style. This continued as a major problem, for the people were now stuttering their songs due to the neglect of the rhythmic aspect of the language.

Discoveries Because of the Workshop

Despite the difficulties, however, the music workshop produced a real watershed and impetus to stimulating the people to create their own songs. The missionaries had demonstrated their belief that God could use a more Senufo-style music to worship him. It was a national lay pastor by the name of Sanga who first grasped what the missionaries were attempting to do and decided that he could do it himself. Through his meager but

---

6. Ibid.
7. Zie, interview.

enthusiastic efforts, the beginnings of authentic Senufo Christian songs that were true to the language as well as the melodic and rhythmic patterns of Senufo music gave birth to a more dynamic expression of Senufo Christianity. An example of one of these early hymn texts that reflects the people's theological thinking at that time states that "Every Day Satan is Walking Around and Fooling People."

Sanga, the lay pastor who created some of the first songs, did not really consider himself a musician. However, in creating these first songs, he set a model that demonstrated to the more musically-capable believers that God could be worshipped with Senufo praise and adoration. The people finally realized that they could compose songs in their own style, and the idea caught fire.

Stepping Stone 3: The First Senufo Songs

Thus, as the new songs were becoming a more genuine expression of Senufo faith, there was also a new movement of the Holy Spirit. In 1960, the first complete translation of the Gospel of Mark was newly available. People were saying, "This is what God's Word says. It's not just what the missionaries are saying."[8] Shortly after that time, towards the end of 1961 and on through 1963, there was ". . . a real people movement. It could very well be that part of the reason for it was that they [the Senufo] began singing their own songs."[9]

For example, during one major surge of this people movement around 1961, there were over 300 people who made confessions of faith within the space of a few weeks. The villages of Nawokaʔa and Kagbanikaʔa located within the Napieolodougou area were the main villages to respond. The people, who spoke the Nafara dialect of Senufo, were being witnessed to by a national evangelist from the other side of the Napieolodougou district. Having requested fields in the Nawokaʔa area, he left his own village of Wapiekaʔa in order to be close to the people where he was ministering. The evangelist was a singer and sang these early Christian songs as a major means to communicating his story about Jesus Christ. The response to the message was amazing, especially when contrasted with the lack of great progress that characterized the earlier work.[10]

---

8. Van den Berg, interview.
9. Skinner, interview, 2.
10. According to the Ivory Coast field chairman, Rev. Merril Skinner, this people movement did not continue on. Many people reverted back to their former way of life. He attributes the lack of trained leadership as the major reason for this subsiding of the people movement (Skinner1986). Also, it appears to me that no basic patterns for Christian living

Thus, it was at this time that there were many new converts who responded to the message presented in the songs and also began singing of their new-found freedom from Satan's bondage in a most spontaneous manner. They were released to sing of their own Christian experience. What was it, then, that characterized these early songs that brought the Gospel home to the people?

Early Song Characteristics

The first songs were built on a simple call-and-response style in which the lead singer calls out the text, and those responding or the congregation imitate exactly what has been sung by the leader. There was no variation between the two sections. Texts were a bit simplistic since the people were not yet totally at home with singing songs to their newly-accepted living God. This is demonstrated in the following song text:

CALL	RESPONSE
Bless my hands	Bless my hands.
Bless my feet	Bless my feet.
Bless my house	Bless my house.
Bless my walk	Bless my walk.
Bless my insides	Bless my insides.
Bless my spirit	Bless my spirit.

As elementary as the song is when one compares it with the contemporary Senufo Christian songs, the fact that it was one of their own songs in a more familiar style and that they could understand it made it very well received. A current song leader from the Zanaka?a church remembers that ". . . When it came out, we thought it was beautiful."

Typical of songs during this breakthrough time was the fact that there was neither clapping nor any instrumental accompaniment. Verification of this comes from a 1974 recording of one of these early Senufo composed songs. It reveals a distinctive lack of basic clapping patterns, a most common feature of current Senufo Christian songs. Perhaps this was due to a hangover from the days of singing only translated hymns, or it was just a major accomplishment to be singing Christian songs in one's own language. Clapping had never been allowed in church before.

---

within the Senufo context were established yet. So, the people simply returned to what was familiar to them.

But the content of the songs mirrored more accurately the people's perspective on life as reflected by the following song text: "Since I believed on Jesus, my home is going to be a place of rest. Our Father gave us rest, so I shall be living with Him in a place of rest." The song, created by a leprous lady who was one of the first song leaders, continues by speaking about God's actions toward the saved in the future. It promises that "After death, things are going to be leveled out," but then warns that among the saved, "This will be worked out in the field of the dead." Here the phrase, "in the field of the dead," reveals the Senufo worldview where the dead are considered to be in the future while the living are not yet there.

First Attempts at Singing Scripture

As these new songs were developing musically, singers were also challenged to add new content to the songs. There was so much singing about freedom from Satan, that some people felt there should be songs that do not always dwell on Satan's work. Dusu Coulibaly, the cook from the Torhogo dispensary referred to above, took up the challenge and started to set scripture verses to song. Some verses were from the newly translated books of Romans and Acts which were not yet in circulation.[11] People who did not read were singing scripture before they had the complete New Testament and the opportunity to learn to read it.

Among the first scriptures set to song were Rev 3:20 and John 14:2. Most of the opening call of the song was taken up with reciting the scripture reference, which became a very long and involved sentence in Senufo. This seemed to dampen the momentum of the acceptance of the song. Dusu, however, makes no mention of including the scripture reference as a problem. Rather she recalls that a certain number of people liked the songs but others were discouraged by them since the songs did not allow for dancing. Although their content was appreciated, the scripture songs did not really catch on at that time. Still restricted in terms of musical style, they were, however, beginning to win an audience.

Results of the New Songs

In general, the immediate results of the newly created songs provided a breath of fresh air in the worship services. The singing became spontaneous, became an integral part of the worship service, and, in contrast to the translated hymns, livened up every meeting.

---

11. Van den Berg, interview.

In addition to this, the songs grew to be a conversion agent in that they started attracting nonbelievers to Christ. One day a Senufo farmer, for example, was out working in his field next to some Christians who were singing their Christian songs while plowing in their field. The man started listening to the song and began moving closer to the Christian group. He found the tune to be catchy, but he could not quite figure out the text. He kept moving closer. Finally, he got so close that he stopped, went over to the Christians, and said, "I'd really like to hear the song that you're singing." The believers responded by singing it for him. Afterwards he asked for an explanation of what it was all about. The Christians told him, "Oh, this is a Christian song." Since he had no idea what that might be, he accepted their invitation to come to a meeting. He attended the meeting, thoroughly enjoying the music and what he heard in the songs. As he listened to the sermon he accepted Christ. Today, he is the pastor of a growing Senufo church.

Other results of the new Senufo songs meant that most of the translated hymns were no longer sung. The time when singing was a foreign experience came to an end. There were exceptions where songs, such as the "Senufo Benediction" based on "One Door and Only One," were retained, since it could be understood and somehow had become meaningful to the people. However, in general, Dusu Coulibaly summarized the situation very well when she remarked, "Once we had our own songs, we abandoned the songs of the missionaries."[12]

Stepping Stone 4: Developing Senufo Songs

Gratifyingly, over time, the production and use of the new songs did not expire but gained even more momentum. The people were growing spiritually. In spite of the persecution that they experienced in their villages, those who were coming to know Jesus Christ in a personal way received Him with joy. They were overwhelmed by their new found freedom from the secret societies and the fetish systems. "When they received Jesus Christ, they had this joy. They had fewer burdens. So this joy pushed the people to make new songs and to dance."[13] As they grew in their faith and understanding of the newly translated scriptures, so did the texts of their songs grow in spiritual depth and insight.

---

12. Coulibaly, interview, 3.
13. Ibid., 4.

Musical Style Innovations

There was also growth and innovation in terms of musical style. The song form no longer restricted itself to the simple call-and-response style cited earlier. Rather, a new section began to be inserted after the presentation of the basic introduction. This new section served as a means to develop the thought presented in the opening. It became a development or exegetical section that allowed the song leader to present in greater detail a further explanation of the basic message of the song:

> Thematic Statement:
>
> We Christians have been relieved of all the old traditions that were binding us in the past.
>
> Development/Exegesis:
>
> 1. When rainy season starts you have to sacrifice a chicken because rainy season start is with chicken sacrifice.
> 2. Rainy season quits, you have to sacrifice a chicken because the end of rainy season is chicken sacrifice.
> 3. If you have a child, you sacrifice a chicken because child birth is accompanied by chicken sacrifice.
>
> Thematic Restatement:
>
> We have rested from all this superfluity of words.

This song, with its additional development section which is more characteristic of the oral tradition storytelling style, is typical of the favorite songs of that time.

In addition to enhancing the musical structure, some of the early songs were so improved that they also took on a more natural and pleasurable manner of singing. Dusu Coulibaly's song based on John 14:2, "In My Father's House Are Many Dwelling Places," was modified by increasing the tempo, and by adding rhythms that were not in the original song but which changed the song sufficiently so that it could be danced to.

Musical Accompaniment Innovations

Once the creation of new songs commenced, there was a desire for some kind of accompaniment. This was at first just a snapping of the fingers on the beat. Even though missionaries initially "raised their eyebrows" at the doing of such a worldly thing, the move towards musical accompaniment continued. This led to the introduction of clapping, the use of the drum, the playing of shakers and of the "*kanrigi*," a metal scraper, and most recently, the addition of the *balafon*, Senufo-style xylophone.

The introduction of musical instruments met with resistance from some missionaries. Around 1965, a missionary challenged the use of the drum in the church, saying, "How can you use an instrument of Satan in the church?" The response to her question by the nationals was a volley of returned questions asking, "Who made the tree that we use for making the drum? Wasn't it God? Who made the skins for the drum head? Wasn't it God? Who made all the things we use for making a drum? Wasn't it God?"[14]

More recently is the introduction of the *balafon* (*jegele*: a wood-frame xylophone common to west Africa and more popularly referred to in French as the *balafon).* The Senufo *balafon* has many similarities to that of the Mandinka and other xylophones found across Africa. For further ethnomusicological studies and information concerning West African *balafon* into Senufo Christian singing has raised questions among the nationals themselves.[15] The issue becomes, for them, one of trying to find ways to show that the Christians are different from the nonbelievers by not using the same instruments as the nonbelievers. However, the *balafon* is well received in many congregations. They are often, but not always, those congregations that are away from direct mission influence. One such congregation is found in the village of Napieolodougou, where no one is against using the *balafon*. They have discovered that their attitude and the way the *balafon* is used for God's glory is the distinguishing factor. They reason for themselves that, "The same mouth that worshipped the fetishes has been changed to worship God. Therefore, when we become Christian, the *balafons* that we took for worshipping the fetishes, we can now seek to use for worshipping our God."[16]

Thus it is that musical accompaniment has been incorporated into the overall musical structure in order to enhance the Senufo Christian worship patterns, thereby making them more authentic and indigenous. The songs have become their own dynamic expression and natural means of communicating God's truths.

Conclusion

We have examined, then, the foundational steps in the historical development of Senufo Christian songs. In tracing this development we have

---

14. Ouattara, interview.
15. See Jessup, *The Mandinka Balafon,* and Knight, "The Style of Mandinka Music."
16. Soro, intervierw, 9.

seen that the initial introduction of translated hymns was not successful. Indeed, the hymns were a detraction from the presentation of Christianity to such an extent that people slept during the singing of them. Both the hymns' musical style and content were out of the frame of reference of the people, making it difficult for them to relate both musically and conceptually.

The movement towards a more meaningful hymnody started when missionaries began challenging Senufo believers to create their own songs. In addition to this, missionaries demonstrated that they felt God could use Senufo musical styles for worship at a music workshop. This idea was caught by a few national leaders who took up the vision by composing new songs themselves even though they did not feel that composition was a natural gift. They modeled the possibilities, and others soon followed their initiative. Since then, indigenous Senufo Christian songs became one of the major rallying cries for the cause of the Gospel.

This new rallying cry through the development of meaningful songs serves as one of the answers to the common missiological question that asks: ". . . how can we present the Gospel message in a way that worshippers realize that Jesus is not a dim figure of the past, a white man's God or Christ, but the Savior of ALL, and therefore of our community today in the peculiar problems that we are facing in this age?"[17]

The Senufo believers were beginning to raise and answer that question for themselves. Their songs have matured and become an integral part of worship, evangelism, and spiritual formation. They have created their own approach to contextualization. Rather than merely adapting or imitating already existent song forms, they have drawn from their cultural, musical repertoire in creating new songs. In the process of developing this, they have avoided a number of the difficult pitfalls—such as associations tied to a form—that are often involved in critical. For further explanations and studies in this area see Kraft and Hiebert.[18]

In seeking to make the Gospel message relevant to their context, they have practiced "creative contextualization." I am indebted to Charles H. Kraft in the coining of this term. Musically, this is a practice where new song forms and music events that are highly indigenous in essence, yet are not merely borrowed customs from the past, are produced and practiced. The result of creative contextualization leads to moving a group of believers further along the path of Christianity.

---

17. Martin, "The Mai Chaza Church," 117.
18. Kraft, *Christianity in Culture*; Hiebert, *Anthropological Insights*, 171–92.

Stepping Stones toward Senufo Christian Songs

What, more specifically, are the musical structures that have facilitated such meaningful communication among the Senufo? That is our next area of investigation.

Part Three

A Musical Analysis

6

Musical Paths to Christian Communication

HAVING PRESENTED THE CULTURAL and historical background to our Senufo case study, we now turn to the music, specifically the songs that the Senufo Christians are singing as they communicate their faith in Jesus Christ. In order to understand the dynamics at work within the production of music, an analysis of these songs from a communicational point of view is required. But let us first catch a glimpse of these songs in performance.

Three Musical Vignettes

Vignette 1

It's a balmy evening as the intense heat of the day begins to drift away from its penetrating and drenching focus on the sparsely-treed hill. Here, just outside of the large village of Napieolodougou, Senufo Christian women have come together for their annual women's conference. The women have sat through three days of Bible instruction. Brimming full with testimonies of God's work in their lives, the women have had insufficient time to share their deep and heart-felt expressions of praise. Now on this Friday evening it is their time to participate fully in the modes of traditional communication that come so naturally to them.

Most of the 120 women are dressed in highly-patterned African clothes that declare their affirmation of the Christian faith. The geometric blue and gold patterns are intermeshed with Christian symbols. The designs include pictorial representations of a cross, a dove, and an opened Bible boldly declaring one of the great "I am" passages of Jesus (John 14:6) in both French and Ceebaara, the prevalent Senufo dialect. The wood benches have been arranged in a large circle out in the middle of the expansive open area between the cement-block eating structure and the chapel. There is a certain sense of expectancy in the air but yet there is no great rush to get the major event underway. A sense of peace, calm, and joy presides as the day fades away.

Eventually, out of the milling crowd emerges a lone voice piercing the air in the first call of a song. As she continues to make her vocal call, the lead singer gradually works her way to the center of the circle that will serve as the arena for the whole evening's event. A few voices pick up the response and call back to the leader what she has just proclaimed in song. Things begin to take shape. A calabash shaker takes up the basic pulse of the song while a complementary clapping pattern is produced by those who have decided to "sit" this first one out. Meanwhile the lead singer and those with the percussion instruments begin to move in a counter-clockwise circle within the interior of a larger circle formed by the major group of women. The song now begins to take on a definite form as the whole group becomes greatly involved in its production. There is a volleying of phrases between the lead singer and the responding group of the outer circle as the calabash shaker and metal scraper add their own rhythmic contrasting and interlocking patterns.

Photo 8: Senufo women dancing their faith with Roberta King joining them.

Musical Paths to Christian Communication

At first, it appears that the women are barely moving, with their feet hardly rising more than an inch off the ground. But as the song develops and progresses, the movements become greatly articulated with the feet keeping one pattern, the knees to the waist creating their own counter but complementary pattern, the arms and shoulders finding yet another rhythmic pattern to delineate, and the women's heads following the lead of their upper bodies. The women are engrossed in the dance, aware of their creating a harmonic unity of movement. Not only are they responding in movement but they are also responsible for singing the musical response to the leader's call. As they do so they are indicating their awareness of and agreement with what she has just stated musically.

There is total involvement, joy, and delight as the dance picks up intensity, the bodies now bending over in an imitation of the particular hoeing action used by these farming women, and then returning to a less demanding upright position. The dance continues on. The dust begins to swirl around them and the repetitive response starts to create a foundational and affirmative drone as the women settle into expressing the measure of their faith through music and movement. Several nonbelieving men from the village have hiked up the hill in order to capture these Christian songs on their radio cassette recorders. Various men from the Baptist churches have also come to make their own recordings. Although this is an event intended mainly for the women, the men cannot stay away.

The night has just begun, the lead singers will change when they become fatigued, but there is joy at knowing that they as believers can worship the true God with all their body, mind, and soul. The women will not be satisfied until the early hours of the morning just before dawn. This musical evening is what "life" is all about: it is a significant part and summatory reenactment of what it is to follow the "Jesus path."

Vignette 2

It is Sunday morning meeting time in the small, rectangular cement building that serves as a church in the village of Zanaka?a. The worshippers have meandered into the building after completing their morning chores. There is no formal call to worship or announcement of the beginning of the church service. A songleader fulfills this role as she leads out in the call of the first song. After the opening introduction of the song, the worshippers take up a number of clapping patterns that are performed while the lead singer extemporizes on the song's theme. There is great involvement in the clapping and, even though they are seated, the song is animated through physical movement of not only the hands but the bobbing of a head and chest and the tapping of a foot. The sense of motion and movement is there in spite of the restrictions of the building.

When the first song is complete, another song leader immediately calls out the opening of a second song without missing a beat between it and the last one. The clapping patterns automatically shift to new ones: they are self-evident to the worshippers and without any need for explanation or reference to a musical score. There is involvement and participation on the part of everyone present, from the adults who sit up front to the children who occupy the back rows with extra enthusiasm in their clapping. The lengthy song service, between 20–30 minutes, draws to a close as they move into a time of personal testimony. The sermon follows and the people begin to doze as it drags on. Suddenly, a song leader with her baby tied to her back interrupts with a song as she stands and wakes the dozing people up so they can return to their efforts to listen to God's Word as it is proclaimed from the pulpit. The song brings them back to attention.

Vignette 3

It has been a good and full Lord's Day in the town of Korhogo. First the three-hour morning service followed in the afternoon by another three-hour service of prayer and fasting. In both services, the pastor and the congregation of around 200 people have requested that Nɔnyimɛ, the former "*sandogi*" (sorceress) and one of the most sought-after song leaders among the Senufo believers, sing the story of the "Man from Torhogo."[1] It is a story-telling song that usually lasts a minimum of 20–25 minutes. Now, at the end of the two-and-one-half hour evening service, the request to sing the "Man from Torhogo" song comes once again. Nɔnyimɛ is the expert in singing this song. Since she does not live in Korhogo, the people are compelled to take advantage of her presence on this warm evening. A grand hush falls over the group as she begins to relate the experience of this man who was duped by Satan promising him all the riches in the world.

The story is true and speaks to the very issues that have confronted the great majority of Senufo believers. It is hot and muggy but that is of no concern to these people, who have turned their full attention to the recounting of this testimony. Exclamations of agreement ring out between the group's sung responses. The song comes to its main point as the "man from Torhogo" comes to faith in Christ. Nɔnyimɛ summarizes its

---

1. See Appendix D.

teaching and rounds off the song with a return to its opening statement. Dossongmon Ouattara, one of the head pastors of the Senufo Baptist believers in Korhogo, turns to me with sweat rolling down the sides of his face and exhilaration beaming from his eyes. He emphatically exclaims," . . . and who says songs do not communicate!" There is no doubt in his mind and it is obvious in the response of the people.

Contexts for Senufo Christian Songs

As may be noted from the three musical vignettes given above, Senufo Christian songs are performed in a variety of situations. They are sung regularly at Sunday worship services, mid-week prayer meetings, wedding ceremonies, funerals, women's conferences, evangelistic services, or whenever there is a Christian gathering. They are not, however, limited to formal Christian meetings. Rather, they have become such a part of the Christian life-style that they are sung while cultivating in the fields, preparing the meal over the fire, or walking to market.

Christian songs, however, are not limited to Baptist believers. Senufo Christian songs created by Baptist composers are also sung by Catholics and at their services as well. Nonbelieving Senufo people listen to them on cassette players while working, also sing them as they travel to market, request that they be sung while working in the fields, play them on the *balafon*, and have used them for newly instituted village rituals such as flag-raising ceremonies. They have even been heard playing on the loudspeaker at the local town bar in Korhogo.

In a real sense, Senufo Christian songs are generic. There is not yet a defined typology of lullabies, work songs, funeral songs, or wedding songs, in contrast to worship songs. At this point all the songs are for worship. This worship may take place at anytime and is not restricted to the church compound. It appears that any of the songs may be sung at funerals, weddings, or in the fields, in addition to the main worship services. The songs are sung in just about any situation other than the Poro society meetings in the sacred forest. Indeed, there is a real concern among the Senufo church leaders for developing appropriate songs for specific occasions, in particular for the important ritual occasions such as funerals. The creation of appropriate songs for specific occasions was one of the main assignments that the Senufo Christian leaders gave me while conducting the song workshops. In general, though, Senufo Christian believers feel that the Christian songs are the ones they are to sing regardless of the occasion. They are adamant that the songs serve as a testimony of their faith or means of Christian identification. This view is held to such an extreme that they are reluctant to acknowledge that they can remember any "secular" songs from their pre-Christian days.

The songs are used mainly for worship during the church service. There is no intended human audience for the songs, except those outside of the church who are going about their daily tasks. They are songs of and for the laity. Each person is a participant and is meant to respond to the call of the song leader.

This description of songs is typical of the village churches. There are no choirs or "professional" musicians. The Senufo church in Korhogo is seeking to create a choir since they have observed them in French-speaking churches. I find this a sad development since, in its attempt to modernize, the choir is taking away from the good worship dynamics of group participation inherent in African traditions. Thus, worshippers are forced to become mere spectators rather than full participants. The song leader may choose to lead the song from his/her seat anywhere in the congregation, or he/she may choose to start the song while seated and then slowly process to the front of the usually rectangular meeting room. No person is meant to be a spectator or serve as an audience. Rather, it is the joining together of everyone in the worship of God.

During the worship service, the songs are often used for a specific functional purpose. A song leader may spontaneously interrupt the sermon by leading out in a song. In this way, the people who are not used to sitting for long, monologue sermons are brought out of their dozing state. Through the relief of singing a song, they are encouraged to follow the rest of the preacher's presentation. Indeed, a song will hold Senufo believers' attention even after a two-to three-hour service. This was the case when the "Man from Torhogo" song was requested at the close of the Sunday evening service (see Vignette 3).

The Multiple Channels of Music Communication

Thus, Senufo Christian songs appear to communicate in a most effective way whenever they are sung. They make a significant contribution to the life of the Senufo Baptist churches of Côte d'Ivoire. How is it that these songs communicate so effectively? What are the dynamics at work within this communication process? We turn our attention now to these two main questions.

In communication terms, music functions as the vehicle or channel for the music communication process. Generally, one speaks of only one

Musical Paths to Christian Communication

channel facilitating the communication of a message. However, my position is that music, and specifically Senufo Christian songs, employ four communication channels at the same time. These highly integrated yet distinct channels include: (1) the linguistic channel, (2) the music channel or actual musical sounds, (3) the movement channel, and (4) the performer channel.

As visualized in the model, see Figure 9, each of the channels simultaneously makes a contribution to the communication process as it provides for transaction of meaning and understanding within the music event. Each channel is working together with the other channels to effect a profound impact on the music event participants. When these channels are appropriately wedded, the sum of their impact is much greater than that of the channels individually.

Figure 9

MULTI-CHANNEL MUSIC COMMUNICATION

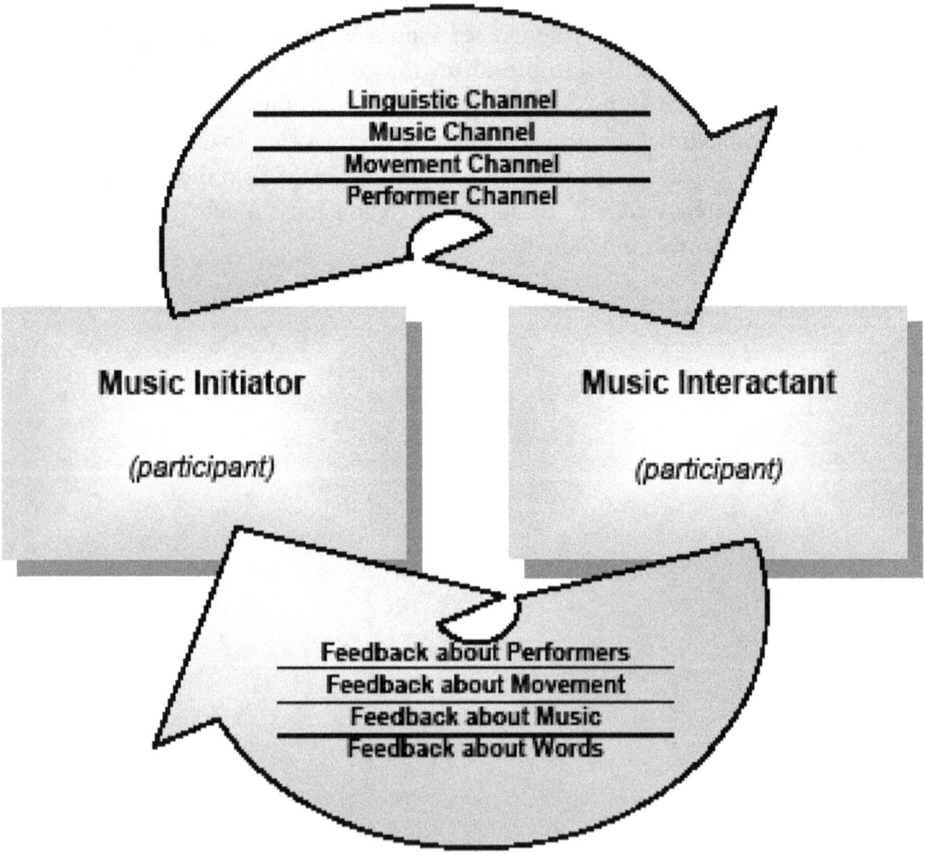

- Linguistic Channel
- Music Channel
- Movement Channel
- Performer Channel

Music Initiator (participant)

Music Interactant (participant)

- Feedback about Performers
- Feedback about Movement
- Feedback about Music
- Feedback about Words

In order to begin to understand the various communication dynamics at work within an actual music event, the presentation of Senufo Christian songs, we will investigate each channel by analyzing the elements or building blocks of which each channel is comprised. Our analysis will be neither a complete formal musical analysis, nor a systematic study in meaning. Rather, we will look at musical sound, behavior, and performers as they relate to the communication process. At times we will draw upon techniques of formal musical analysis and/or symbolic interaction as they are able to contribute to the understanding of "how and why" music communicates.

The Linguistic Channel

Since language is the predominant and main generative factor in the creation of Senufo Christian songs, our discussion begins with the linguistic channel. The main element in the linguistic channel is the actual text of a song. If we had been discussing songs from the Western tradition, it would have been natural to start with the music channel first. Although songs in the western tradition are also highly influenced by concern for a clear presentation of the text, there is much more freedom in approaching melodic, harmonic, and rhythmical patterns. The musical patterns of African songs and more specifically Senufo Christian songs, however, are much more shaped and determined by the exigencies of their languages than songs from the Western traditions.

The Priority of the Text

The importance of the text in Senufo Christian songs will keep revealing itself throughout the course of this study both in its meaningfulness and attraction to the receivers of the text and in its molding of the musical structures and forms. The fact that songs are treated as speech utterances reveals the intimate nature between music and language. Songs, based on language, communicate powerfully. This was underlined for me as I was talking with a Senufo friend who had come to visit me. I had been working on some cassette tape recordings of Senufo Christian songs shortly before she arrived but turned them off as I saw her approach my house. We had been talking for a while when I somewhat absent-mindedly turned on the tape recorder. Immediately my friend's attention was riveted to the tape recorder. It was as if another person had entered the room, picked up a new topic of conversation, and I could not get a word in edge-wise, nor could I get my friend's attention back. The recorded Senufo Christian song had usurped the original conversation; it had taken over the situation, since it was functioning as a speech utterance.

This interaction with the song text as a speech utterance and its importance in music communication is not unique to the Senufo, but appears to be a characteristic feature of traditional African songs. In his study of Mandinka *jaliya*, a song form found north of the Senufo, Knight chose to focus more attention on the vocal aspect, since it is "this part that holds more interest for the African listener despite the complexity and appeal of the instrumental part."[2]

A further demonstration of the importance of song texts to the Senufo believers was their constant return to stating that all the musical elements such as clapping, the use of instruments and their volume must be kept in control so that the text may be understood. Even in terms of length of the song, they are more interested in what the song is saying than completing a song within a certain period of time. If the text of the song is especially meaningful, then it should be long and continue on for quite a period of time.

Elements in the Linguistic Channel

There are several elements that can be discussed within the linguistic channel, in general. Each plays an important role in facilitating effective communication and is essential in avoiding distortion of the intended message of the song. The relationship between the music and linguistic codes reveals the need to investigate such areas as the relationship between melody and text, and between rhythm and text. Considerations in the areas of text load, imagery, and style also contribute to or detract from the effectiveness of the linguistic channel. Finally, the actual languages used such as the vernacular languages, dialects, trade languages, and foreign languages are essential factors in the linguistic channel. To sum up, then, the elements for consideration within the linguistic channel may be diagrammed as follows:

---

2. Knight, "The Style of Mandinka Music," 5.

Musical Paths to Christian Communication

**Figure 10
Elements in the Linguistic Channel**

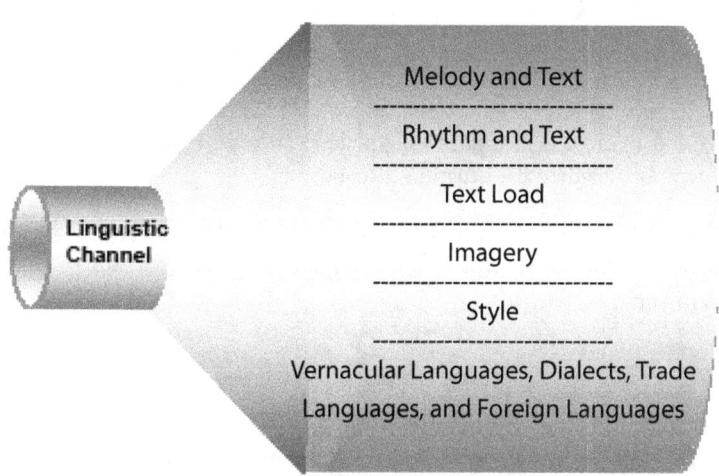

Rather than discuss each of these elements separately at this point, we will be referring to them more specifically throughout this and the next chapter as we relate the language to the development of musical structures. Briefly, we will be noting how the language influences the melodic and rhythmic structures of the songs so that there is an intimate relationship between the "melody and text" and the "rhythm and text." The "text load" component refers to the amount of text that is incorporated in a song. For example, some songs use one or two basic phrases and then repeat them several times; whereas, other songs incorporate many thoughts and phrases with very little repetition. The "imagery" and "style" components refer to the analogies and the way in which thoughts are put together. Finally, the "language-dialect" component deals with the particular language or dialect that is used in the song.

Since language is so intimately integrated with the musical structure and elements of a song, it is difficult to distinguish them from one another. This fact is very similar to what Von Hornbostel maintained about songs in general: "Words and music come into the singer's mind as one."[3] This certainly is true for the Senufo. Even when attempting to elicit a discussion with the Senufo composers with basic musical question—"How do you know what pitch to start the song on?"—they lead you right back to the text. Their response is, "You have to know the words of the song."

3. Blacking, *Venda Children's Songs*, 155.

The text, then, along with various linguistic considerations, takes priority in determining the theoretical basis for musical pitch and the production of songs. Although musical patterns are so highly shaped by the linguistic channel, this is not viewed as a major constraint in music making.

> Traditional African musicians do not consider the mold that language provides for song structure limiting. On the contrary: they use it because it facilitates song making and makes it easy to extemporize where the situation demands it.[4]

We turn our attention, then, to the music channel, keeping in mind the foundational, generative role of language in the creation of Senufo Christian songs.

The Music Channel

Just as we have noted a number of elements mutually at work within the linguistic channel, so there are several elements that must be considered within the music channel. The breakdown of elements includes form, melody, harmony, rhythm, instruments, tempo, performance patterns, and tone qualities (see Figure 11).

Each of these elements makes a significant contribution to the production of a song. They combine to form a composite of ingredients necessary in the song making process. Since musical analysis is central to an ethnomusicological study, there is a wealth of material to be covered. Therefore, we will comment only briefly on each element within a Senufo song in this chapter. My objective here is to show the music channel's relationship to the other communication channels. A more detailed musical analysis will be made in the following chapter. A brief overview follows.

---

4. Nketia, *The Music of Africa*, 188.

Figure 11
Elements in the Music Channel

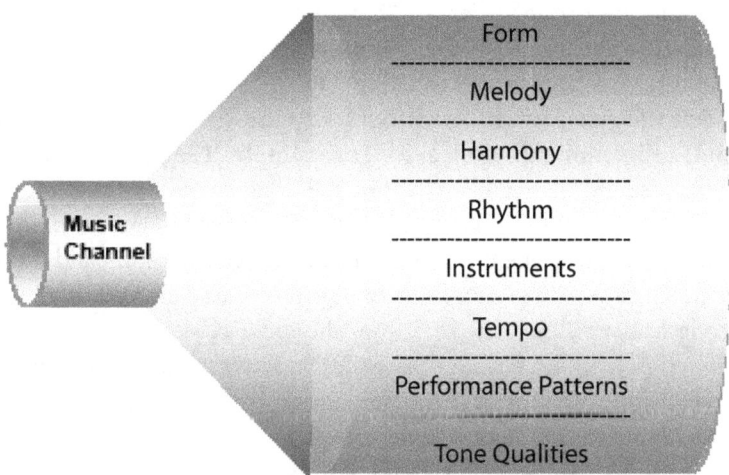

The first element in the music channel is form. Form is the way in which a song is structured and draws on available resources for making songs. For example, the Senufo rely on a main leader, who calls out the lines of the song, and the song participants sing back a one-line response. The opening Senufo call-and-response form of Christian songs is unique within Senufo singing traditions. Yet the form definitely draws from these Senufo traditions and is not something that has been imposed on them.

Both melody and rhythm are intimately related to the language. The melodic contour, for example, basically follows the tonal patterns of the language, so that a spoken high-tone is sung high in relationship to the other sung tones. The rhythm of the words is also followed in the singing of the song. Naturally, there is allowance for elongation of a syllable, but the overall pattern recognizes the spoken rhythm of the words. Additional and contrasting rhythms are created through the incorporation of clapping and instrumental accompaniment. This provides some of the main musical interest in the song.

Harmony, where several tones are combined in order to create chords as is so characteristic in Western music, is not an essential feature of Senufo songs.

Musical instruments provide another arena of musical interest for the Senufo. Any number of instruments may be added to a song to enhance it as long as it does not detract from clear communication of the song text.

The tempo (speed at which a song is sung) determines the mood or character of a song. A fast or "hot" tempo, according to the Senufo, facilitates movement and dance while medium tempos help people learn new songs.

Performance patterns refer to the ways in which a song is sung and/or musical instruments are played. For example, a song leader will very often stay seated at her place within the congregation as she leads the song. Other times, she will start at her place and slowly move towards the front of the church where she will continue to lead the song and bring it to its conclusion. When singing at an outside evening evangelism meeting the song leader will usually sing from the inner circle that is most often composed of song leaders and players of various percussion instruments. Meanwhile, the other participants are moving and singing in a larger circle that encompasses the smaller circle.

Finally, tone quality refers to the aesthetic standards for a good singer. Among the Senufo believers, a good singer must have a clear, strong voice that will carry a long distance. Tone quality also may influence the meaning and reception of a song.

The Movement Channel

Intimately related to the music channel is the movement channel. The movement channel can and does serve as its own independent nonverbal channel of communication. Yet, it is deeply interwoven with the production of traditional African music. This is true for the Senufo as well. Indeed, the primacy of motion in Senufo societies in general is a major theme in art forms outside of the music event. In reference to Senufo plastic arts, Glaze emphasizes:

> There is an unvoiced criterion that assumes the elements of time and motion. An appreciation of the kinetic factor in Senufo aesthetic criteria, form, and symbolism is essential to an understanding of their art. In the Senufo world, sculpture dances, moves in processions and participates in ritual, worship, work and spatial ceremonies.[5]

Movement, more commonly referred to as dance, is an essential ingredient to the whole process in African music. Senufo believers have not separated

---

5. Glaze, "The Religious and Metaphysical," 14.

themselves from this important avenue of communication. As one church leader explained: "If our voices are not singing, our arms and legs are singing."[6] Motion and movement are essential, then, to Senufo singing.

The importance of movement and dance to the Senufo believers inadvertently made an impact on me as I first attempted to dance with the women at their annual conference. From my studies in African music, I was aware that the dance usually delineated the deep-lying rhythmic structures with their contrasts and interplay between groupings of two and three beats. So, in my desire to try to understand the musical structures of Senufo song, I decided to join the circle of dancers. The women were moving in a slow "shuffle," as the other missionaries fondly identify it. The women were delighted and amazed as I began moving in a definitely articulated rhythm along with them, madly trying to imitate every move they were making. There was a definite pattern to their movements. Instantly I no longer felt that I could find the beat: it was different from what my own western-trained perceptions had allowed me to map cognitively. Caught up in the thrill and extreme challenge of actually participating in praising God in this manner, I was not aware of what was being said about my participation. In talking with two missionary women with over 20 years of experience speaking the language and living among the Senufo, the Senufo women told them that I, this new missionary, put them to shame. (Fortunately, these missionary women were very gracious, not offended, and pleased to see the impact I was making.) The point is, though, that in one act of dancing with these African women, I had gained rapport that equaled 20 years of experience. I had become appreciated for dancing. Ever since that first women's conference, the tradition has developed that whenever I am working among Senufo believers, the most common greeting I receive is "*Yelifiige, fo yolo na!*" "Yelifiige (my Senufo name), greetings on the dance!"[7]

I would like to point out a number of significant aspects of dance for Senufo believers. In Africa, dance is often a religious expression and incorporates spiritual dynamics and interchange.[8] This is also true for Senufo believers. Dance for them is an act of worship and especially important since they are now worshipping "the true God." As one lady explained, "When I was a pagan everyone said that I knew how to dance but now this

---

6. R. King, Senufo Field notes.
7. Although a thorough investigation of dance as communication is beyond the scope of this study and my capability at this point, a very helpful resource on dance as communication can be found in Hanna, *To Dance is Human*.
8. See Hanna, *To Dance is Human*.

(believer's dance) is real joy!"[9] Indeed, for many Senufo believers participation in dance reveals the measure of their faith. One who cannot dance due to ill health is concerned that others perceive it as a "bad testimony." Dance becomes an essential part of their identity as Christian believers.

Dance for Senufo believers functions in much the same way as clapping in that it expresses the believer's joy in "coming to Jesus" and "what he has done." In their lives. In a real sense it is a form of spiritual work. This need to express one's spiritual joy through dance is carried into the church building, where actual dance is not possible due to the limitation of benches and the restricted area. Thus, just a minor movement of the body becomes "dance." In a limited sense. Rather than the full dance, one moves their head or feet. For example, one believer shared: "But this song, My Friend, Jesus is Calling You, pleases me a lot and when I sing it, if I cannot dance, I move my head a little."

Regularly articulated movement although done while seated in a building qualifies as dance for Senufo believers and a necessary aspect. Music and movement are integrally intertwined to such an extent that neither can exist without the other.

In addition to providing a visualization of musical structures, dance, like clapping, is important for visually expressing one's relationship with God and works not only in aesthetic and affective terms but in terms of spiritual transaction. For Senufo believers, dance allows the whole person to become involved in the communication event: "Dancing and clapping the hands is the same thing, it is joy! We *must* [emphasis mine] praise the Lord with all our instruments and all our thoughts."[10] Their full participation in this spiritual form of communication becomes heightened and much more appropriate in terms of effectively negotiating spiritual exchange. This is in agreement with other African traditions where, "Response and conscious involvement in music can be intensified on the individual level through movement or dance activity, and this, in African terms, is just as valid as listening to it contemplatively."[11] For the Senufo believers, there is indeed an intensification of their response and conscious involvement through movement. It is rare that while a Senufo believer is listening to songs, they do not move. For them, music and movement walk hand in hand.

---

9. R. King, Focus Group Interview, Dessingbo, QIII-8.
10. R. King, Focus Group Interview, Foro, QIII.
11. Nketia, *The Music of Africa*, 49.

Performance Channel

The final communication channel that must be discussed is that of the performance. In this channel, I am referring to the way in which the performers, themselves, become a channel of communication working in relation to the other three discussed above; the linguistic channel, the music channel, and the movement channel.

Communication theory alerts us to the fact that the communicator/performer is also a channel.[12] Ethnomusicologists would generally prefer to treat the performer as one who plays an important music-making role in correlation with the dynamics of form and texture of the musical product itself. I have, however, chosen to include the performer/s as an additional channel in the music communication process, since musical skills cannot be separated from the performer/s' personhood as they are relating to a group or society.

Both the song initiator (song leader) and the song interactants are necessary to the successful presentation of a song. However, especially crucial to the effective presentation of Senufo Christian songs is the song leader, the initiator of a song. Without the song leader a song cannot be presented at all. There is a certain set of requirements that make for an effective song leader in terms of musical skills, personal credibility, and spiritual development.

First, among the Senufo, one must be able to perform and lead a song with great skill. This ability requires freely creating textual musical phrases without interrupting the flow of the rhythm and also working within the restrictions of its framework (time span). The rhythmical framework, or time span, is an established set number of beats within which a phrase must be completed. This is self-evident to the Senufo, yet among Senufo believers, it is a skill that must also be developed. Interestingly, all the composers with whom I worked claimed that they could not "sing" (lead in songs) before they became Christians. They developed the skill afterwards. A good song leader must be able to remember the text, understand its ramifications, and extemporize on the spot, adapting the song to the needs of the moment, the occasion, and/or the audience. Song leaders develop a repertoire of phrases from which they may increase a song's length and content. This is perhaps one reason why so many phrases keep referring back to their former way of life, with references to sacrifices and fetishes. These phrases have formed the basic core of their musical skill repertoire since the development of Christian Senufo songs.

---

12. C. Kraft, *Communication Theory*, 195–240.

A song leader must also have the necessary voice quality in order to present the song in a meaningful way. Although someone may have the ability to compose and create songs, they may not feel adequate to present the song in performance. One of the composers who participated regularly in the New Song Workshops did not consider herself adequate to present songs in the larger, more formal song presentation settings. She would sing a song in order to teach and share it with others, but when it came to making a more professional recording with all the instruments and increased number of singers involved, she backed down from participating. Her voice did not have the proper qualities: she sang with a cracking and trembling of her voice that did not let it ring out clearly and effortlessly.

The song leader will also determine the length of the song. It is up to the leader to notice if the responding participants are too tired to continue or if the participants are especially pleased with the song. If pleasure is expressed, signaled through positive response and by the degree of clapping, then the song leader knows to lengthen the song. If there is not any positive response or feedback, the leader judges that the song should be made shorter. Thus, the song's performance will often determine its meaningfulness and pleasure. Just as in their speaking patterns, the length of a communication event reveals the importance of its message; the length of a song partially determines a song's significance to the people involved. It is then up to the leader to be responsive to the group's signals and determine the actual performance length of the song.

Photo 9: Senufo song leaders, who are also composers: Jɛniba, Nɔnyimɛ, Flaca, and Sandɛɛn with a mother and child looking on.

Musical Paths to Christian Communication

Second, a song leaders' ability to effectively lead in songs will also depend on their personal credibility. A striking example of this is the song leader, Nɔnyimɛ, who was formerly a *"sandogi"* (sorceress). Having given up her sorceress responsibilities when becoming a Christian, she still maintained her status and role, which already involved her participation in the spiritual realm. Transferring this status in a positive way to singing about Jesus Christ, people, and especially non-believers, will come from miles around to hear her sing in the all-night evangelistic meetings which are made up of singing and dancing. She is called out to do all-night Christmas festivals anywhere from December to February, sacrificing her need to do the crucial work in her fields in order to have food for her family. Nɔnyimɛ's songs and messages impact the people because she knows how to relate the Christian message within the frame of reference of the Senufo, often calling upon well-known proverbs. For example, she uses "Faith is like an egg" to indicate that faith is fragile and must be guarded. The proverb, then, becomes a meaningful device for beginning her musical interpretation of the Christian message. She makes the scriptures come alive within the Senufo world with explanations that are understandable and easy to comprehend.

In contrast to Nɔnyimɛ's credibility, Flaca has a more difficult time commanding an audience due to her barrenness. She is not considered a mature woman. Although it is not the actual case, she is automatically perceived as not having significant wisdom to offer in her songs.

Third, the spiritual development of a song leader is a crucial element in their functioning as a communication channel. This is one of the marked qualities of Nɔnyimɛ discussed above. She is focused on spiritual development of her own relationship with the Lord. Sɛnyɛnɛgatɛnɛ, a blacksmith by trade, and Jɛniba a business woman, both have this particular quality which results in people requesting their music leadership.

In both the song leader's personal credibility and spiritual development, the purpose of African music finds fulfillment since it provides "a framework through which people may relate to each other."[13] Senufo Christian songs and their presentation create an opportunity to take advantage of this particular characteristic of African music where people relate to people, influencing each other. The Senufo Christian song leader is significant in respect to communicating the Christian message:

> There is a sense in which we can say the communicator is the message that he seeks to communicate, especially with respect to messages such as those that Christians are expected to communicate.

13. Chernoff, *African Rhythm*, 154.

For those messages are expected to affect lives. And life is affected by rubbing against other life.[14]

Without skilled, credible, and spiritually-developing songleaders, Senufo Christian songs have no opportunity to communicate both within the Christian community or to reach out to those outside of their community, calling nonbelievers to participate in the interaction provided by song.

The elements that play a significant role in communicational impact within the performer channel may be summarized as follows:

**Figure 12
Elements in the Performance Channel**

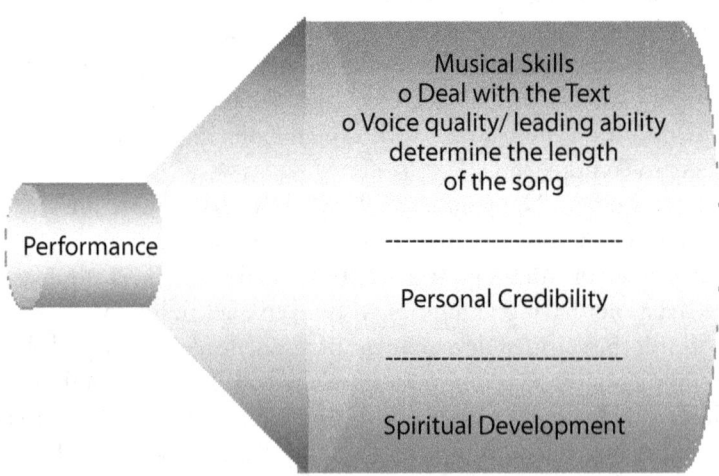

These are essential elements in the overall communication process and are required in order to transmit effectively the Christian message.

Summary

We have analyzed the various elements involved in facilitating the actual communication of a message via Senufo Christian songs. In contrast to rhetorical or monologue communication methods, music communication employs not just one channel but several channels simultaneously, each of which is reinforcing and supporting Christian communication of specific messages. There is a multiplication of impact. When each of these four

---

14. C. Kraft, *Communication Theory*, 161.

channels, (linguistic, music, movement, and performer), are skillfully wed, the resulting impact on the receptors is significantly increased to such a degree that total participation and involvement is demanded.

The significance of this contrast between monologue (rhetorical) and musical communication can be observed in the active participation of Senufo believers within a Sunday morning service. While singing everyone is awake, participating and receiving the messages presented in a song. During the sermon, however, the majority of people battle to stay awake and often use a song to wake themselves up before returning to less active attempts to catch the message of a sermon. The songs are sermons themselves.

Having considered the four channels involved in the music communication process among the Senufo, we turn to a more detailed analysis of the music channel.

7

The Music Channel on the Path

WE HAVE IDENTIFIED THE multi-channeled characteristic of music communication as being four-fold. The linguistic, music, movement, and performer channels are wedded to create an impact communication event. Having discussed each of these channels from a communicational point of view, we want to focus more directly on the role of the music channel as it participates in communication. As we have suggested in the previous chapter, the music channel is composed of eight musical elements that are utilized and integrated in the music making process (see Figure 11). We turn now to a more in-depth analysis of the first six of these, since the final two have already been dealt with in the performance channel. Our objective is to observe each of these elements as they contribute and relate to the communication process.

Form

The form of a song reveals the overall organization and plan. Senufo Christians have developed a new song form drawing from the repertoire and resources of their own musical traditions. The creation of this new song form has emerged as a result of meeting the demands and requirements of the newly established church, and is based on the church's desire and intention to effectively communicate the Christian message. The main preoccupation of Senufo Christian songs is precise presentation of the text, causing the musical resources to become subservient to this overriding intention. In spite of this fact, the musical complexity and aesthetic concerns do not suffer.

The songs have drawn from the rich Senufo tradition by relying on the basic call-and-response form so typical of African songs in general. With its own sort of musical dialogue, this form allows for the necessary involvement and participation of the whole community, a basic requirement in African music-making. Traditionally, a lead singer calls out a line or phrase, with the rest of the group responding by singing back the very same phrase in exact imitation; the "A" phrase is repeated back by the group with the same "A" phrase. This was the initial form in the early stage of Senufo Christian songs and is somewhat reminiscent of Senufo entertainment songs, where a dialogue takes place between the group of singers and the Senufo xylophone, jegele. The main difference in Senufo Christian songs is that the dialogue takes place between the lead singer and the responding group of singers.

The form that has developed out of this basic call-and-response form is related but modified. The opening line or lines become a thematic statement that introduces the song and serves as a thematic introduction, both musically and textually. The opening section is then repeated in its totality by the responding group. There is a repetition of the whole unit between the lead singer and the responding group. The final result is that the thematic statement is presented a total of four times. Then, as the lead singer moves into the next section, the final line of this opening unit becomes the repetitive response that continues throughout the duration of the song.

A development section follows, which functions as a type of exegesis and application of the opening statement. As the lead singer presents this development, the group continues to respond to the presentation of new material with its repetitive response—in most cases the "A" phrase—that keeps the opening theme continually before them. Throughout the development, the lead singer is free to repeat as many of the exegetical phrases as desired and to introduce new material.

Take, for example, the song, "Aleluya, Aleluya, Zyezu Bariga," based on Revelation 4:8, where the opening line states, "Alleluia, Alleluia, thank you Jesus." After this opening thematic statement has been presented and responded to twice, the lead singer then begins to elucidate it by stating, "God, the master of blessing and of all power, you are holy and good, without fault." After the group's response, the lead singer goes on to state, "God, master of blessing and of all power, you are perfect." There is a repetition here but also an additional description of God. A third statement says, "Daddy, you are really holy, holy, holy." This third phrase is then used another eight times throughout the development section, revealing the main emphasis of the song.

This development section not only serves as an exegetical section but also provides a means of musical elaboration and extension of the song, as judged by the song leader. It is at this point that the leader may choose to lengthen the song by repeating the basic textual phrases and/or adding new insights of explanation.

Once the development section is complete, there is a return to the opening thematic statement. This signals to the group that the song is ending and allows for another four final presentations of the main theme, where the now concluding thematic statement is also repeated as it was in the opening.

This general form may be typified by and derived from the song, "Aleluya, Aleluya Zyezu Bariga."

Figure 13
Senufo Christian Song Form #1

	Thematic Statement	Development (Exegesis)	Thematic Statement
Soloist 	A	B B' C C' D C E C	A
Group 	A	A A A A A A A	A

Key: Each letter represents a musical phrase/statement.
"B'" and "C'" indicates a variation within phrases B and C.

In Figure 13, I have not indicated every phrase that one can possibly include since this will change with each performance. There is, however, always a core of material for presentation that can be used and/or adapted, as indicated above in "B" and "C."

This song form, with its elasticity in the development section, allows for adapting to the context of the situation. If the occasion, for example, is one of festivity, or if there are nonbelievers present, the song leader will adapt the content. This is accomplished through personalizing the message; the names of those participating or references to specific life situations are added to the text. More specifically, the text may be saying, "Jesus is calling you." The song leader may adapt and personalize it by including the names of the people responding to the song, such as "Ngana, Jesus is calling you." Thus, the song form is flexible and allows for adaptation to the constraints and concerns of the people at a particular music event, whether it be a church worship service, an outdoor festival, or an evangelistic event.

The Music Channel on the Path

The development of a second and more common form in current Senufo Christian songs reflects a concern for including an increased amount of informative material in the beginning section of the song. The opening thematic section is further developed in that the lead singer does not limit the opening statement to one phrase, but rather extends it to include three phrases. The third phrase is the same as the first phrase, so that the form of this opening section becomes "A B A." In this case, the "A" phrase still becomes the response by the participating group of singers repeated throughout the duration of the song.

Figure 14
Senufo Christian Song Form #2

	Thematic Statement	Development (Exegesis)	Thematic Statement
Soloist 	A B A	C C' D A' A' D E	A B A
Group 	A B A	A A A A A A A	A B A

Key: Each letter represents a musical phrase/statement.
"A'" and "C'" indicates a variation within phrases A and C.

In the opening statement, the "B" phrase already starts to give clarification to the opening "A" phrase, and does not wait to be stated in the development section. For example, in the Senufo song version of Psalm 23:1–3 the opening statement claims:

> The father, Jehovah, is my guide.[1]
> He takes care of me.
> People, David said it in the Psalms.
> The father, Jehovah, is my guide.
> He takes care of me.

---

1. The Senufo term used is actually *nya*[glottal]*anfolo* and refers to the one who carries the child on his/her back as a baby is growing up. It carries strong implications of an intimate relationship.

At this point, the composer chose to clarify the origin of the opening statement concerning God, indicating that it comes from scripture, God's Word.

Unique to this form is its clearly defined opening and ending sections. This stands in contrast to some African song forms where the ending, especially, is not clearly defined. However, as was described in the second musical vignette, it is possible to create an immediate transition into other songs, thus avoiding a stop in the flow of musical output.

Melody

The melodic features of Senufo Christian songs are closely related to the structure of the language. This is due once again to the major intention of the song to communicate in a clear, precise, and comprehensible way. It is not within the parameters of this study to do a detailed analysis of the relationship between the tonal aspects of the language and the creative processes that take place in melodic production. The need for such a study is indeed recognized. Elizabeth Mills has written a scholarly work on Senoufo phonology that could form the basis for a beginning approach to this needed area of investigation.[2]

We note, however, that the Ceebara dialect of the Senufo language group has three discrete tones (high-tone, mid-tone, and low-tone). These three tones largely generate the melodic contour of a song. This was graphically reinforced during one of the New Song Workshops, where, after reading a scripture portion, Psalm 150, a participating composer summarized the text. The response to her summary came from another composer, claiming, "Ah-ha! That's already a song!" In re-stating the text, the basic melodic contour had been developed and it was now a matter of determining the actual pitches and intonational rhythm for each word.

More specifically, the melodies are characteristically full of large intervallic jumps of fourths and fifths in combination with thirds. These large jumps are the result of both linguistic considerations and the anhemitonic pentatonic scale (five-tone scale without half steps), which forms the basis for melodic development. The melodies are not immediately descending in nature, but rather, due to the interplay of the three tones, are characterized by an opening jump upward followed by a movement downward to a low point and returning to a middle level, usually a fourth or fifth below the opening tone. En route from the high tone to the final home tone of

---

2. Mills, *Senufo Phonology*.

the phrase via the lowest tone are a series of jumps utilizing interlocking and pendular intervals.

Figure 15
Interlocking and Pendular melodic Intervals

Song Title: Bariga Saʔa

Such interlocking and pendular melodic intervals are most likely in response to the tonal structure of the language. When we look at the spoken phrase, "Aleluya, Aleluya Zyezu Bariga," we note that there is a high tone in the third syllable of the word "Aleluya" and also a high tone on the last syllable of "Zyezu," followed by low tones on the word "bariga." Observe in the melodic pattern above that it is true to the high tones of the words. This is also the case with the thematic statement from the song "Bariga Saʔa," where there is a high tone on the first syllable of "saʔa." The influence of the language structure also apparently influences the range of the melody, which is wide and often spans up to an octave and a fourth.

It is important to maintain the relationship of the tones in the language in order to understand the message of a song. The most fundamental of these relationships is that of the tones of words. The Senufo languages are "tone languages," where the three tones serve a phonemic function. A group of words may have the same vowels and consonants, but distinguish different meanings through the varying tone levels. The following sets of words exemplify this.

 kólo [¨] to give approval
 kolo [- -] to be wrong
 kòlo [_ _] chair
 kólogo [¨¨] to lack
 kologo [- - -] a road, path
 kologò [- - _] to roll
 kòdo liqo [_ ¨ - -] a person wearing funeral clothes
 kodo lōq [- ¨¨ _] a grass skirt of the *Poro*

Tones not only function in a semantic role, as above, but also perform grammatical functions such as signaling positive and negative statements.

For example, a high tone at the end of the sentence negates the positive version of the same statement:

> *Wo lapie ní Zyezu ní* [- - - ˙ - - -] We will be with Jesus.
> *Wo lapie ní Zyezu nií* [- - - ˙ - - - ˌ] We will not be with Jesus.

Another feature of melody in Senufo Christian songs is the dependence on the interplay between the leader and the responding singers. This interplay provides the structural continuity of the melody produced through this singing dialogue. The lead singer and participants are dependent on one another in order to maintain the presentation of the song. This reflects a call to participate on everyone's part. There is no place for the spectator; rather, each person becomes involved with the production of the song. The singing of a song is not a passive experience but one of interaction. People must act out their roles.

There is a parallel between the interplay of the song leader and the responding group, and the names attached to the two dialoguing parts. The leader's call, *gokpori,* literally refers to "the one who kills the chicken for the fetish," while the group's response, *sandogi,* refers to the fetish itself. The basic song form, then, is reflective of Senufo worship forms of sacrifice. However, in the case of the believing Senufo the song has become a new type of "spiritual work," in that it has become a sacrifice of praise.[3]

Thus, there are two major dynamics of communication occuring within the melodic form of Senufo Christian songs. First is the preoccupation with comprehensibility of the text as the language shapes the melody. Second, there is the call to participate in the responsibility for producing the song's melody where participants must work together. This call to participate is also related to traditional worship forms where the leader and people work together in preparing a sacrifice, but Senufo Christians have transformed their songs into sacrifices of praise.

Harmony

Harmony, per se, is not characteristic of traditional Senufo songs, and possibly points, once again, to the song's main intention of communicating a message in a clear fashion. The vocal parts of Senufo Christian songs are characteristically monodic in that they are single melodies with no accompanying harmonic vocal parts. There is occasional singing in parallel octaves or fifths in order to meet the limitations of a person's particular vocal range. Occasional divergence of isolated tones also often occurs at

---

3. Heb 13:15.

the end of the phrase, where a singer is not exactly on pitch, but appears to be within the allowable range for the overall melodic contour of the song. This divergence of pitch is not intended as a harmonic effect.

Rhythm

The rhythmic aspects and relationships within Senufo Christian songs are complex. As Nketia points out about African songs in general, there are both musical and speech considerations to be taken into account.[4] Senufo rhythmic structure reveals the same complex interplay of rhythms based on alternations between units of duple and triple beats. This occurs in melodic phrases as well as complex rhythmic interplays between the vocal and instrumental parts.

Among the various rhythmic interplays is the element of clapping. Clapping plays a significant role in the overall rhythmic structure of a song by helping to define the basic pulse underlying this somewhat fluid form. It also allows the responding group to be constantly participating and giving expression to their agreement or relation to the song text. More pertinent to our discussion of music's contribution to the communication process, however, is the role that clapping plays in relation to the participants. Clapping is not restricted merely to adding musical interest and complexity to the total musical event, as aesthetically pleasing and challenging as that may be. For Senufo Christians there is no real discussion about the complexity and sophistication of clapping patterns, or focus on whether a particular pattern is especially enjoyable. Rather, for the song participants, clapping serves as a rhythmic expression and visualization of one's spiritual relationship to God.

The major dynamic involved in clapping is that it expresses joy. This expression of joy reveals the vitality of the Senufo believer's walk on the "Jesus road." Believers repeatedly stated that joy "pushes" them to clap their hands. In fact, clapping is so important that one believer explained: "Yes, I clap my hands because of joy. My hands have been damaged due to illness but I clap my hands anyway even though they don't make a large noise."[5] It is important to clap one's hands, even they have bee damaged and are incapable of doing it well, since clapping serves as a means of "proving" one's joy.

For the Senufo believers, clapping is a visual signal that reflects their spiritual state, to such a degree that when a person does not clap their

---

4. Nketia, *Music of Africa*, 169–176.
5. R. King, Focus Group Interviews, Foro, QIII-7.

hands others believers perceive that something is wrong and/or the person is not happy. On the other hand, clapping for joy is a means of manifesting one's complete contentment in relationship with God as compared to one's former life:

> When I was a "pagan," I used to go around looking and searching for a certain joy. It was a joy that was not perfect. But the joy that I have in the Lord is a perfect and total joy. Therefore, in order to prove it one must clap their hands.[6]

At the same time that clapping reflects the believers' relationship with God, it also serves as a means of direct, spiritual communication: clapping is a way to praise God. In order to adequately praise God, Senufo believers must clap their hands. This is so important to some believers that one lady exclaimed, "It really bugs me if someone does not clap their hands when we're singing!"[7] Within this approach to praise is the expression of gratefulness to God for the way He has acted in their lives, whether it be solutions to problems of infertility, deliverance from the tests of Satan, or blessing of marital relationships. Praise, through clapping of the hands, is a way to show their gratefulness to God, to bring him pleasure, and to do it with "all their heart."

Finally, clapping in Senufo secular society is a natural means of communicating pleasure and interest in what is being said, and also a means of showing honor and respect. This concept has been transferred over to Senufo Christian songs, and is explained as one believer expounds the felt imperative to clap on behalf of God: "We see that when an important person speaks, such as a mayor of the town or a government official, that people applaud him if he says something that interests them. In this case, we're applauding just people. However, in our case, we must clap even more for God."[8] Clapping, then, allows Christians to show their interest in what God is saying to them, to give him respect and honor, and to underline the importance of God's ways in their lives. It provides a major means for them to praise God with "all their heart."[9] Clapping, then, also contributes to their new-found "spiritual work," which is to offer God a "sacrifice of praise."[10] It plays in integral role in the communication process.

Senufo believers caution, however, that as important as it is to them, in the total production of song clapping plays a subservient role to com-

---

6. Ibid.
7. Ibid.
8. Ibid.
9. Ibid.
10. Heb 13.

prehension of the text. They maintain that one must be able to understand the song before they participate in clapping, and that if they cannot understand the message of the song, then the song is useless. The message being communicated must be heard and understood before they can clap in agreement as praise to God.

In terms of communication dynamics, we see that the two main elements in the production of a song are (1) the actual singing of the song, with its call-and-response dialogue and (2) clapping by the group. Clapping is essential to the song form. While there may be a varying number of instruments accompanying the song, or none at all, the element of clapping cannot be omitted. In relation to the song's form, clapping is not performed during the opening thematic statement. However, the singers do clap during the development/exegesis section whenever the lead singer is calling out the next phrase.

Figure 16
The Relation of Clapping to the Melodic Structure

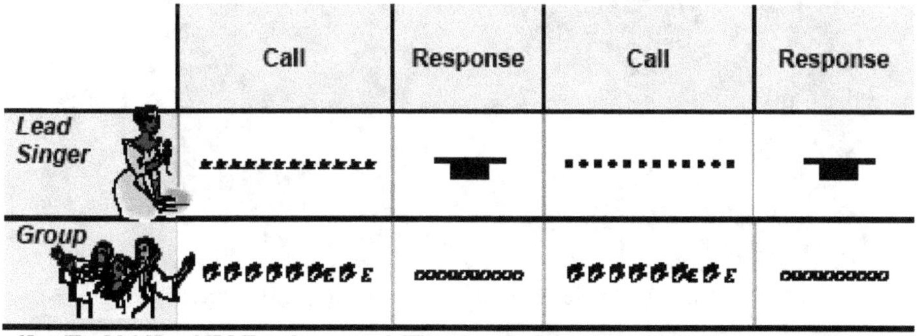

	Call	Response	Call	Response
Lead Singer	★★★★★★★★★★	▬	• • • • • • • • • •	▬
Group	♪♪♪♪♪♪♪♪	oooooooo	♪♪♪♪♪♪♪♪	oooooooo

Key: The "★★★" and "• • •" each represent different musical phrases that are sung by the leader. The "ooo" represents the sung response. The clapping pattern alternates between the responses for the responding group while the song leader rests between phrases.

From this figure we note that during the development/exegesis section the group is involved in both clapping and singing the response; the group participates on a continual basis. They are always involved in the creation of the music channel, actively participating in the musical product and the message carried by the song. There is no time to become inattentive, as the whole person participates.

Instruments

Although Senufo Christian songs as they are sung today require a minimum of the vocal parts plus clapping, other instruments have slowly worked their way into the song presentations. In the early stages of development, the believers hardly felt free to even snap their fingers, as they asked themselves if this was acceptable for the worship of God, "*kolocoloo.*" Today an ensemble of instruments may be employed in the presentation of song, depending on the availability of the instruments and sufficiently developed instrumentalists.

Photo 10: Singer with *caliw* (a calabash gourd shaker)

The ensemble of instruments that the Senufo Christians have incorporated into their forms of worship on a regular basis include the *caliw* (a calabash shaker with cowry shells strung on the outside), the *kaanrigi* (a cylindrical metal scraper), and the *jegele* (*balafon*). Other instruments that are beginning to work their way into the ensemble include drums and an open calabash gourd with cowry shells strung on the outside.

The Music Channel on the Path

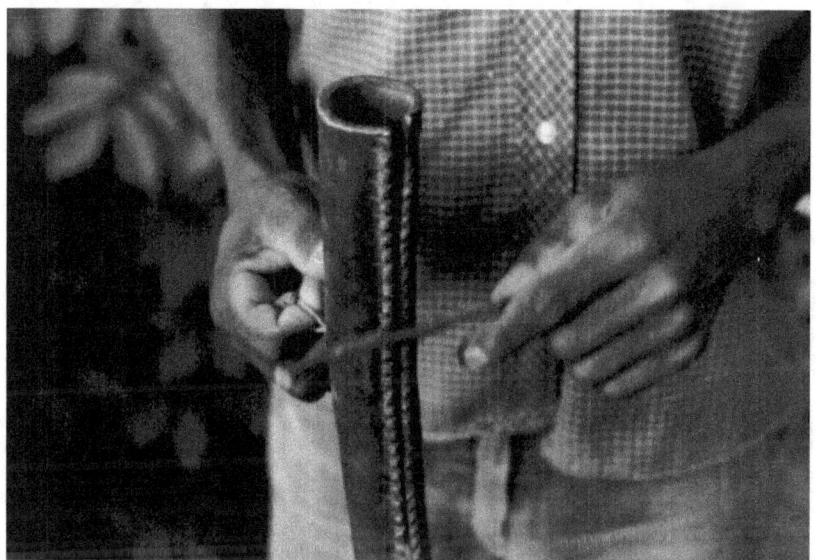

Photo 11: *Kaanrigi*, a Senufo metal scraper

Senufo society, in general, offers a wealth of instruments to draw from. Zemp maintains that Senufo musical life revolves mainly around the activities of the secret societies such as the *Poro* and the *Sandogo*.[11] For the women's *Sandogo* society, instruments used include a hand-struck four-footed drum, or the water-drum, "formed from a half-calabash filled with water in which an upturned calabash floats, which is struck with a spoon-shaped half-gourd." The men's *Poro* society uses double-headed cylindrical drums and wooden anthropomorphic trumpet ensembles.[12] A full array of other musical instruments, including harp-lutes, flutes, and various types of drums, complete the ensemble.[13]

Rigid rules regulate when the sacred instruments of the *Poro* may be played. They are usually reserved for special initiation events.[14] Interestingly enough, the *jegele* (*balafon*) that is used along with the Christian songs does not traditionally belong to this group of sacred instruments, and is actually considered to be of low rank. It is an instrument that can be played

---

11. "Ivory Coast," 434.
12. Ibid.
13. Knops, *Les Anciens Senufo*, 171–78.
14. Glaze, *Art and Death*, 95.

and practiced on at any time, and thus appears to be more appropriate for church activities and less offensive to the requirements of the *Poro*.

The *jegele*, however, is not without its own "stigma." Its use in the church with Christian songs has been a topic of great debate among national believers. Oral tradition attributes the origin of all musical instruments to either monkeys or "bush spirits." The "bush spirits" are the owners of each village's *jegele* orchestra,[15] composed of three *jegele* and two drums. Before a *jegele* is put into performance, chicken sacrifices are made to the spirits and sacrificial blood is applied to the instrument.

Photo 12: Believers playing Senufo Chrisitan *balafons*

Senufo believers have dealt with this problem by having new *jegeles* made, for which there has not been any chicken sacrifice. The *jegele* is then dedicated to praising God. Indeed, in contrast to the sacrificial blood being found on the instrument, I've often noticed a series of Christian stickers in French making various types of statements such as "God is love." This points towards a type of functional substitute for the sacrifice and identifies the purpose of the *jegele* in use.

A word about Senufo believers' theological position on the incorporation of their own instruments into worship is in order at this point. One of the most important themes in evangelism among the Senufo people is the creation story. This repeatedly makes an impression on them. As they

---

15. Kientz, *Dieu et les Genies*, 114.

have come to understand that God is the creator of all things, they have realized that they can offer to God all he has given them. When asked about the difference between a "Christian" and non-Christian *jegele,* a church leader at the village of Kissanka? explained:

> We know that everything on earth was created by God. On this earth we also worship the fetishes with the *jegele*. But it is God who created everything and that is why we can worship God with everything. Everything that we play, no matter what we used to worship Satan we can now also use to worship God. Even the drums from the *Poro* if you beat them in the name of the Lord you can praise God with them. . . . We play the *jegele* in the name of Jesus, with the name of Jesus we worship our God. It is God who created them. That's why we are very unhappy to leave these things to Satan. (King 1985: Kissanka?a)[16]

Thus, for many Senufo believers, the use of the instrument depends on the one to whom it is dedicated. The *jegele* may be used if it is played in the name of Jesus and offered to him. As a church leader from another village explained, "So I think that it depends on the use of the instrument or the master that the instrument serves."[17] In this way, then, an instrument is empowered by the usage to which it is put. If a *jegele*'s master is God, then it is empowered by him and given spiritual sanction to be used in his service. Thus, the source of the spiritual dynamics involved determine the validity of its use in worship.

Another distinctive feature of the *jegele* as used by Senufo believers is that they claim it is both different physically from the non-Christian one and played in a different style. The traditional *jegele* played in the "*balafon* bands" (three *balafons* and two drums) at funeral celebrations and for entertainment has twelve keys, whereas the *jegele* used by the believers has seventeen. The reason for this requirement centers around the predominant concern and intention in Senufo Christian songs of making the text clear; their ultimate goal and emphasis is on communication of a message.

The *jegele*, in general, is capable of imitating the Senufo language itself, due to the tonal nature of the language, and is often used to send messages in the village. In fact, it is said that the wood used for the keys that sound the notes never dies since the keys are always speaking.[18] They are always speaking the language; they are communicating. Thus, when

---

16. R. King, Senufo Field Notes, 1985.
17. R. King, Focus Group Interviews, Foro, QIII-9.
18. R. King, Senufo Song Survey.

a Christian song is played on the *jegele*, it is done in such a way that people can also understand the textual message of the song, usually the "A" phrase.

Since the *jegele* is also communicating the text of the song, the actual performance style and manner of playing the *jegele* is important. Briefly, the *jegele* is not played by merely imitating and accompanying the melody with a supporting chordal structure, as in western hymn accompaniment. Rather, two *jegeles* are normally played, with one player at each instrument. The lead player will perform in the lower range of the instrument. Each hand plays its own *ostinato* pattern (a repetitive, constantly recurring circular-type pattern that never changes). For example, in the song, "Alleluia, Alleluia, Zyezubariga," the left-hand ostinato of the lead player is the full length of the "A" phrase of the song, while the right-hand ostinato is half the length of the left-hand ostinato. The right-hand ostinato will then be repeated twice by the time the left-hand has finished playing its ostinato once. Meanwhile, the second *jegele* player performs in the upper range of notes with a left-hand ostinato that is half the length of the "A" phrase and a right-hand ostinato that is a fourth of the "A" phrase. Graphically, it would look as depicted in Figure 17.

We note here that the texture is very dense. Significantly though, each of these individual ostinato patterns interlock together in such a way that the textual phrase of the song is heard and understood. The melodic line is not contained in one ostinato pattern alone, but is the result of combining each of the patterns together (see Appendix E for full notation of this song).

One final remark about the uniqueness of the believers' *jegele* concerns the general community's response to it. On the whole, the Senufo Christian songs, especially at Christmas celebrations, are well received and people are naturally attracted to them. The *jegele* adds an additional dynamic to the atmosphere and mood of the song. There have been occasional complaints that the nonbelieving Senufos do not appreciate that the believers are incorporating this instrument into their worship practices.

The Music Channel on the Path

Figure 17
Jegele (Balafon) Performance Patterns

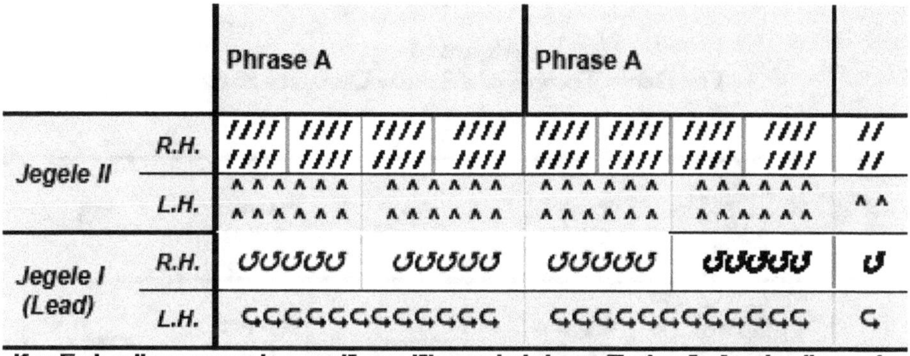

		Phrase A				Phrase A				
Jegele II	R.H.	//// ////	//// ////	//// ////	//// ////	//// ////	//// ////	//// ////	//// ////	// //
	L.H.	∧∧∧∧∧∧ ∧∧∧∧∧∧		∧∧∧∧∧∧ ∧∧∧∧∧∧		∧∧∧∧∧∧ ∧∧∧∧∧∧		∧∧∧∧∧∧ ∧∧∧∧∧∧		∧∧
Jegele I (Lead)	R.H.	ʊʊʊʊʊ	ʊʊʊʊʊ		ʊʊʊʊʊ		ʊʊʊʊʊ			ʊ
	L.H.	ϛϛϛϛϛϛϛϛϛϛϛ				ϛϛϛϛϛϛϛϛϛϛϛ				ϛ

Key: Each pattern represents a specific repetitive musical phrase. The length of each pattern varies and is indicated by the vertical lines.

Evidently, the spiritual dynamics of playing it are so distinctive and disruptive in terms of general atmosphere that one Sunday a village chief requested that the believers not play their *jegele*, since the *Poro* society would be performing a funeral. This was not a concern over having too many music groups participating at the funeral, since all instrumental groups perform simultaneously but also independently from one another. The problem was that the believers' *jegele* performance would disturb the activities of the funeral, which is highly involved with both the bush spirits and the spirits of the ancestors.

In discussing the *jegele* to such a degree, we have bypassed the two other rhythmic instruments that are used on a regular basis. The *caliw* (a calabase shaker with cowry shells) and the *kaanrigi* (an iron friction instrument played with an iron baton) both support rhythmic structures of the song, and usually restrict themselves to short rhythmic ostinatos that help to define the basic pulse. They contribute to the creation of the intricate rhythmic configuration and the complexity of the song, with its use of cross rhythms and polyrhythms, characteristic features typical of traditional African music.

If we combine all the instrumental parts together with the vocal parts, we note that a very dense texture is created (see Figure 18). This dense texture created by the instruments enhances and heightens musical interest. The instrumental parts support and define the rhythmic structure of the song, while the *jegele* also provides a melodic re-creation of the song text itself. The combination of each of these musical elements adds to the unique and distinctive mood created by the Senufo Christian song style. It is a sound that is distinctively Senufo and yet also comes to be identified with the Senufo believers and the name of Jesus Christ.

Figure 18
The Dense Texture of a Senufo Christian Song

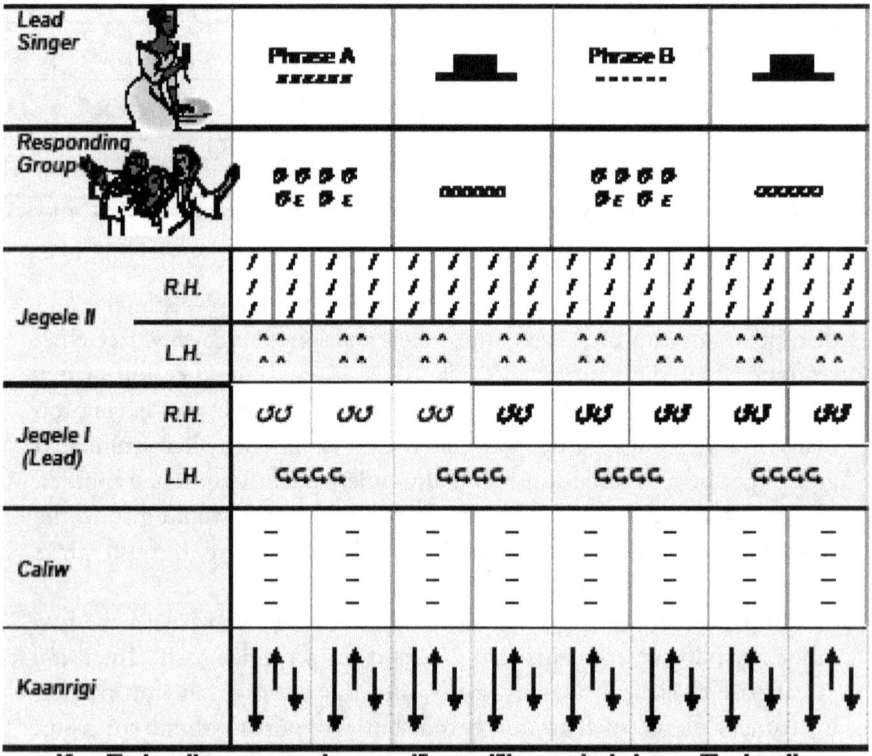

Lead Singer		Phrase A		Phrase B	
Responding Group					
Jegele II	R.H.				
	L.H.				
Jegele I (Lead)	R.H.				
	L.H.				
Caliw					
Kaanrigi					

Key: Each pattern represents a specific repetitive musical phrase. The length of each pattern varies and is indicated by the vertical lines.

Tempo

The tempo of Senufo Christian songs will vary according to a song's particular composition character. In relation to communication, comprehension of the text still has priority. Senufo believers feel that a song should not be too fast: one must be able to understand what is being sung and to sing together as a single unit. They specify that a "medium" tempo will allow them to understand the text and also enjoy the music.

New learners of a song request that it be performed slowly so that they may be able to listen, whereas others say that a slow tempo will put them to sleep. In general, the youth, with their high energy levels, prefer the songs in a fast or "hot" tempo so that they may fully enjoy the dance. The women at their annual conferences, in contrast to the youth, take their songs at more of a "medium" speed. The "medium" tempo songs are the ones that both hold interest and allow for comprehension, which is perhaps a higher priority for the more mature women than for the youth.

Performance Patterns and Tone Qualities

We have briefly discussed performance patterns and tone qualities in the previous chapter. I have dealt with performance patterns in greater detail in the performance channel and have also defined it briefly in the discussion on the music channel. The area of tone quality and its relationship to communication is in need of further investigation. However, due to the focus of this investigation and the restraints on researching this aspect, I was not able to research any further than what I have already discussed within the context of the performance channel. For an introductory study on vocal tone qualities in African music, see Rose Brandel's book, *Music of Central Africa*.

Summary

We have, then, analyzed six elements within the music channel and highlighted aspects of the remaining two. Each of these musical elements plays a significant role in the music making process. If any one of these elements is not employed appropriately and correctly, a distortion of the message and a hampering of facility in performance may occur. The complexity of the music communication process reveals the many possibilities for miscommunication of a message. At the same time, however, the complexity of the music channel also adds greater impact to the communication event when meeting the formal musical requirements of Senufo Christian songs.

PART FOUR

A Study of Song Texts

8

Song Texts: A Path to Worldview Discovery

Having studied each of the four music channels within the communication process as found among Senufo Christian songs, we turn now to an investigation of the verbal contents of the songs. Song texts communicate most directly and specifically within the linguistic channel and are at the center of the communication process. The analysis of their content is the task that is presently before us.

Song Texts as Guideposts

Song texts often function as guideposts or signals to deeper issues in life. For example, there was a typical Senufo, non-Christian woman, who was mad at her husband. Yet, she was not free to talk about it with him. However, as her Senufo tradition had taught her, she found herself singing a song alluding to this husband of hers who had angered her. She never included his name in the song, but he nevertheless recognized himself in it. In order to show the depth of her anger, the woman began to include derogatory remarks about her husband's family. In fact, as she sang expressing her anger, she decided to take the final step to an open fight: she started singing derogatory remarks about his mother.[1] The message had been communicated through the song text, serving its purpose of invading the world of her husband. Its contents were oblique and indirect to the outsider but very obvious to those involved in the situation.

As I have sought to learn and understand the texts of Senufo Christian songs, I found myself often feeling very much like an outsider. Yet, as I have discussed the texts with informants, I have found myself naturally moving into the underlying assumptions of a people in their everyday life. One of my most vivid recollections of this was when I was working with a young girl about to be married. She was helping me transcribe and translate a number of songs I had recorded at her church in Boundiali. We had already translated several songs that had typically referred to all the things from which Jesus had saved the Senufo believers; for example,

---

1. R. King, Focus Group Interviews, Coonyɛʔɛn.

doing harm to other people, lying, being jealous of other people's possessions, and stealing. I was beginning to feel I knew some of their problems and felt needs.

Then came a song that addressed sorcerers, admittedly an area that is naturally foreign to me. The text revealed several of the practices of sorcery, including a reference to the "eating of people." What was meant by that phrase? Is it a literal practice or a belief on the part of people concerning sorcerers? This signaled an area for investigation that I would not have naturally pursued based on my western background. The song text revealed a deeper issue that is not openly observable to the outsider.

Song texts, then, provide a path for discovering the underlying assumptions and cognitive understanding of a people. For Senufo believers the song texts are the most important element of a Christian song. The purpose of the present two chapters is to do a content analysis of the song texts that have developed within the emerging Senufo church of Côte d'Ivoire. We will seek to show that song texts reflect a people's worldview, developing theological understandings, and approach and attempt to integrate the Christian message within their own cultural context.

Blueprints for Song Text Analysis

Blueprints or methods for analyzing song texts may be drawn from several fields. Within ethnomusicology, for example, the study of song texts takes one beyond the structural analysis of the music. It serves as a "means of expanding knowledge about music to knowledge of other and wider human behavioral processes."[2] The uniqueness of studying song texts is that they raise to the surface deeply embedded issues, concerns, and perspectives that are not easily obtained. Thus, the singing of songs allows for the expression of ideas, values, and concerns that would not necessarily be allowed in normal conversations or discourses. Merriam summarizes this point in his convincing discussion about song texts:

> What is important . . . is that song itself gives the freedom to express thoughts, ideas, and comments which cannot be stated baldly in the normal language situation. It appears, then, that song texts, because of the special kind of license that singing apparently gives, afford an extremely useful means for obtaining kinds of information which are not otherwise easily accessible.[3]

---

2. Merriam, *Anthropology of Music*, 187.
3. Ibid., 193.

Song Texts: A Path to Worldview Discovery

With this in mind, ethnomusicolgists often study song texts by delineating the basic themes of songs within the total musical repertoire of a people. Nketia affirms this approach: "In addition to songs of a personal, topical, and historical nature, one should take note of those that deal in a general way with philosophical and religious themes, or with specific problems of man's existence in the universe."[4] A specific example of following this approach can be found in Knight's discussion of Mandinka music, where he points to the main textual themes found within *jaliya* songs, a specific genre of Mandinke songs. These basic themes revolve around death, bravery, religion, and praise,[5] and allow for investigating worldview issues.

An additional field that studies content is that of intercultural communication research, where both quantitative and qualitative content analysis is practiced. Quantitative content analysis focuses on a quantitative-spacial metaphor, which assumes that whatever "means" takes up more space and/or time.[6] This appears to be true in everyday Senufo discourse. According to Elizabeth Mills, in the practice of the Senufo the greater the importance of the idea stated, the greater number of words and space devoted to it. Thus, a straight-forward quantitative content analysis of song texts can be helpful to us in determining significance.

However, qualitative content analysis goes beyond the mere compilation of the occurrences of references within a text. Rather, it strives to relate key terms used within a given context with the objective of determining a communicator's motivation. This is done as a means of searching for an understanding of the communicator's intended meaning. Context becomes the grid through which words are interpreted. Based on this, then, Sarosta asserts that "meaning resides in phrases, kernels, and collections of symbols within a context, seldom within isolated terms," and that "culture provides a context, high or low, which undergirds all cultural interaction."[7] Meaning is derived within particular contexts.

Therefore, the method of content analysis of song texts used in these two chapters is based on the disciplines of both ethnomusicology and intercultural communication research. This is pursued in an effort to learn about the Senufo's worldview and their perceptions of the Christian message.

---

4. *The Music of Africa*, 199.
5. Knight, "The Style of Mandinka Music," 9.
6. Starosta, "Qualitative Content Analysis,"185.
7. Ibid., 192.

The greatest emphasis is put upon qualitative content analysis. In presenting the material, I have chosen to create taxonomies based on various cultural domains as revealed through the song texts. As Spradley advocates, a taxonomy indicates the relationships among the things inside a cultural domain as they relate to the culture as a whole.[8] Thus, in these taxonomies, I am seeking to determine the relationship between key terms and the cultural context. I freely recognize that the use of content analysis to suggest cultural patterns does indeed create an "etic" construct. However, I also pursued information from cultural informants concerning "emic" perceptions of words and phrases as they relate to the specific context.

Scope and Limitations

Fifty song texts were selected from a total of 172 collected during my four stays in the Korhogo area. In an attempt to acquire a diachronic sense of the growth and development of content, songs were selected from three different collection periods: Songs Before the 1986 Workshop, the Current Senufo Repertoire, and the Most Popular Songs of 1987.

The first set of song texts analyzed are those collected in 1986 at the beginning of the Senufo New Song Workshop. These songs existed before the workshop. A total of thirty-seven Senufo Christian songs were recorded at the workshop. From these, eighteen song texts were selected for analysis. The selection criteria was three-fold. The first ten songs analyzed are those initially presented at the workshop. These songs were selected on the assumption and practice that the most popular and most meaningful songs are those that come first to a singer's mind. In addition to this, they serve as a type of random sample, since the singers were free to sing songs of their choice. The remaining eight songs were selected based on personal observation that the songs are regular standards in song services. This collection of songs is referred to in the following charts as Songs Before the 1986 Workshop.

The second set of songs, entitled "Current Senufo Repertoire," comprises those determined to be the most popular by eighty-nine Senufo Christians in the song survey of 1987. Although there was an overwhelmingly large number of songs indicated as favorites, the nine texts selected received the highest number of votes. The tenth song in the group is the one that was used in the Focus Groups interviews conducted in 1988.

Finally, the third set of song texts used in the analysis are those considered to be the most popular songs created at the 1987 workshop. A total

---

8. *Participant Observation*, 112.

of fifty-six songs were composed at that time. From these, twenty-three of them have made their way into the regularly-sung Senufo repertoire. These songs serve as an indication of current theological concerns and everyday needs of the believers. I refer to this set of songs as the Most Popular Songs of 1987.

This last set was selected according to three criteria. First, the composers indicated which songs they had sung most frequently throughout the year. Second, my main translator and informant examined the list and tapes of songs, indicating the ones sung on a regular basis in the Korhogo area. Third, songs that were popular enough to have had a *balafon* accompaniment developed were also included in this collection. Let us now focus on discovering a people's worldview through song texts.

Song Texts as Windows on Worldview

As we begin a more specific study of song texts as a means to discovering worldview, we must reaffirm that song texts may serve as a means to gaining information that might not otherwise be immediately accessible. This is particularly true with regard to worldview. Particular areas of a people's worldview currently posing difficulties in the integration of the Christian message in the lives of believers will also surface in song texts. However, we must note that song texts merely point to Senufo worldview assumptions, and do not attempt to elucidate a precise definition of what each concept signifies. Song texts allow one to catch glimpses, as though viewing through a window, of the reality of a people's needs and assumptions concerning their particular life situation. They do not necessarily give access to the totality of a particular worldview concept. Although song texts cannot indicate the precise rate of occurrence or degree of seriousness of a specific problem or concern, they do raise to the surface particular felt needs and serve as indicators for further investigation that the culturally sensitive communicator may pursue.

A Brief Definition of Worldview

Before actually looking at the Senufo Christian song texts, we need to briefly define worldview. The anthropological study of worldview falls within the cognitive domain of cultural study and analysis. It attempts to seek out the deep level of a people's perception towards reality rather than merely dwell on the aspects of a society that are more readily observable.

During my stay in the village of Zanaka?a, for example, I was able to immediately gain a sense of the daily village routine, including sweeping the courtyard, fetching water from the well, going to the fields to cultivate, bathing in the morning and evening, pounding maize in order to prepare the evening meal, and school studies in the evening by the gas lamp. I could also observe when songs were sung, such as the children's songs and games that were sung and played on evenings where there was a full moon. However, I was restricted in my understandings and approach to these activities since I did not have a total grasp of the language. I was, admittedly, limited in interacting with the people in gaining their perceptions about such activities. I could see them working in their fields, for example, but I could not observe their concern for pleasing the "bush spirits" as they hoed their tomatoes. Nor could I understand all the innuendos and deeper lessons that were involved as the children played their singing games.

Such deep-level concepts and perceptions of reality that act as an "unconscious system of meanings"[9] serve as a people's worldview. Worldview reflects the way a people look at the reality of their world. Worldview, then, is composed of "the basic assumptions the people have about the nature of reality and of right and wrong."[10] Although theory concerning world view is extensive, worldview is a main area of study within anthropology. Further in-depth study into worldview may be pursued in Kearney[11] and in Kraft.[12] We will use this definition of worldview as the basis of our discussion.

Song Texts and Worldview

Song texts relate to worldview in that they allow the people a medium of expression of their everyday concerns, perspectives, and assumptions not otherwise permitted. Indeed, "in song the individual or the group can apparently express deep-seated feeling not permissibly verbalized in other contexts."[13] The study of song texts, then, is a means of "getting at" worldview. Kraft has aptly asserted: "In a large number of cultures one would look to fables, proverbs, riddles, songs, and other forms of folklore for overt and covert indications of the worldview."[14] It is my contention that keys to the Senufo worldview are available to us through the study of their song texts, both secular and Christian.

---

9. Sapir, "The Status of Linguistics.
10. Hiebert, "Culture and Cross-Cultural Differences," 49.
11. Kearney, *World View.*
12. C. Kraft, *Christianity in Culture*, 53–63.
13. Merriam, "Anthropology of Music," 190.
14. C. Kraft, *Christianity in Culture*, 55.

Ideally, the intercultural Christian worker should study both the non-Christian and Christian song texts of the people in order to facilitate a fuller understanding of their worldview. I was most determined to do this, however, the majority of the Senufo Christians with whom I had the most contact and to whom I reported would neither allow me to collect non-Christian songs nor willingly share many of the songs they had known before they were Christians. There was a fear that they would betray themselves as Christians or give a bad testimony if they did reveal knowledge of such songs. Thus, in the 1987 song survey, very few Christians would state that they even knew any non-Christian songs.

One especially poignant non-Christian song text that I was able to collect, however, may serve as an example of discovering traditional Senufo worldview. The song text, offered by a former singer for the *Poro* society, discusses a philosophy of death. It declares that:

> Death is like a river bed. If it rains, the water always follows the same path picking up and carrying the branches along. When there is a root in the river, some of the branches are caught while others go on down the river. So it is with death. When she arrives, she follows the same path.[15]

This song text provides advice and condolence offered to a family when they have lost a family member. The general theme is that all dead ones follow along the same path or river bed. They are all going the same direction with some family members getting caught on roots earlier in the river while others continue on further. The river appears to have no final destination but simply continues on. From this we see that the perspective on death within the Senufo worldview is distinct from that of Christian teaching. Thus, the text deals with an essential ontological question and is of ultimate concern to the cause of God's kingdom when presenting the Christian faith.

Activities that Christians Abandon

In addition to the secular, traditional Senufo songs, the texts of Senufo Christian songs also reveal aspects of their worldview. The predominant worldview domain that has surfaced in the Christian song texts is mainly concerned with a sense of right and wrong, categorized here as "Activities that Christians Abandon." Although the song texts allude to other aspects of worldview, we will limit our discussion to this particular domain due

---

15. R. King, Senufo Field Notes, 1987.

to its predominance. Let us look at an investigation of the activities that Christians must abandon as explained in the song texts.

A Typical Senufo Christian Song Text

We begin by focusing on one specific song text. This, the most popular song in the "Current Senufo Repertoire," based on John 14:2, serves as a prime example for revealing keys to the Senufo worldview:

"In My Father's House"

Thematic Statement:

There are many dwelling places in my Father's house. If it were not so, I would have plainly told you. But I am going there to prepare one for you. When I finish, I will come and take you. You will live in the dwelling place of my father.

Response: You will live in the dwelling place of my father.

Development:

(1) Abandon lying, Jesus is calling you.

(2) Abandon doubts, Jesus is calling you.

(3) Abandon sadness, Jesus is calling you.

(4) Abandon the "lɔɔsunyi," Jesus is calling you.

(5) Abandon the "coto-beeri," Jesus is calling you.

(6) Abandon the "fani-wiiw," Jesus is calling you.

(7) My fathers, Jesus is calling you.

(8) My mothers, Jesus is calling you.

(9) My brothers, Jesus is calling you.

(10) Abandon sadness, Jesus is calling you.

(11) Get up and walk, Jesus is calling you. Come!

Thematic Statement:

There are many dwelling places in my Father's house.
If it were not so, I would have plainly told you.
But I am going there to prepare one for you.
When I finish, I will come and take you. You will live in the dwelling place of my father.

Song Texts: A Path to Worldview Discovery

From this song text we learn of the problems and activities that are perceived as needing to be abandoned. Notice that activities dealing with relationships with others, such as lying, must be given up. Personal problems, including doubt and sadness, must be given up if you respond to Jesus' call. One must also abandon traditional customs such as the *lɔɔsunyi* (the worship of bodies of water), the *coto-beeri* (the initiation into the secret *Poro* society), and the *fani-wiiw* (the specially woven cloth attached to a person or thing that serves as a fetish). Although there is a call to abandon these things, there is also a promise that, in a sense, in getting up and walking with Jesus these burdens and difficulties will no longer exist.

From this one song text, then, we may pose several questions in relationship to worldview. There are references to traditional customs, relational problems with other people, and personal problems. Each of these areas may be investigated. Beyond this, an overall picture of such concerns and activities that need to be abandoned discloses four major domains. These are drawn from the compilation of all fifty texts and include the domains of traditional customs, relationships with the spirits, relationships with other people, and personal problems.

Table 1
Activities that Christians Abandon
("SINS" – Shows a Sense of Right and Wrong)

DOMAIN	Total Number of References
TRADITIONAL CUSTOMS	
SORCERY	3
USE OF FETISHES	29
OX'S TAIL	5
FANI-WIIW (woven cloth)	2
NANBW YI (used to harm one's neighbor)	2
SANDO?O (women's sorcery society)	7
CONSULT THE SORCERESS	1
WORK OF TRADITIONAL HEALERS	1
MARABOUTAGE (the work of the marabouts)	3
WORSHIP	
SACRIFICES	1
CHICKEN SACRIFICE	1
COLA NUT SACRIFICE	1
THINGS	
THE WOODEN SNAKE	1
ANIMALS	
CHICKENS	1
PLACES	
BODIES OF WATER (rivers/ponds)	5
PEOPLE	
THE DEAD	2
TRADITIONAL INITIATIONS	1
INITIATION INTO THE PORO SOCIETY	2
THE BAD PORO	1
FUNERAL CEREMONIES	4
TRADITIONAL CUSTOMS SUB-TOTAL	**73 (46%)**

DOMAIN	Total Number of References
RELATIONSHIPS WITH SPIRITS	
SATAN	4
HIS WORK	1
SATAN'S INSOMNIA	1
SPIRITS	
DISCUSSION WITH SPIRITS	1
IN THE HANDS OF THE SPIRITS	1
RELATIONSHIPS WITH SPIRITS SUB-TOTAL	**8 (5%)**

Song Texts: A Path to Worldview Discovery

Traditional Customs

The traditional customs definitely create the largest group of activities that Senufo Christians feel they must abandon. Forty-six percent of the references made concerning these activities dwell on sorcery, worship practices, traditional initiations, and funeral ceremonies.

Sorcery

Sorcery heads the list as the activity that most definitely needs to be abandoned, with 71 percent of the references made about the traditional customs referring to sorcery. Among sorcery practices, the use of fetishes or charms continues to pester believing Senufos. They appear to have the strongest hold on the people. From the song texts we learn that fetishes among the Senufo include objects such as ox tails and woven cloth, and that they may be used to harm one's neighbor. They may also be used as *yawiiri*, protective devices prescribed by the *sando* (sorceress), and also for sacrificial worship (*yasunyi*).

Not unrelated to the use of fetishes is the sorcery society known as the *Sandogo*, an association of diviners. It is:

> . . . a powerful women's organization, a village institution found throughout the Senufo culture area. *Sandogo* society members are charged with two broad areas of responsibility: first, safeguarding the purity of matrilineage and, second, ritual maintenance of good relationships with the hierarchy of spiritual beings through a particular technique of divination (*tyele*).[16]

The *sando* diviner's main source of power comes from the bush spirits, who are solicited for aid in dealing with supernatural misfortune or requesting help with effective hunting, good harvest, or successful pregnancies.[17] Practices within the divination ritual often require ritual abstinences, prayers, and sacrifices, a few of which are referred to in the song texts.

The work of the *marabout*, an Islamic holy man who deals with a spectrum of power including sorcery, is also mentioned in the song texts. Although the *marabout* apparently does not possess anywhere near the prominence that the Sandogo (sorcery) society displays, he does have a long tradition within the Senufo traditions dating as far back as the sixteenth century. Thus, its practices of Islamic-style divination may also be found among the Senufo, but on a less influential basis than the *Sandogo* society.

---

16. Glaze, *Art and Death*, 57.
17. Ibid., 61.

Worship

Senufo worship practices are not separate from the overall sorcery/divination system, but rather intricately intertwined. Indeed, they are often prescribed as a means of appeasing the spirits or soliciting their favor. Such sacrifices as chickens and kola nuts are related, as well as the worship of the wooden snake. According to Glaze, the python (*fo*) is the primary emblem used by the *sando* diviner and is considered to be a messenger between the spirit world and human beings.[18]

Based on the song texts, the worship of bodies of water (*lɔɔsunyi*) such as ponds or streams is discussed most often. The Senufo protective spirits inhabit such bodies of water, as well as the forests and fields. Known as *madebele*, these bush spirits are considered as "quasi-human spirits . . . malevolent and unpredictable beings who demand constant propitiation; they work harm but are not considered wholly evil."[19] It appears that each Senufo has his own particular *lɔɔsunyi* that is passed on as an inheritance from father to son. Also, it is common for Senufo people to ask others about their *lɔɔsunyi*, desiring to know if they are on good terms with the spirits that are worshipped in the body of water.

Worship of the dead also plays a role in the overall cosmological structure of the society. Ancestors function as "mediators between the human and the supernatural. Left angry or dissatisfied with relatives and the home village, the dead one remains a dangerous threat to all succeeding generations."[20] Thus, it is important to pay homage to the ancestors through such practices as animal sacrifice. The Senufo refer to sacrifice as worship. Such worship carries heavy value in assuring that there is peace in the village, that there is success, and that disaster and misfortune are avoided.[21]

Traditional Initiations

Initiation into the *Poro* society is a universal given for Senufo males. As we have pointed out earlier, the men's *Poro* societies weave together social relationships between kinship lines and household ties, thus functioning as a "stabilizing and unifying force at the community level."[22] Initiates are taught to "walk the path of *Poro*" that becomes the Senufos' educational training for meeting the demands of life. Since the head of each *Poro*

---

18. Ibid., 256.
19. Ibid., 258.
20. Ibid., 149.
21. Ouattara, interview.
22. Glaze, *Art and Death*, 11.

organization possesses and commands powerful and magical secrets for protection of the initiates, Christians believe that they cannot be a part of the *Poro* society. They are adamant that they cannot be involved in the spirit worship practiced within the *Poro* society since they have abandoned the spirits in order to "follow the Jesus road."

Funeral Ceremonies

Funeral ceremonies play a principal role in establishing the dead person as an ancestor in order to maintain good relations with those who are still living. Glaze explains:

> The entire series of events that form the funeral are undertaken for one encompassing purpose: to mark the completion of the spiritual, intellectual, and social formation of the individual member within the group and to create the necessary conditions under which the dead one will not leave this world of the living. The funeral is the final rite of passage, one that transforms the dead into a state of being that is beneficial to the living community, thereby ensuring a sense of continuity between the living and the dead. Only in the "village of the dead" can the dead one function effectively and safely as an ancestor.[23]

Because of their associations with the spirits, Senufo Christians have chosen not to participate in all the activities of the funeral ceremonies. Currently, the act of dancing at the funeral, for example, is especially taboo for the Christian community. The dance is the practice that actually establishes the dead person as an ancestor.

Relationships with Spirits

Another important area of discussion in the song texts is the Senufos' relationships with the spirits. It is imperative to the Senufo to maintain right relationships with the spirits. The worship of spirits at bodies of water is just one way of maintaining this balance. Discussion with spirits and getting out of the hands of the spirits are among the references to the spirit world. A shift in discussion of the spirits is starting to take place among Senufo believers where they have incorporated Satan into their taxonomy of spirits.

Apparently, Satan is not a term or concept indigenous to Senufo culture. This is revealed in a song text that explains: "People who are living and working for Satan do not realize that it is Satan they are working for,

---

23. Ibid., 149.

that he is ruining them by what they are doing."[24] The response to the song states it more directly when they sing, "They don't know who Satan is." Within Christian song texts, then, Satan has come to be the one accused of any type of spirit activity. He is perceived as the one who made them suffer so much, including the "insomnia of Satan."

Relationships with Other People

Although the Senufo worldview appears to be predominantly concerned with maintaining order between the natural and the supernatural worlds, they are also very concerned with relationships with their neighbors and fellow human beings. Some thirty-six percent of the references made to activities that need to be abandoned are concerned with horizontal relationships between people. Indeed, the purpose of traditional customs and interactions with the spirits is intertwined with interpersonal relationships on the human level. Interaction with the spirits may call for extreme action—even killing one's child.

While adultery rises to the top of the list of unjust actions, verbal behavior such as lying, gossip, deceiving people with words, speaking badly about someone, quarrels, mocking, vain discussion, and negatively judging others permeates the themes of the wounding activities that damage relationships. Theft and murder dominate the remaining two categories, with an elucidation of a few methods of murder. These include acts of poisoning, assassination, and killing one's child, who may be sacrificed ritualistically for consumption by the *sandogo* (sorceress).

Personal Problems

Finally, personal problems surface on the list of activities that Christians should abandon where an individual must deal with her or his own particular life. The theological term "sins" solidly positions itself in this area. Individual sins for the Senufo Christian believer include drinking alcoholic beverages, bad conduct, malicious activities, and the pursuit of money and things of the world.

Overcoming worries and attitudes are also ideals for the Senufo Christian, as doubts, troubles of the heart, sadness, and things that haunt are common everyday occurrences. Meanwhile, jealousy, anger, and boastfulness are the major personal attitudes that must be dealt with. Poor attitudes often lead to poor relationships with other people. Jealousy, for example, controlled the family of one Christian composer. Her husband

---

24. R. King, Senufo Field Notes, 1985.

Song Texts: A Path to Worldview Discovery

was becoming too wealthy as a merchant. The extended family sought out a *sandogi* to kill him by manipulating both lightning and cobra snakes. Yet, they were not successful. After several unsuccessful attempts to kill him, the husband discovered, through a friend, the power of Jesus Christ to protect and save him. He became a Christian believer.

Although illness is referred to only twice in this list, good health remains a major concern of the Senufo. As we will see later from the focus group interviews, the concern for illnesses to be cured has served to bring many Senufo Christians to the Lord through the medical mission services at the dispensary in Torhogo and the hospital in Ferkessedougou.

Summary

In summary, we have seen that texts of culturally appropriate songs work within and reveal a people's worldview and assumptions about life. Among the Senufo, we have found from the song texts that the predominant worldview concern is the maintenance of balance between the natural and supernatural realms. This is accomplished through the observance of traditional customs and interactions with the spirits. Two other major worldview concerns are the maintenance of justice between neighbors and others and dealing with personal problems relating to moral conduct, attitudes, and physical health. Song texts have provided a beginning path for initially unmasking and discovering various aspects of the Senufo worldview.

We turn next to investigating song texts as they disclose the theological understandings of Senufo Christians.

9

Song Texts: Pathway to a Developing Theology

IN THE PREVIOUS CHAPTER, we investigated how Senufo Christian song texts reveal below-the-surface assumptions about the Senufo's worldview and approaches to life. We turn now to contemplate pictures of an emerging church's concepts and understandings of God as presented in the Senufo song texts. In the process of creating songs, theological understandings are incorporated in the texts. These theological concepts serve as a source for initial investigations into understanding Senufo theological concepts at the grass-roots level.

Lyric Theology

Since communication of a message is at the heart of Senufo Christian songs, they indeed serve as a storehouse of knowledge typical of oral methods of communication. Thus, they disclose popular understandings about God and his work among a people. This is somewhat parallel to what we find in the Hebrew Psalter, where there is a broad spectrum of experiences and concepts of God expressed in a popular theological mode. Such theology "is not the abstract and philosophical theology limited to the intelligentsia, but that theology or knowledge of God which emerges out of a life lived in relationship with God."[1] This implies that theology, properly understood, is done in several modes. The Israelites did much of their theologizing through the creation of psalms, a mode that was highly valued.

Likewise, the Senufo believing community has chosen to theologize in a mode that is culturally appropriate to their society. It is highly valued over other forms of literature, especially since they are a predominantly oral society. Senufo Christian songs become confessional statements of their faith in God. They are theological statements that serve simultaneously as individual and collective affirmations of faith and as a witness to the society at large. Theology, viewed as "divine revelation understood in

---

1. Craigie, *Psalms 1–50*, 40.

Song Texts: Pathway to a Developing Theology

human contexts,"[2] is contained in the song lyrics. It is in this sense, then, that we may speak of "lyric theology."[3]

Christian song texts provide a logical resource for theological analysis. In our analysis in this chapter, we are following a path that leads towards the development of an "ethnic theology,"[4] a path that proceeds from the Senufo encounter with the Good News of Jesus Christ.

Christian Songs as a Theological Index

The analysis of hymns as a theological index in across-cultural situation is not unique to our study. In his work on *Solomon Islands Christianity*, Tippett presents an analysis of the frequency of hymns that are sung as an index to determining the theology of a people.[5] It is his "very carefully considered opinion that . . . Christian hymns have been the dominant formative for popular belief."[6] With this statement, Tippett underscores the importance of songs in the Christian formation process. Likewise, in our study here, it is my conviction that hymns, or Christian songs, when culturally appropriate, are significantly formative as well as informative in the Christian maturation process.

In contrast to Tippett's study, however, our song texts here are not mere translations of imported hymns from the West. They are culturally appropriate songs that have been formulated by Senufo believers. Nor are we analyzing the frequency of usage of a song. Rather, the frequent usage of the Senufo songs has already been taken into consideration during the selection of songs to be analyzed. We are attempting to focus on the specific content and perceptions about God that are presently sung and heard throughout Senufo territory. The song texts function as valid theological indicators due to their "home-grown" nature, originating from the people themselves as they interact with Christian teaching.

Based on the above, then, we are posing the following question: What would one understand about God and the Christian faith if the Senufo Christian songs were the only means of effective communication of the Christian message among the Senufo? This question is particularly relevant to the Senufo context, where literacy falls far short of playing a major role in the communication of information. Of the eighty-nine respondents surveyed in 1987, only 48 percent considered themselves

---

2. Hiebert, *Anthropological Insights*, 198.
3. Ibid., 32.
4. C. Kraft, *Christianity in Culture*, 404.
5. "Hymns as a Theological Index," 186–196.
6. Ibid., 186.

literate. Christians, in general, maintain a higher literacy rate, and a major reason for this is their motivation to read the Bible. Overall census figures claim a 10 percent literacy among the Senufo.[7]

As we consider the theological implications of the song texts, we will analyze the texts from a diachronic perspective by comparing the three collections of song texts: Songs Before the 1986 Workshop, the Current Senufo Repertoire, and the Most Popular Songs of 1987. Since these texts represent a historical progression of lyrical theology, we will be able to contrast early theological understandings with later, more developed theological concepts.

Senufo Lyric Theology

Based on the compilation of fifty Senufo Christian song texts, five main theological categories come to the forefront of Senufo Christian perceptions: (1) the names of God, (2) the characteristics or attributes of God, (3) what God has done in the past, (4) what God does in the believer's life, and (5) the believer's relationship to God.

Names of God

The names of God fall into two main categories, those for God and for Jesus, the son of God (see Table 2). *Kolocɔlɔɔ* is the Senufo term used for God, and is traditionally considered one of two principle Senufo deities referred to as the Creator God. *Kolocɔlɔɔ* is non-visible and completely good in nature.[8] The term has historically included the meaning, "far-distant woman." Within the Senufo Christians' vocabulary for God is the term Jehovah, a foreign word that has been introduced to Senufo believers and has had meaning put into it. There is also the concept of God as father/ancestor (*toow*), where any male who is older and also an adult is considered a father to the rest of the community. God is also referred to as *Baba* ("Daddy"), implying an intimate relationship, where *Baba* is the actual father and source of one's life.

The second person of the godhead, Jesus Christ, appears in the most prominent position, with the greatest number of references being made to Jesus. Other related names, such as Lord Jesus, Jesus Christ, Christ, and Lord, do not appear as often. A further description of Jesus is added in the most popular song of 1987, in which he is described as "our father Jesus," in the sense of being a father (*toow*) to the larger community.

---

7. Republique de Côte d'Ivoire, "Recensement General de la Population," 44.
8. Glaze, *Art and Death*, 257.

Song Texts: Pathway to a Developing Theology

One of the major theological areas that has not been developed in regards to the godhead is that of the Holy Spirit. The song texts reveal no direct references made to the Holy Spirit's work or place in the godhead.

However, comparing the analysis of the three song collections, the early church picture presented by the Songs Before the 1986 Workshop shows Jesus as the central figure in the godhead. Eighty percent of the references focus on him and only 20 percent speak of God as either the Creator God, *Kolocɔlɔɔ*, or as the intimate father, *Baba* or *Aba*. There is a trend towards more references to God as father-figure, *Baba*, as the church starts to mature. This is exemplified in the Most Popular Songs of 1987, with 15 percent of the references specifying God as *Baba* or *Aba*, growing to 22 percent in the Current Senufo Repertoire. Overall, Jesus continues to play the most prominent role in Senufo Christian thinking, with references made to him comprising 63 percent in the Most Popular Songs of 1987 and 67 percent in the Current Senufo Repertoire. However, at the same time there is a greater emphasis on God as either *Kolocɔlɔɔ* or *Baba*, as these accounted for 37 percent of references in the Most Popular Songs of 1987 and 33 percent in the Current Senufo Repertoire.

Table 2
Names of God

SONGS BEFORE THE 1986 WORKSHOP	Total Number of References	% in each Collection
GOD (*KOLOCL*)	19 (10%)	
JEHOVAH	8 (4%)	20%
FATHER/ANCESTOR (*TOOW*)	5 (3%)	
"DADDY" (BABA, ABA)	5 (3%)	
JESUS	120+ (64%)	
LORD JESUS	18+ (19%)	
JESUS CHRIST	6 (3%)	80%
CHRIST	5 (3%)	
LORD	2 (3%)	
TOTAL	188+ references	

CURRENT SENUFO REPERTOIRE	Total Number of References	% in each Collection
GOD (*KOLOCL*)	2 (2%)	
JEHOVAH	8+ (7%)	33%
FATHER/ANCESTOR (*TOOW*)	5+ (2%)	
"DADDY" (BABA, ABA)	24 (22%)	
JESUS	65 (60%)	
LORD JESUS	5+ (5%)	
JESUS CHRIST	1 (1%)	67%
CHRIST	1 (1%)	
LORD	1 (1%)	
TOTAL	105 references	

MOST POPULAR SONGS OF 1987	Total Number of References	% in each Collection
GOD (*KOLOCL*)	58+ (16%)	
JEHOVAH	10+ (6%)	
LORD JEHOVAH	1 (0.2%)	37%
FATHER/ANCESTOR (*TOOW*)	2 (0.6%)	
"DADDY" (BABA, ABA)	53+ (15%)	
JESUS	150+ (42%)	
LORD JESUS	45+ (12%)	
JESUS CHRIST	9 (2%)	
CHRIST	7 (2%)	63%
LORD	14 (4%)	
NOTRE PERE JESUS	2 (1%)	
TOTAL	361 references	

The "+" indicates songs that also use the term in the response but the number of times sung is not included in the total number of references since it will vary.

Song Texts: Pathway to a Developing Theology

The emphasis on Jesus over *Kolocɔlɔɔ* or *Baba* appears to be indicative of initial presentations of the Gospel message that centered on the uniqueness of Jesus. With increased Christian teaching, there is a greater comprehension of Jesus as the incarnation of God (*Kolocɔlɔɔ* and *Baba*). Thus, the terms are used more interchangeably throughout the song texts. For example, Jesus is often referred to as *Baba* in the sense of God, the Father.

Characteristics of God

The early glimpses of the nature of God portrayed in the Songs Before the 1986 Workshop are very limited indeed (see Table 3). Besides referring to Jesus as the "Jesus of love" throughout one song, there are only two other references to Jesus: as the good savior and as our "Dad," who is great and beautiful. This leaves us on average with slightly more than one reference (1.3) per song to the character of God.

On the other hand, there is a great increase in references to the character of God in the Current Senufo Repertoire, a combination of the songs before 1986 and popular songs from the 1986 and 1987 workshops. Sixty percent of the songs have a biblical base, which accounts for a fuller explanation of God's characteristics. They are the song texts that make the main contributions in this area. The most popular song from the 1986 workshop, which is based on Rev 4:8 and focuses on the holiness of God, accounts for 86 percent of the references in this category. The remaining 14 percent of the references come from a 1987 song based on Psalm 23. These two songs have resoundingly earned their position in the Current Senufo Repertoire due to people's response to them. This response may be viewed as indicative of the Senufo believers' desire to know more about the God they worship.

The Most Popular Songs of 1987 are naturally interwoven with our theme of the characteristics of God due to the fact that they are more directly based on scripture. As was noted in the earlier songs, the major emphasis (24.6 percent) is on the love of God. God is credited with originating, owning, giving, and practicing *taamadelegi* (true love). This term originally meant true friendship, but has had more of an *agape*, sacrificial meaning built into it through new usage in association with Christianity.

Other major understandings about the nature of God are that he is the owner of the new Jerusalem, the new earth, the heavens, and especially his "village" (21.7 percent). In addition to this, he also owns one's habits. He is acknowledged as the author or source of blessing, eternal life, forgiveness, patience, power, and the world, in addition to love (13 percent). Finally, there is an emphasis on his power and the claim that he is the God of power (13 percent), a reflection of the people's particular worldview orientation towards power.

On the whole, then, we see a major growth in the song texts as they start to describe the nature of God. Although the early songs were definitely lacking in this area, there is a trend toward the acceptance and appreciation of singing about God and who he is. This is reflected in the growth of refrences to God from the Most Popular Songs of 1987, averaging three references per song, to the Current Senufo Repertoire, with an average of 4.2 references per song.

Song Texts: Pathway to a Developing Theology

Table 3
Characteristics of God

	Total Number of References	% in each Section
SONGS BEFORE THE 1986 WORKSHOP		
THE JESUS OF LOVE	10	
OUR GOOD SAVIOR	2	
OUR "DADDY" (<u>BABA</u>)	1	
GREAT	1	100%
BEAUTIFUL	1	
NO ONE HAS MORE IMPORTANT LOVE THAN HIM	5+	
FATHER OF TRUE LOVE	5	
TOTAL	25+ references 1.4 ref per song	

	Total Number of References	% in each Section
CURRENT SENUFO REPERTOIRE		
GOD/"DADDY"		
REALLY/TRULY HOLY (WITHOUT FAULT/SIN)	23	
LORD OF BLESSING	2	
OF POWER	2	
GOOD	3	100%
PERFECT	4	
JUST	1	
WAS FROM A VERY LONG TIME	1	
MY GUIDE	5+	
THE AUTHOR/OWNER OF PEACE	1	
TOTAL	42 references 4.2 ref per song	

	Total Number of References	% in each Section
MOST POPULAR SONGS OF 1987		
GOD/"DADDY"		
IS LOVE	3	
AUTHOR OF LOVE	3	
AUTHOR OF TRUE LOVE	1	
HIS LOVE NEVER ENDS	1	
LOVE BELONGS TO HIM	1	24.6% refers to love
LOVES THE WORLD	5	
HIS LOVE IS GOOD/BEAUTIFUL	2	
TRUE LOVE/FRIENDSHIP	1	
OWNER OF		
THE NEW JERUSALEM	1	
THE NEW EARTH	1	
THE HEAVENS	1	21.7%

145

HEAVEN BELONGS TO HIM	1	refers to ownership
MY HABITS	1	
HIS VILLAGE	10	
AUTHOR OF		
- BLESSING	2	
- ETERNAL LIFE	1	
- FORGIVENESS	1	13% refers to authorship
- PATIENCE	1	
- IS PATIENT	1	
- POWER	1	
- THE WORLD	2	
HAS A GREAT POWER	8+	13% refers to power
GOD OF POWER	1	
OTHER QUALITIES OF GOD		
HE HAS DISCIPLES	3	
IS MERCIFUL	2	
A GOD OF SELF-CONTROL	1	
PEACE	1	
FAITHFUL	1	27.5% refers to other qualities
IS TO BE WORSHIPPED	2	
IS MY GUIDE (SHEPHERD)	2	
JESUS – THE GOOD WITNESS	1	
IS RESURRECTED	1	
WORTHY OF SPLENDOR	1	
WORTHY OF POWER	1	
KING OF KINGS	1	
TOTAL	69 references 3 ref per song	
{In this table the "+" indicates that there are songs that also use the term in the response but the number of times sung is not included in the total number of references since it will vary.}		

Key: The "+" indicates that there are songs that also use the term in the response, but since the number of times it is sung in the response will vary, it is not included in the total number of references.

What God Has Done

The frequency of discussion about God's acts, as well as the range of things he has done, is much more limited than the names and characteristics of God (see Table 4). In the early songs there was a great sense of freedom from the slavery of Satan. Thus, 62 percent of the song texts proclaim that Jesus chased away the bad works of Satan and their accompanying enslavement. Indeed, these songs claim that Jesus made all of this possible.

At the same time, 25 percent of the songs focused on Jesus' death as the means of salvation, so that there is a growing awareness of the significance of Jesus' death on the cross. This is seen in the Most Popular

Songs of 1987, with a 47 percent focus on this topic. Sixty-nine percent of all songs combined refer to Jesus' death and the salvation made possible through his death. Significantly, the only mention of God's work in the Current Senufo Repertoire is that "Jesus died for us."

Other topics include the teachings that Jesus is the one who made us, who created the earth, who came to earth, and who resurrected Lazarus. We also learn that God took Enoch to heaven and that he chose us, two statements that show a growing understanding of the role of God in the lives of Senufo believers.

Table 4
What God Has Done

	Total Number of References	% in each Section
SONGS BEFORE THE 1986 WORKSHOP		
JESUS		
WHO SAVED ME	11	
SUFFERED IN THE WORLD	1	
BEATEN, LADEN WITH THE CROSS, NAILS POUNDED IN	1	25% refers to salvation
TOOK AWAY/FREED FROM BAD WORKS	1	
HE CHASED AWAY BAD WORKS	19	61.5% refers to freedom
SAVED US FROM ALL THE BAD THINGS OF SATAN	7	
MADE IT POSSIBLE TO LEAVE ALL THESE THINGS	6	11.5% refers to other things
THE ONE WHO MADE ME	4	
THE ONE WHO CREATED THE EARTH	1	
HE HAS COME	1	
TOTAL	52 references 2.9 ref per song	

	Total Number of References	% in each Section
CURRENT SENUFO REPERTOIRE		
JESUS DIED FOR US	16	100%
TOTAL	16 references 1.6 ref per song	

	Total Number of References	% in each Section
MOST POPULAR SONGS OF 1987		
GOD/"DADDY"		
TOOK ENOCH TO HEAVEN	1	67% refers to God's work
GAVE JESUS TO DIE (FOR US)	3	
HE CHOSE US	6	
JESUS		
HE DIED FOR US TO SHOW HIS LOVE	3	33% refers to Jesus' work
HE SAVED US	1	
HE RESURRECTED LAZARUS	1	
TOTAL	15 references 0.66 ref per song	

69 percent of the combined references refer to Jesus' death and the salvation made possible through his death.

Song Texts: Pathway to a Developing Theology

What God Does

Having reviewed Senufo understandings about the acts of God, towards God's present working in a believer's life they show a higher degree of growth, understanding, and concern. Beginning with the limited but important understandings of the Songs Before the 1986 Workshop (1.7 references per song), and proceeding to the Most Popular Songs of 1987 (3.9 references per song), the peak is discovered among the songs of the Current Senufo Repertoire (8.4 references per song) (see Table 5).

While the two main categories in the Songs Before the 1986 Workshop proclaim that salvation is in Jesus (52 percent) and that his hand of protection and blessing is on us all the time (48 percent), new concepts emerge pointing toward the gifts that God offers. In the Most Popular Songs of 1987 these range from freedom, to patience, rest, eternal life, peace, love, gifts, blessing, faith, joy, and bestowing authority to the husband. These topics represent 46 percent of such references made in these songs. God's intervention on our behalf, as well as his care for us, rises to second position (29 percent), with God entering into relationship with us in order to save. Love follows this category with 9 percent. Although we learn that Jesus loves the church (4 percent), performs miracles including healing (3 percent), and forgives by "closing debts" (2 percent), there is not a high degree of emphasis on these acts in the songs. These apparently are new concepts that are beginning to come into focus and will grow with deeper Christian experience and maturation.

The Current Senufo Repertoire (8.4 references per song), on the other hand, reveals the most pressing felt needs in the lives of the Senufo people. Here we note that two-way communication with God is given utmost priority (38 percent). The second most pressing concern is that God has victory over Satan, who is the source of suffering, because he is able to "chase away Satan with his bad deeds" (30 percent). God's intervention on our behalf is carried further with his constant watching and care of us (17 percent). There is, interestingly, only a minimal awareness of God's forgiveness (2 percent).

Table 5
What God Does

	Total Number of References	% in each Section
SONGS BEFORE THE 1986 WORKSHOP		
JESUS		52% refers to salvation
WILL SAVE YOU	6+	
ONE FINDS TRUE SALVATION IN HIM	5+	
ALL THE TIME HIS HAND IS ON YOU	5+	48% refers to blessing
ALSO HIS BLESSING	5+	
TOTAL	21 references 1.7 ref per song	

	Total Number of References	% in each Section
CURRENT SENUFO REPERTOIRE		
WATCHES/SEES ME AND MY ACTIVITIES	9	17% refers to God sees
KNOWS EVERYTHING WE DO/ WATCHES US	4	
HE TAKES CARE OF ME	1	
COMMUNICATES WITH US		
JESUS CALLS US TO HIM	19	38% refer to communication
COMMANDS US TO LOVE ONE ANOTHER	8	
TALKS WITH US	5+	
CHASES AWAY SATAN AND HIS BAD DEEDS	9	30% refer to God chases
DELIVERS US FROM OUR SUFFERINGS	16	
GIVES US		
REST	5+	12% refer to God's giving
ETERNAL LIFE	4	
PROVIDES FOOD	1	
HE FORGIVES OUR SINS	2	4% refer to other things
LIVES IN ME	1	
TOTAL	84 references 8.4 ref per song	

The Believer's Relationship with God

Finally, we want to look at one final area of theological concern: the believer's relationship with God. How do the Senufo Christians view themselves in relationship to their new-found Lord (*kafɔwʔ*)? There are two aspects of this relationship; (1) the believer's position before God/Jesus, and (2) the believer's interaction with God.

Song Texts: Pathway to a Developing Theology

The Believer's Position before God/Jesus

Although the early songs have very few references to the believer's position before God (0.39 references per song), the one song that does discuss this theme speaks of the unworthiness of the Christian to enter into relationship with God (see Table 6). The song explains that they are not worthy to talk with God since they, the Senufo Christians, are small before Him—sinners, bad, disobedient, and responsible for the crucifixion of Jesus by hitting him and pounding the nails into him. There is, then, a great sense of humility before God.

Understandings about their relationship to God mature and grow as we note from later songs that one will stay in their father's house, they will be with Him, and live in his presence (see the Current Senufo Repertoire, with 1.3 references per song). We also observe that Senufo Christians have come to perceive that they are God's children and belong to Him. They also realize that they are his disciples as they follow the "path of Jesus," and that they will receive an inheritance that is reserved for them, as specified in the Most Popular Songs of 1987 (1.3 references per song).

Table 6
The Believer's Position Before God/Jesus

SONGS BEFORE THE 1986 WORKSHOP	Total Number of References
UNWORTHY TO ENTER IN RELATIONSHIP	
SHOULD NOT BE ABLE TO TALK WITH YOU	2
SMALL BEFORE GOD	1
SINNER	1
BAD	1
DISOBEDIENT	1
WE HIT HIM POUNDED THE NAILS INTO HIM	1
TOTAL	7 references 0.39 ref per song

CURRENT SENUFO REPERTOIRE	Total Number of References
WILL STAY IN MY FATHER'S HOUSE	3
WILL BE WITH HIM	10
TOTAL	13 references 1.3 ref per song

MOST POPULAR SONGS OF 1987	Total Number of References
WE ARE HIS CHILDREN	9
WE BELONG TO JESUS	1
WE ARE HIS DISCIPLES	3
WE RECEIVE AN INHERITANCE	
HE RESERVES OUR PART	17
TOTAL	30 references 1.3 ref per song

The Believer's Interaction with God

The early picture of the believer's interaction with God was much more developed than their awareness of their position before God/Jesus (see table 7). In the Songs Before the 1986 Workshop there was a higher average of references about interacting with God (2.3 references per song) than to their position before God (0.39 references per song). They were aware that they could dialogue with him, that their prayers would be heard, that God is approachable, and that they could put their hope in Jesus since He lives in them. Surprisingly, the Current Senufo Repertoire is lacking in this area, where there are very few references (0.7 per song) that focus on communicating with the Jesus who is calling them and speaks to them. This situation improves slightly in the Most Popular Songs of 1987 (1.56

references per song), yet still does not attain the earlier emphasis on interaction with God.

Table 7
The Believer's Interaction with God

SONGS BEFORE THE 1986 WORKSHOP	Total Number of References
GREET/TALK WITH GOD	7
CHRIST LIVES IN ME	5
PUT YOUR HOPE IN JESUS	5
COME TO JESUS	22
HE IS APPROACHABLE	1
PRAYERS ARE HEARD	1
TOTAL	**41 references** / **2.3 ref per song**

CURRENT SENUFO REPERTOIRE	Total Number of References
JESUS CALLS YOU	3+
JESUS SAID	4
TOTAL	**7+ references** / **0.7 ref per song**

MOST POPULAR SONGS OF 1987	Total Number of References
WE KNOW GOD	4
BE IN AGREEMENT WITH GOD	3
WE SEE GOD	15
WE ARE ACCEPTED BY HIM	4
WE WILL BE WITH HIM	5
GRAB HOLD OF JESUS	5
TOTAL	**36 references** / **1.56 ref per song**

Additional Theological Themes

Thus far, we have observed five main areas of theological understandings among Senufo believers. We have compared the growth and development of these understandings over a period of time. Our analysis does not presume to be exhaustive. However, it does serve to indicate major concerns, felt needs, and starting points for further and more effective Christian communication.

Less frequent but important themes that could be examined include the return of Jesus, salvation, weariness in Satan, rest found in Jesus, suffering, the love of God and its implications within the Senufo worldview, peace—with its distinction of appearing cool on the outside, patience that includes being cool from the inside, specific everyday problems, and all that Christians possess. We will limit ourselves, however, to looking at three additional themes: heaven, Satan and his role in the nonbeliever's life, and worship.

Heaven

I have chosen to discuss the theme of heaven because of its surprising lack of emphasis in the Senufo Christian songs. This stands in great contrast to the emphasis on heaven in the songs of East Africa. In Kenya, for example, one receives the impression that at least 50–60 percent of the songs composed by Kenyan Christian composers revolve around the theme of heaven and the promise that there will be no more pain, tears, sickness, or death. Although the repertoire of one Africa Inland Church choir includes only ten songs on heaven out of eighty-five, these ten songs are the ones performed most often. Explains Scott, the initiator of the Africa Inland Church School of Music:

> What this indicates, to my mind, is a realization of how tough things are here for them, and heaven is therefore something very much to look forward to when things will be different. It may be partly a legacy of colonialism—having on display around them so much that is wealthier and more privileged than their own life situation. But for some people at least—like the Maasai—the afterlife is a discovery which is very exciting as traditionally the dead simply die. Now as Christians they see the end is not death, but a wonderful future has opened up through Christ's resurrection, and therefore in their own. It's worth singing about.[9]

What, then, is the concept of the afterlife for the Senufo? Earlier, we discussed the song that likens death to a river bed flowing on without any definite destination. Likewise, we have noted above that there is the concept of the "village of the dead" where the dead go to act as mediators between the supernatural and the living. Also, inherent in Senufo thought is the idea of a paradise (*kusegi tecenge*) for those who do well in life and a hell for those who do poorly (*moa sasogi*). When one dies then the individual departs for the appropriate place that has been accorded.

---

9. Scott, personal correspondence, 1.

Song Texts: Pathway to a Developing Theology

Interestingly, heaven is a rare concept among Senufo believers. There is, however, one song in the Current Senufo Repertoire that happens to be among the earliest Senufo Christian songs created. It is the song discussed in the chapter on worldview and based on John 14:2, which proclaims that there are many dwelling places in the Father's house. Although this is stated in the thematic section of the song, there is no further discussion of the Father's dwelling place in the development section. Rather, this section dwells on the need to abandon one's actions, since Jesus is calling them. We may assume that this is the topic indicating the action that must be taken in order to live with the Father. However, it does not dwell on heaven as an escape from the present situation. This is in spite of the suffering and different life-style that is experienced in Senufo life.

Allusions to heaven are made in the Most Popular Songs of 1987, where there is reference to a "new earth" and to a new Senufo Christian concept of a "village in the sky." As in the former song, there is a desire to live in the "village in the sky," and in order to do so one must work for it.

Perhaps most intriguing though is the song, "My Father Has Everything." The original intention of the song was to sing about everything that the Father gives us. Yet, the composer chose to dwell on the inheritance we have in heaven. He describes heaven as the "village of our Father's peace," the "village of love," the "village without sickness," the "village without death," the "village without famine," the "village without sadness," and the place of eternal life. He has created a new image in the Senufo mind as an alternative to the traditional concept of the "village of the dead." It is a "village" that offers hope whether one has done well or not.

Satan

A theme frequently recurring in the Senufo Christian songs is that of Satan. Satan is described as the "bad" one who brings many problems into a person's life and who causes a great deal of suffering. The term *fɔrɔ* means both "to be tired out" and "to suffer." Satan is the one who brings such weariness into their lives that they seek rest *(nodaali)*. *Nodaali* literally means "to catch one's breath." Freedom and rest from such a manipulator of one's life is an overwhelming theme throughout the songs. Although only 50 percent of the songs, both in the Songs Before the 1986 Workshop and the Current Senufo Repertoire, speak of Satan, the impression one receives while participating in song services is that the singing dwells almost constantly on the theme of Satan. This is due to the reality of Satan and his demands in their lives. A common complaint when discussing songs is that the songs praise Satan too much. The situation is improving, with only 13 percent of the Most Popular Songs of 1987 mentioning the name of Satan or dwelling on his pervasive influence.

Satan plays multiple roles in the people's lives. His greatest influence is that he forces people to work for him through the use of fetishes, at funerals, in adultery, and anything that is evil. He is also accused of bringing a great deal of suffering in the form of insomnia. Satan has not quit working in the Senufo Christian's lives since it is acknowledged that he brings temptation into people's lives.

It is significant, though, that the people often sing as a means of power encounter, where they order Satan out of their lives. They sing "Satan get away from us," and inform him that they now belong to Jesus. In addition to this, the songs call for a change of allegiance: "Abandon Satan, the Devil," and make a plea to "offer Yourselves to Jesus." Songs are a means of spiritual exchange among the Senufo. It appears, then, that such songs are used in power encounters, so a certain portion needs to remain within the Senufo repertoire (see Appendix F).

Worship

When perusing the song texts that we have used for our analysis in this section, it is striking that only nine out of fifty texts speak of worshipping God. They acknowledge God by giving thanks to God (*Bariga Sa?a*) and by showing appreciation for what He has done and the gift of his Son. Included in these direct verbal approaches to worshipping and praising God is the idea of "greeting God," the basic Senufo concept behind prayer. One of the major strengths of Senufo believers is their ability to pray fervently and for long times. They pour out their hearts before the Lord with great intensity and sincerity. There are no short prayers since a short prayer would probably function as something of an insult before God. Rather, communication with Him is highly important and there is a great flow of words of supplication.

Senufo worship, then, includes the above means of praising God directly through prayer. Yet, there appears to be more than mere verbal praise at the core of Senufo practices. Two areas need to be explored further.

First, as mentioned before, a common feeling among Senufo believers today is that they do not like their songs that praise Satan. Their desire is to eliminate such songs from the repertoire. In actuality, no song says that Satan should be exalted. Many songs do speak, though, of the influ-

Song Texts: Pathway to a Developing Theology

ence and control that he has in both the life of the nonbeliever and also the believer. The effect received is that Satan, at the mention of his name and the way he works in people's lives, is given glory and thus worshipped. Indeed, among my initial impressions when first listening and learning the Senufo Christian songs remains the fact that it appeared I was learning much more about Satan and how he works than about God and Jesus Christ. Thus, just the mention of either Satan or God gives praise to them and becomes a form of worship.

When one looks at the song texts from this perspective, we may note that 99 percent of the Senufo Christian songs are indeed songs that worship God or Jesus Christ through the specific mentioning of their names. There is an early song that advises people to leave the work of Satan, such as the "*sando?o*," but never mentions the name of God or Jesus. A change of allegiance from Satan is called for, but the personage of new loyalty is not named.

Secondly, worship for the Senufo appears to be much more closely associated with specific actions that are completed in response to a set of requirements. This is exemplified in the song texts that stipulate activities that need to be abandoned by Christians. For the Senufo, such activities as chicken sacrifice, speaking with the spirits at ponds or bodies of water, and practicing divination are considered acts of worship. My limited understanding of this was revealed when I kept asking informants what worship was for them. They kept responding that sacrifices, talking with the spirits, and divination are worship. Worship, then, is also a concrete act.

Worship based on acts performed in acknowledgement of a deity is not without biblical precedent. W. E. Vine elucidates for us that

> Worship of God is nowhere defined in scripture . . . (nor is it) confined to praise. . . . Broadly it may be regarded as the direct acknowledgement to God of His nature, attributes, ways and claims, whether by the outgoing of the heart in praise and thanksgiving or by deed done in such acknowledgement.[10]

Thus, worship may be composed of "deeds done in acknowledgement" of God. This is similar to the Senufo approach to worship.

We may observe the Senufo Christians developing their own approaches to worship of the true and living God as expressed in their song texts. In Table 8, Positive Activities for Christians, we note that there is a lack of specific worship activities for the Senufo Christian, especially in the earlier songs. In these songs, the believers are rejoicing that they no longer

---

10. Vine, *An Expository Dictionary,* 1248.

have to perform ritual sacrifices. They relate this new freedom. Yet, there is very little reference as to what they are to do now that they are Christians. They dwell, then, on what they have done in the past. This reveals a major developmental need in their spiritual lives.

Looking at the texts from the Songs Before the 1986 Workshop, there was a general call to work for God and to walk with him. Working for God is not elucidated at all, but it does serve as an acknowledgement of a change of allegiance since they formerly worked for Satan. There are no specifics given as to how they are to work for God other than the statement that "God is working with you in all things." The way to walk with God is specified more clearly in the songs that emphasize prayer as greeting or talking with him (67 percent of all references). "Giving of oneself to Jesus" calls once again for a change of allegiance and also reflects a biblical basis[11] for spiritual worship. Obedience to God also becomes a major goal in the Christian life.

With the growth of the church and its development in teaching, the song texts reflect an increased number of ways to worship God through actions and deeds. Walking with God becomes the main worship theme (68 percent in the Current Senufo Repertoire and 76 percent of the Most Popular Songs of 1987). In the Current Senufo Repertoire, we are told to "rise up and work for God" by believing on Jesus, accepting the teaching of his Word, and, as always, praying. Prayer remains the main worship activity of the Senufo Christian. In the Most Popular Songs of 1987, walking with God expands even further with such additions as "following the Jesus road in order to know God," worshipping God by giving thanks, and "running the race" that includes walking, eating, and being together with Jesus.

The new activity introduced in both the Current Senufo Repertoire and the Most Popular Songs of 1987 is in the area of relationships with other believers. As Christians, they should learn to love one another sincerely in order to (1) fulfill Jesus' commands and (2) be his children. Learning to forgive your neighbor by not returning a bad deed, and doing good to your enemy, highlights major spiritual growth in interpersonal relationships. This emphasis serves not only as an indicator of spiritual growth in understanding God's work in their lives, but is also a most appropriate functional substitute for the various relational problems of lying, thievery, and adultery documented in Table 1, Activities Christians Abandon.

Thus we note that positive spiritual growth in the area of worship is indicated. This takes place especially in those song texts that adhere more

---

11. Rom 12:1.

to a scriptural base. One concern remains. The majority of the "Positive Activities for Christians" continues to speak, for the most part, in generalities. Obedience, accepting God's teaching, and loving one another sincerely are among these generalities. How, for example, does one sincerely love another person within the Senufo context? What concrete activities does the Senufo Christian now follow? Undoubtedly, the practices of these questions are still in a developmental process. There is a need to develop specific acts that Christians may perform as a means of concretely acknowledging the power and greatness of God, in order to worship meaningfully within the Senufo context.

Table 8
Positive Activities for Christians

	Total Number of References	% in each Section
SONGS BEFORE THE 1986 WORKSHOP		
WORK FOR GOD	5	15%
NO SPECIFICS GIVEN		
WALK WITH GOD	1	
PRAY	7	
GREET/TALK WITH GOD	9	
IN ORDER TO BE CLOSE TO GOD	5	85%
BE OBEDIENT	2	
GIVE OURSELVES TO JESUS	5	
TOTAL	34 references 1.9 ref per song	

	Total Number of References	% in each Section
CURRENT SENUFO REPERTOIRE		
RISE UP AND WALK WITH GOD	1	
BELIEVE ON JESUS	6	
ACCEPT GOD'S TEACHING	5	68%
PRAY TO GOD	9	
RELATIONSHIP WITH OTHER BELIEVERS		
LOVE ONE ANOTHER SINCERELY	5	
A WAY TO FULFILL JESUS' COMMANDS	3	
IN ORDER TO BE A VILLAGE ON THE MOUNTAIN	1	32%
IN ORDER TO BE A LIGHT TO EVERYBODY	1	
TOTAL	31 references 3.1 ref per song	

	Total Number of References	% in each Section
MOST POPULAR SONGS OF 1987		
WALK WITH GOD	1	
IN ORDER TO KNOW GOD	16	
IF YOU SEE JESUS, YOU SEE GOD	18	
ACCORDING TO HIS WORD	6	
IN ORDER TO BE HIS DISCIPLES	3	
WITHOUT SINS (FAULTS)	3	
BE IN AGREEMENT WITH GOD	3	
COME TO JESUS	9	
BELIEVE IN JESUS	4	
GRAB HOLD OF FAITH (HANG ON)	15	76%

Song Texts: Pathway to a Developing Theology

WORSHIP HIM	2	
BY GIVING THANKS	4	
RUN THE RACE	4	
MUST WALK WITH JESUS	1	
EAT WITH JESUS	1	
WORK TOGETHER WITH JESUS	1	
SO YOU WILL BE WITH HIM	1	
SO YOU WILL BE JOYFUL	2	
RELATIONSHIP WITH OTHERS		
PRACTICE TRUE LOVE	13	
IN ORDER TO BE CHILDREN OF GOD	4	
FORGIVE YOUR NEIGHBOR	2	24%
DO NOT RETURN A BAD DEED	7	
DO GOOD TO YOUR ENEMY	3	
TOTAL	123 references 5.34 ref per song	

Summary

In summary, then, we have observed the various stages of theological growth within the Senufo church through the analysis of song texts. The early picture of Christianity formulated from the Songs Before the 1986 Workshop displayed glimpses of the potential of freedom from slavery to the spirits. Adhering to regulations made by the spirits came to be perceived and designated as working for Satan. Concepts of God and growth in relationship to Him have developed and are revealed in the later songs. These later songs are composed from a more direct biblical base. Likewise, as the people have grown in their theological understandings, they have also grown in interpersonal relationships with their neighbors, especially other Christians.

Senufo Christians have started without any background in Christianity. As they have come to understand more about God, their song texts have also grown in depth and theological wisdom. The situation among the Senufo Christians believers is like the process of focusing a zoom lens. Upon initially sighting an object from a long distance the image is small and lacks clarity, but after zooming in and focusing, one can see the object with greater detail and appreciate it more fully. We have seen that as they have grown in their relationship with God and learned more about Him through the scriptures they have developed a greater understanding about him.

In no way do the song texts represent a full picture of all Senufo theological concepts. Yet, it is my opinion that they mirror the most prevalent and popular theological understandings. Not only may we come to know the major theological interests of the Senufo people through their song texts, but we may also begin to discover theological gaps or misunderstandings through the texts. For example, the song texts reveal no major teaching on the Holy Spirit as having penetrated the laity, an area that should develop as the church matures.

Senufo believers are also attempting to integrate their worldview with biblical teachings. The development of their theological approaches to heaven, Satan, and worship are representative of this. They are theologizing at a grass-roots, popular level (see Appendix F) in the creation of Senufo Christian songs as they continue on their encounter and pilgrimage with God.

Having analyzed both the musical and textual aspects of Christian songs, we turn now to a study of the impact of these songs in the lives of both Senufo believers and non-believers.

PART FIVE

Music as Communication

10

The Pathway of a Song

THIS SECTION IS DEVOTED to an examination of the receptors in the music communication process. We will be addressing two main questions: 1) How do Senufo Christian songs work in the lives of Senufo people? 2) How do these songs influence and affect their decisions and life-styles? In order to understand the communication process in its totality one must investigate the ways in which the receptor accepts and acts upon the communication of a message—for, as Engel maintains, the "receptor is sovereign."[1]

The pathway of a Senufo song, the way in which it communicates within the lives of Senufo people, is complex. It does not follow a straight progressive line, but rather may take sweeping turn-arounds, often appearing to almost return to a place already visited. Yet, there is a movement toward or away from understanding the teachings of the songs. It is like a progressive spiral in its effect upon the song participant, either moving in a positive or negative direction towards the beliefs, values, or ideals presented in a song.

The singing of a Senufo Christian song provides an opportunity for dealing in the dimensions of time and space. It creates an event where, through active participation within a group, one may contemplate and reflect upon one's particular life-situation. In a sense, the singing of Senufo Christian songs is a type of "slow motion" communication. Time is expanded, and participants are allowed to see complex parts of an action, analyze it, reflect upon it, and then make their own decisions as to its particular application.

In order to grasp and begin to delineate its spiraling path, we will investigate three major areas that integrate and interact within the overall music communication process—the pathway of a song. These three dimensions are the affective, cognitive, and behavioral. As may be noted in Figure 19, they do not exist in isolation from one another; rather, they are mutually interrelated and mutually influential.

---

1. Engel, *Contemporary Christian Communication*, 57.

Briefly, the "affective" dimension includes a person's attitude, which may be either positive or negative "toward undertaking a given 'action' consistent with beliefs in a particular set of circumstances."[2] It functions within the full arena of emotions and feelings towards a decision or action. The "cognitive" dimension, on the other hand, incorporates a person's main storehouse facts and knowledge, including "those things that people hold to be true with respect to a given subject matter or action."[3] The final, "behavioral" dimension, deals with the intention of the person to act upon the attitudes and beliefs under consideration within a communication event.

Let us examine first the affective dimension as it contributes to developing the pathway of a song among the Senufo.

**Figure 19
The Three Dimensions in the Song Pathway**

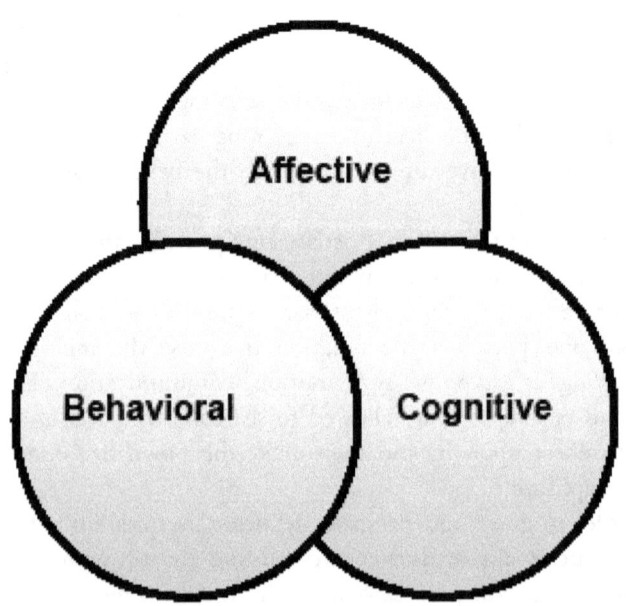

---

2. Ibid., 181.
3. Ibid.

The Pathway of a Song

The Affective Dimension

The most readily recognized area where song is influential is in the affective dimension. A song's strong-suit remains initially in this dimension where general yet profound emotions are elicited and attitudes shaped. Indeed, it is here that the pathway of a song first begins.

The ability of song to influence participants in this affective dimension is certainly true among the Senufo. The response to song is almost immediate and spontaneous. A typical example of this occurred at the end of our second annual New Song Workshop in February 1987. With all their new songs jostling around in their heads, the Senufo composers and I headed out to the annual Women's Conference, which had become the traditional sight for presenting new songs for the coming year. The group of one hundred twenty-five women, predominantly over thirty-five years of age, were praising and worshipping God as the evening meeting opened. Those who arrived after the singing and dancing had started simply made their way up to a seat by joining in the slow shuffle that the Senufo Christians have developed as a dance style. The women were joyfully participating in delightful praise to God. Everyone participated spontaneously and enthusiastically, as all the percussion instruments that could be found were added to the clapping and swaying bodies.

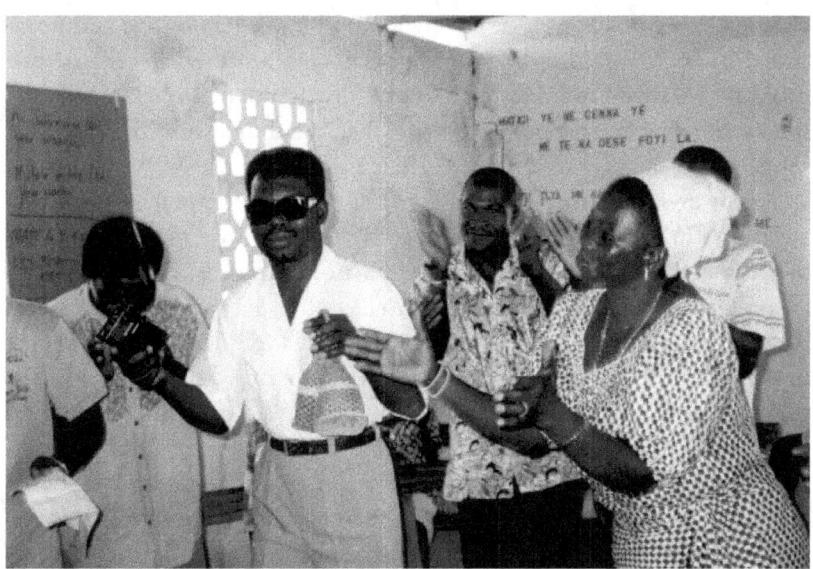

Photo 13: Clapping is an integral feature of Senufo Christian songs.
It serves as a testimony of the believer's faith.

167

The time of opening worship came to a close and each of the four composers were asked to come and present one of their new songs. Sɛnyɛnɛgatɛnɛ, the blacksmith, came forward with his metal scraper, the *kanrigi*. Everyone sat in their seats expectantly waiting to hear and sing the new song that God had given. Even though it is not natural for them, the church has emphasized that the congregation refrain from clapping when they are hearing a song for the first time. Thus, they sat quietly. Sɛnyɛnɛgatɛnɛ, as lead singer, lifted his scraper and began to call out in a piercing and voluminous voice that "The Lord is my "*nyaʔnafolo*" (the one who provides for and protects me, carries me on his back, and knows me intimately), based on Psalm 23. Within ten seconds the whole congregation of women was on their feet singing enthusiastically, clapping joyfully, and dancing delightedly. The atmosphere was electric as they learned of God's care for them.

How was it that these women responded so instantly and overwhelmingly? The attitude toward the presentation of the song was more than resounding. Indeed, to ask questions about a Senufo Christian's attitude toward their Christian songs is not really a question for them. They are so positive toward songs that a positive attitude is more an unspoken assumption than an evaluation. Attitude is more readily observed in their response and willingness to participate in the song event. But even so, they choose between two levels of positivity, not between a positive and negative attitude. It would ordinarily not occur to a Senufo believer that one could be negative toward a song. As one lady responded when asked why she liked a particular song, "Why do I like the song? Huh! Because it's a song!" Or, as another responded, "There is no bad song."

However, the issue is more complex than first appears. When discussing attitude in Christian music communication we must distinguish between attitude towards two different actions. There is, first of all, one's attitude toward the musical sound itself and all its various dimensions. Among the Senufo this can be measured by one's willingness to participate in the actual production of music (the music event). For example, when the early Senufo church was limited to singing western hymns translated by the missionaries, the people fell asleep. This attitude or lack of participation stands in great contrast to the women's response to the song based on Psalm 23, described above, where the musical style itself facilitated the women's spontaneous participation in the song event.

In addition to measuring one's attitude towards the musical style, there is, however, the need to measure one's attitude towards the message or intent of the song's text. Although the song may be attractive musically, the text of the song may be either accepted or rejected. These two areas of attitude may either be in harmony at the time of the song presentation or, as is often the case initially with non-believers, in conflict. Thus, a two-fold attitude towards the songs, one towards the musical style and the other towards the text, must be considered.

Believers' Attitudes

In order to grasp the various ways in which Senufo Christian songs work in the lives of the participants, it is necessary to distinguish between believers' and non-believers' attitudes. We turn first to the believers' attitudes.

THE PLEASING NATURE OF SONGS

The Christian songs among the Senufo are highly pleasing and very important to Senufo believers. Indeed, it seems rather overwhelming that throughout my research, whether in the survey, the focus groups, or formal and informal interviews, no believing Senufo stated that they did not like their Christian songs. The main emphasis is on the fact that the songs are pleasing and the question becomes about the degree to which a song is pleasing. When asked how much they liked two of the most frequently performed new songs, the one based on Psalm 23 and the Alleluia song based on Revelation 4, 97 percent of the respondents said that it pleased them a lot (*gbanʔama*), with the remainder only liking it a little (*ceeri*). However, a song that is not sung frequently and is therefore assumed not to be as effective, still received a 90 percent vote that it was highly pleasing.

When songs are pleasing, they are received enthusiastically and the believer feels compelled to become totally involved with the song. For example, one lady explained: "God has helped me. I can praise him in the songs. There are many Christian songs that when I sing them, I dance. . . . No one can tire of singing them."[4] Indeed, the impetus toward involvement with the song can be so forceful that one must stop his/her work. For example, one woman told of how she sings songs while hoeing in the fields. In referring to a favorite of hers, she explained, "when I sing it, I have to put down my hoe in order to clap my hands as I sing. Only afterwards can I continue with my work." Thus, the mark of pleasing and compelling songs is that the people are spontaneously compelled to respond.

---

4. R. King, Focus Group Interviews, Foro, QI-1.

Songs Are Pleasing Due to Their Meaning

Senufo believers repeatedly emphasized the meaning of the texts as the main factor in determining the attractiveness of a song. This represents, then, a positive attitude in the second area—the text. Throughout my research, example after example was given that a song was pleasing because of what it stated. It seemed that whenever I tried to pose a question that would stimulate discussion of the musical style rather than the text, I would invariably be told about the content of the song. Indeed, figures from the survey show that on the average 59 percent of the people found the songs pleasing due to the meaning of their text.[5]

The next highest reason for a song's popularity was that it glorified or praised God, a reason that is also text related. Thus, in total 78 percent of the respondents found the songs pleasing due to their content.

The texts that are so meaningful to Senufo believers play a vital role in confirming their beliefs, expressing their spiritual experiences with the Lord and/or Satan, stimulating joy, and fortifying their faith. One believer, typical of many others, affirmed this in the following manner:

> Yes, we like them (the Christian songs) because of their meaning. There are some songs that when we sing them they fill us with great joy and build us up in the faith. These songs help us like the Word of God so that we wish to hear them all the time.[6]

Thus the Senufo Christian songs are especially pleasing to believers due to their text. The text takes precedence above and beyond the believers' appreciation of the musical style, with its compelling call to participation. When the songs are meaningful to their lives they "wish that the songs would just go on and on." In this way, then, the songs serve as a dynamic expression of their Christian experience.

The musical style, in spite of its importance in creating interest and serving as a vehicle for communication, appears to be below the level of awareness. It does not necessitate discussion since it is culturally appropriate and does not call attention to itself. Rather, the musical style functions more as a gateway for allowing the participants to interact with the verbal content of the song. When the music is culturally appropriate, the Senufo believers naturally focus much more on the cognitive content of the song. This confirms the fact that the central function of a song for Senufo believers is communication of a message. However, an appropriate musical

---

5. R. King, Senufo Song Survey, 20a, 44a, 52a.
6. R. King, Focus Group Interviews, Foro, QIII-1.

The Pathway of a Song

style remains crucial to the overall song event even, though its importance remains below the level of awareness.

Thus, we can deduce that Senufo believers have positive attitudes toward both the musical style of their songs and the text or content of the songs. As shown in the diagram below, the musical style, if pleasing and appropriate, leads to the positive reception of the song text. It is in this way that the musical style serves as a gateway to the greater perceived importance of the song text. When both attitudes towards the songs are positive (shown as "+" in Figure 20) then the overall experience also rates highly positive.

Figure 20
Believers' Attitudes Toward the Songs

	TEXT	MUSIC
Attitude	+	+
Focus	primary	secondary

Non-believers' Attitudes

Non-believers come to the production of music from another direction. They appear to emphasize the musical sound over the lyric content.

An Appropriate and Pleasing Musical Style

In contrast to the believers' emphasis on the meaning of the text in Senufo Christian songs, the non-believers' response to the same songs focuses on the attractiveness and importance of the musical style. Large numbers of non-believers enjoy the Christian songs for their musical style and will seek out occasions where they can go listen to them.

It is quite common for non-believers to request copies of audio cassette tapes of the Christian songs. Indeed, their demands are quite emphatic and insistent. After completing our New Song Workshop in 1988, for example, Pastor Zie was listening to his cassette copies of the new songs in the courtyard of the church. On hearing the songs, the pastor's non-believing neighbor from across the street came and begged him to let him take the cassettes. Pastor Zie said that he would make him copies of the songs if he would bring some blank cassettes. The neighbor agreed but then demanded to borrow one of the recorded cassettes until he could purchase the blank cassettes. He took it back to his courtyard and played it at a volume that all the neighborhood could hear and enjoy.

Furthermore, the musical style is so attractive and easy to learn that the non-believers often come to church for the music. A believer in the village of Foro tells of the non-believers learning their songs:

> Yes, one day they came to church in order to listen to and learn our songs. Then as they walked to market they sang our songs. And if someone heard them singing they would think that they are Christians but they are "pagans." They simply come to church in order to listen to the songs.[7]

Some songs are so popular that they have made their entrance into the secular repertoire of the Senufo *balafon*. According to informants, the non-believers sing the Christian songs "even at funerals. They play them on the *balafon* and dance to them."[8]

The Christians actually refer to the "pagan" *balafon* as "singing" their songs and can name the various songs that are frequently "sung" on the *balafon*. Among them are "Come, Believe on Jesus Christ," "My Friend, Jesus is Calling You," and "Come, Come Brothers and Sisters, Come and Let Us Rejoice!" They are songs that carry a definite call to and witness about Jesus Christ.

Initially Unacceptable Texts

Where the texts are the most important facet to the Senufo Christians, the very same texts pose problems for many of the non-believing Senufos. Exceptions do occur, however. One example is that of a village outside of Ferkessedougou that had just received its national flag. They had never had a flag raising ceremony before, but decided that they should sing a song during the raising of the flag. They pondered over what they should sing and selected one of the well-known Christian songs. When asked why they had selected that particular song, they responded, "Because we like what it says." Two conclusions can be drawn here. Non-believers are definitely able to understand at a surface level what is being sung. Secondly, it follows that they are beginning to process the content of the song. We will deal more specifically with those dynamics later.

---

7. Ibid., QII-3.
8. Ibid.

The Pathway of a Song

In general, however, the attitude of the non-believers is that, although the songs are pleasing, they do not agree with the messages of the songs. A non-believing Senufo does not immediately want to believe in Jesus or to convert to the Christian path. They enjoy listening to the songs. Some non-believers are offended at even hearing the name of Jesus mentioned, whether it is sung or spoken. However, the more common reaction is that the song is interesting and attractive but the message can be convicting (*touchant*). This is similar to the contrast between the attraction of songs and the actual preaching of a sermon.

One non-believer expressed it as follows: "If you see us coming close to you in church when you are singing [it is because of the songs], but when it is the time for the Word of God, we go home because this word touches us."[9] In other words, the songs will attract them to church, and even though they listen to the songs that essentially carry the same Christian message as a sermon, they are not offended by them. But to stay on at church and listen to the sermon is too threatening and convicting. The message of the songs as well as church sermons is initially rejected.

Thus, the non-believing Senufos have a disparity in attitude. They are highly positive towards the music yet negative towards the message of the songs, in terms of making a change of allegiance towards Christ (see Figure 21). Despite this disparity in attitude, the songs at least win a hearing since the people will listen to and even sing the songs in spite of their initial dislike for the message. A sermon, in contrast to this, does not even gain an audience. This is repeatedly confirmed at evangelistic meetings or all-night Christmas celebrations where non-believers will come for the music and singing but then leave at the time of preaching. The musical style, then, is the main focus for the Senufo non-believer, while the content of a song is more out of focus yet remains an integral part of it.

Figure 21
Non-believers' Attitudes Toward the Songs

	TEXT	MUSIC
Attitude	-	+
Focus	secondary	primary

---

9. R. King, Focus Group Interviews, Sɛʔɛlʔ, QII-3.

In actuality, the content of the songs has won a greater hearing than it appears. The problem lies in outside social influence, where one is concerned about his/her relationship to the village and family. A typical response from a non-believer is, "The Christian songs are really good, but if we believe we will be persecuted" by the family. This includes being hated by the whole village and suffering persecution.

Indeed, another example of hearing the message and not responding to it is found in the answer given to the questions, "You love our songs, don't you? But don't you also love God?" A group of non-believers responded, "We love God but your way of life is difficult."[10] This presents a problem that can defy even the powerful influence of songs.

Yet, in spite of the lack of agreement with the texts and the possibilities of persecution, if one's allegiance is turned to Christ, non-believers are known for their enthusiasm for the songs. They readily participate in the presentation of the songs through singing the response and joining in the dance. They participate at such music events as all-night Christmas celebrations, evangelistic meetings, and church worship services, or in the fields, at home, and wherever songs may be heard. A good emic description of their position in the conversion process is that the non-believers "say they like our songs, but they can't see Jesus with their eyes,"[11] a response that is typical of those who have not yet responded to the Gospel message.

Summary

However, Christian Senufo songs do win a hearing of the Gospel message among non-believers and provide opportunities to allow their content to begin to permeate their thought. The message of the songs can become important to them. For example, one believer related:

> I know a non-believer who is a carver of statues. Now this carver, when he cuts wood for carving the masks takes his audio cassettes and tape player with him. Then he turns it on and when it plays, he forbids his children from playing loudly or yelling in order that he can understand the words of the song. He does this to his "own" children.[12]

Indeed, the songs can start to convince them of the truth of the message. A common response after participating in an all-night evangelistic meeting or Christmas celebration is, "Really! If I could accept Jesus Christ it would

---

10. Ibid.
11. R. King, Focus Group Interviews, Dessingbo, QII-3.
12. R. King, Focus Group Interviews, Coonyɛʔɛn, QII-1.

be thanks to the these songs," because of what they say.[13] Here a paradigm shift has begun to take place, because the non-believer is becoming more aware of the content of the songs as it interacts with his/her own belief systems and worldview. The songs are beginning to work more directly in the cognitive dimension, to which we now turn our attention.

---

13. Ibid., QII-2.

11

Moving Further Along the Pathway of a Song

THUS FAR WE HAVE analyzed the pathway of Senufo Christian songs by focusing on the affective dimension in the song communication process. The cognitive and behavior dimensions as they interact with each other and are crucial to the communication process become the focal points of this chapter. We consider the cognitive dimension first.

The Cognitive Dimension

Communicating within the cognitive dimension is crucial to Christian communicators, for our goal is to offer life-changing alternatives. Before these life-changing alternatives may be acted upon they must be understood. This creation of understanding, then, becomes the overriding purpose of communication, including Christian music communication. D. K. Smith underscores this well when he explains that:

> The whole point in communication is to achieve understanding. It is easy to miss the purpose, thinking that communication is to get a favorable response, to get people to do what you want them to do. That is not at all adequate; that is not why we communicate. We communicate to get understanding.[1]

The cognitive dimension, traditionally the area where understanding is sought, deals with beliefs and systems of knowledge that people consider to be true. Senufo Christian songs, with their main intent of communicating a message, operate most profoundly in the cognitive dimension, and, contrary to popular thought, not merely in the affective dimension. Ultimately, the pathway of a Senufo song must pass through or in-and-out of the cognitive dimension. With such importance attributed to the songs due to their content, we are forced to ask questions, such as, how are the people actually interacting with the song texts? What is happening in the cognitive dimension?

---

1. Smith, *Make Haste Slowly*, 5.

Senufo Christian songs work in several ways. It appears that, in the overarching scheme, there are two sides to a Senufo Christian song as they work within the cognitive dimension: a song can (1) send a message, and also simultaneously (2) express the thoughts or experiences of the participant/singer. The intention of a song as sending a message is highlighted by one informant in the context of influencing a believer towards Christ: "When we sing our Christian songs for the non-believers, the words that are sung may one day lead a non-believer to convert because it is a message that we send in the song."[2] Thus, the content of the song is intended to convey a message with the purpose of creating understanding, in this case, the call to faith in Jesus Christ. It is meant to influence the receivers and their thinking as they receive new information.

At the same time, however, another effect of the song may be that the participants/singers find that they are singing their own thoughts. "There are also songs that when we sing them, we sing what we are thinking ["nos penses"]: those things that we reflect upon or contemplate."[3] The thoughts in the song appear to speak to one's very own experiences and questions; they reflect one's own personal history. This is where the song appears to "expand time," since it raises to the level of awareness one's multiple and various experiences in terms of which one will interpret the message of the song.

How, then, does the pathway of a song progress within this cognitive dimension among the Senufo? For the purpose of further analysis, we want to delve deeper into each of these two sides of Senufo Christian song: (1) how its content expresses and reveals real-life situations, and (2) how its content functions like the Word of God in sending a message.

Relates to Real-Life Situations

In my attempts to elicit discussion about songs in the cognitive dimension, my focus group leaders would first play a song and then ask the respondents in the group to tell what the song was talking about. Invariably, the respondents would tell their own personal experiences that related to the basic content of the song text. These stories would often involve deep and sensitive issues in the lives of the respondents, told with great passion and attention to detail.

---

2. R. King, Focus Group Interviews, Coonyɛʔɛn, QII-1.
3. R. King, Focus Group Interviews, Sɛʔɛlɛ, QI-8.

One brief example typical of the other responses shows how the respondent is relating the text of the song to her own personal situation.[4] The main theme of the song to which she is responding states: "I pray to you, our father, Jesus. I pray to you. Because you are the one who died, we have been delivered from the sufferings brought by Satan." The song continues by listing a series of the various sufferings that Satan can cause in a believer's life. Tyetin, from the village of Foro, responded in the following way to the question, "What does the song say?":

> This song has helped me a lot because when I was still a "pagan" [a non-believer], I suffered a lot. I was extremely ill. Ever since I was a child, I could never help my mother with the housework because of my illness. I went to many traditional healers. I washed with all sorts of leaves [as they instructed] but nothing would help me. I went to many different medical dispensaries, and still nothing would heal me. Then I was at the American dispensary [at the Torhogo mission station]. They told me to give my trust to the eternal God and they prayed for me. I thought about it but I did not understand. So I asked them, "I have followed the instructions of many people and have never been healed. But you say that I should follow [Jesus] and I will be healed. What are you going to do?" They prayed to God and I was healed. I'm just a new believer, but what the song says pleases me very much.[5]

Notice that Tyetin has not given a mere repetition of the text but has taken its main message and applied it to her own situation. This shows her own interaction with the song and personal identification with its content.

Interpretations and applications of the songs may vary greatly according to each person's own individual history. However, my research shows that the Senufo Christian songs relate to people's lives in three main areas: (1) their personal beliefs, (2) their past experiences, and (3) their contemporary life-situations and problems. Let us briefly focus on each of these areas.

Personal Beliefs

The song texts affirm what the respondents have found to be true in their own lives, especially in the area of belief:

---

4. For a complete listing of responses in this area, refer to Appendix C, Focus Group Interview Samples, Section I, Questions 1–2, Samples 1 and 2.
5. R. King, Focus Group Interviews. Foro, QI-1.

1. Everyday I think about these songs because (as one song says) "If someone who is suffering comes to Jesus, he'll find rest." Now that is the truth![6]

2. We sing a song that says "Satan comes with lots of affliction and punishment, but Jesus saves us from this." This song pleases me a lot because, for me, if we had not believed on Jesus, Satan would have come with lots of affliction such as the eternal fire, diseases, the Poro, the "sandogi" . . . but we've been saved from all that.[7]

3. (This song) pleased me a lot because of its invitation . . . It shows the way in which one can have salvation.[8] (Referring to the song "Come, believe in Jesus Christ so that He can give You Life.")

These examples refer to beliefs concerning salvation, what Jesus saves one from, and how believers are at peace (rest) because of their relationship with Jesus Christ. The respondents are in agreement with the text of the song and the song then reconfirms the spiritual principle that is stated.

PAST PERSONAL EXPERIENCES

The song texts speak to specific life situations in which the respondents were formerly involved. These texts raise these situations to the participants' awareness. The participants then contemplate, process, and put their experiences into perspective. For example:

(1) One lady suffered a lot. Since she was a child she suffered a lot. But the Lord helped her and she was able to have a child. Therefore, just as the song says "All the time, the blessing of God is on you," she saw that in her misfortunes and in her sufferings, God was always blessing her. That is why she likes the song.[9]

(2) And one [song] that really pleases me is "That is why I came to Jesus." [She sings the song.] This song pleases me a lot because when I was sick, I believed in Jesus and he saved me from the sickness.[10]

In the first example, the lady is able to take a spiritual principle and see its development in her own life, whereas the second example serves as both a reminder of the reason she came to believe in Jesus and a testimony to the power of Jesus in her life. Their relating of past experiences to the

---

6. Ibid., QI-3.
7. R. King, Focus Group Interviews, Korhogo, QI-3.
8. R. King, Focus Group Interviews, Torhogo, QI-8.
9. Ibid.
10. R. King, Focus Group Interviews, Dessingbo, QI-3.

thoughts expressed in the songs allows them to reinterpret their past situations as well as to interpret the song's content through their own grid of experience.

Contemporary Life Situations and Problems

The text of a song may enter into the contemporary concerns and problems of one who may be just listening, as well as the singers. For example, my main translator and informant, Ngana, was singing a Christian song recently while working as a brick layer and house builder. One of the lines caught the attention of a non-believing man in the village who healed people with charms (a *feticheur*). The phrase of the text that caught his attention said, "Everyone is a sinner." This thought came into the midst of the *feticheur's* current situation where, as a man with six wives, twenty-five children, and a usually thriving business of healing sterile women, found himself incapable of healing his own children as well as a woman with sterility problems. He told Ngana that this phrase started him thinking and questioning. He sent the woman to the Christians for healing in recognition that the Christians have an "idol" more powerful. This *feticheur* is now considering becoming a Christian.

Here we see that a person may process the message of a song in relation to his/her current situation and make a decision to try something new, such as a new alternative in Jesus Christ. The Senufo are so high-context oriented that the song's generalization about being a sinner with no specific reference to healing nevertheless triggered in the *feticheur's* mind the area in which he was experiencing difficulty. High-context, in this situation, refers to a person being so involved with their own immediate context that they interpret a message in light of their own specific situation. They are not aware of a more general interpretation.

Thus far, we have seen how the contents of a song may work within the cognitive dimension by creating relevance to real-life situations in the three major areas of personal beliefs, personal past experiences, and contemporary life-situation and/or problems. Let us now look at the other side of the effects of Senufo Christian songs, that of the message sent.

Moving Further Along the Pathway of a Song

Photo 14: Contextualized music in worship on Sunday morning

Equivalent to the Word of God

One of the questions included in the 1987 New Song Survey was open-ended, asking, "Do you have a story to tell us about how the songs have helped you in your walk with Jesus?" In speaking to the issue of how songs help them in their lives, 11 percent remarked that songs functioned like the Word of God in their lives. It was an analogy in no way suggested by the question, and which I personally found surprising. Among the responses were:

1. All the songs that we sing strengthen me like the Word of God.

2. For me all the songs are like the Word of God, so that all the songs help me.

3. Since all the Christian songs are the Word of God, that pleases me a lot.

4. Yes, the Christian songs help me in my Christian life during times of distress, times of fear, when I'm troubled about something that is approaching or during times of material [need]. They help me to take heart and resist [temptations] in my Christian life as much as the Word of God. Songs help me as much as the Word of God.

5. Songs help me as much as the Word of God.

6. I think that the songs can serve like the Word of God in evangelism.

7. The songs help me like the Word of God.

8. There are those songs that if I enter into temptation or my heart is troubled or I have little faith, they help me. They are truly the Word of God.

9. The Christian songs help me. If I listen to them its as if one is preaching the Word of God to me.

10. The Christian songs help me because they teach me the Word of God. It pleases me to invoke the name of the Lord.[11]

These initial responses raised new questions. Was the indication that songs were as effective and influential as the Word of God in their lives limited demographically, or was this a broad-ranging opinion that had not been verbalized by others? If the songs are equivalent to the Word of God, how then do they resemble the effect of God's Word in their lives?

My research the next year followed up on these questions during the focus group interviews. Out of seventy-nine participants, only one responded that he did not think the songs were like the Word of God. The remainder indicated their agreement with other groups, such as the young people from Korhogo, who exclaimed, "That's it! That's it exactly!" It was as if someone had finally hit upon the correct expression that agreed with their deepest concerns. Senufo Christian songs function like the Word of God in three main ways: (1) they are instructional, (2) they bring joy in the midst of difficulties (calm/balance the emotions), and (3) they preach to their felt needs (see Figure 22).

SONGS INSTRUCT LIKE THE WORD OF GOD

The believers consider the songs to function like the Word of God in that they teach them how they should live and point out the truth to them. Expressions that were used included "teaching that goes to the depths of our hearts," "counsel," "advise," "speak and show the way we should walk, and "teach us new things that we have not yet learned." One speaker combined it altogether in the following way:

> The songs help us as far as they teach us, showing us the path of truth and praising the Lord. Their teaching goes to the depths of

---

11. R. King, Senufo Song Survey, 55a.

our hearts, teaching your heart if you are good or bad. Then they tell you what you should do about it.[12]

Here we note that the songs teach at a deep level, touching them at the core of their cognitive reasoning and revealing to them where they are right or wrong in their Christian life and conduct. They do not stop at just merely passing on information, but they bring about understanding in their own personal lives, giving them advice and counsel to which they are receptive.

Songs Bring Joy like the Word of God

Just as the Word of God can bring instruction into the lives of the believers, the Senufo Christian songs also speak to the emotional dimensions of the people's concerns as they relate to their particular problems. This may include occasions when one's "heart is troubled," when one is angry or vexed by a situation, in distress, or concerned about physical needs. As one respondent explained:

> Yes, the Christian songs help me in the Christian life during times of distress, of fear, when I'm troubled about the future or physical needs. The songs help me to take courage, to resist [temptation] in my Christian life as much as the Word of God.[13]

---

12. R. King, Focus Group Interviews, Sɛʔɛlɛ, QI-8.
13. R. King, Focus Group Interviews, Korhogo, QI-8.

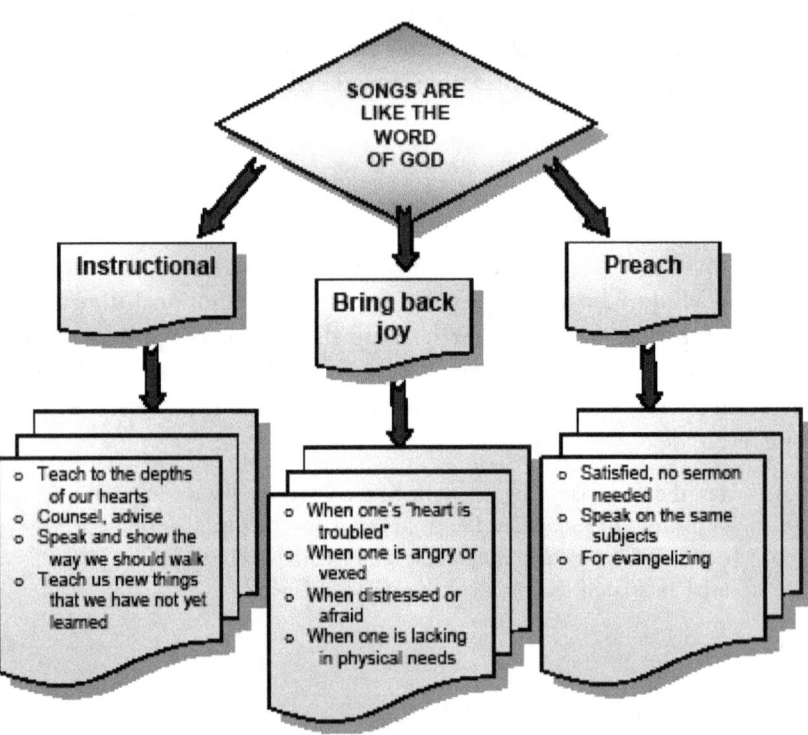

Figure 22
Songs Are Like the Word of God

Not only do the songs speak to specific issues, they also bring emotional equilibrium into the lives of the believers, expressed as "bringing back joy." This then gives them courage to continue in the Christian faith. They have the ability to remind them in the midst of their emotional turmoil that there is order to their world. This stabilizes them and returns them to a state of balanced "joy" in the same way that hearing God's Word does for them. There is a cross-over, then, between the cognitive and affective dimensions where a song will "bring joy." It will speaking to a person simultaneously on both levels, into their particular situation, reassuring him/her concerning a particular concern or need at a deep emotional level.

Songs Preach

The final main way in which songs are like the Word of God is that they preach. In a sense this final function summarizes and reiterates the foregoing two functions of instruction and bringing joy. I have included it here, though, to point out that, as far as the Senufo Christians are concerned, songs proclaim God's Word just as preaching is the proclamation of God's Word. That is not to say that preaching or the proclamation of God's Word is not important to the Senufo Christians. On the contrary, it is very important. However, they are not limited to proclamation of the Word coming in monologue form.

Rather, they seem to indicate that there are more effective ways of communicating or that there are, at least, alternative ways for accomplishing the same task. The are songs that are so effective that, as one respondent indicated, when they are sung, "it is useless to preach."[14] Taking it a step further, it is useless to preach because when one sings some songs, ". . . one finds that one is somehow satisfied. It is not worth the effort for the speaker to give a message from the Word of God. In this way, one sees that the songs are the equivalent of the Word of God."[15] Senufo Christian songs, then, can speak and communicate at such an effective level that a sermon or preaching based upon scripture is not needed. The proclamation of the Word of God has already taken place.

Thus we note that , in their ability to function like the Word of God and to speak to real-life situations, generate two dynamics within the cognitive dimension: an influential dynamic (the sending of a message) and an expressive dynamic (the raising to awareness of past or current experiences) (see Figure 23). These two sides of the cognitive dimension of songs simultaneously send a message and express the thoughts of the participants, allowing them to interact with the message and interpret it in light of their previous or current experiences.

The questions, then, become: How do these two sides of the songs interact with one another? How do they affect each other? Do they somehow work together to create understanding? We cannot discuss this interaction without moving into the final dimension of the communication process, behavior.

---

14. Ibid.
15. R. King, Focus Group Interviews, Coonyɛʔɛn, QI-8.

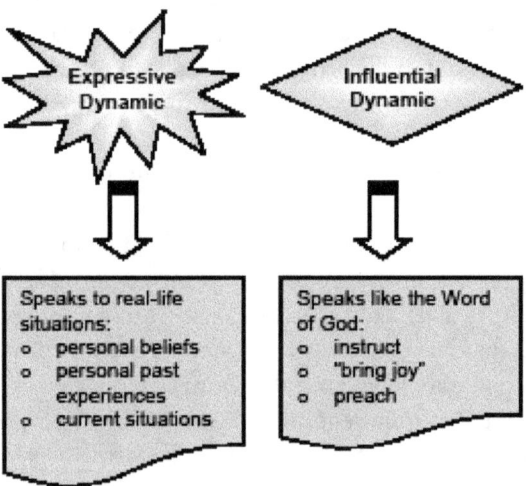

**Figure 23
The Cognitive Dimension**

The Behavioral Dimension

In communication terms, the behavioral dimension presupposes the possibility that beliefs and attitudes can be acted upon. In other words, if a receptor has a positive attitude toward the message that has interacted with his/her belief system, it is most likely that this will be acted upon and a decision made to incorporate the new understandings.

Our question, here, with reference to Senufo Christian songs, is whether Senufo Christian songs have influenced their receptors towards incorporating the instruction and information that has been passed on in the songs. How have these two sides of the cognitive dimension interacted and influenced the person toward making a decision? In order to further trace the pathway of Senufo Christian songs, let us focus on two types of decisions–those that lead to initial conversion and those involved in the spiritual formation process.

Decisions for Initial Conversion

Since the Christian songs are so popular among the Senufo, it was assumed that surely the songs must have played a significant role in persuading people to make a commitment to Christ. Initial results in the 1987 Senufo Song Survey showed, however, that only one respondent out of eighty-nine indicated that a song was the major factor in his coming to Christ. Evidently, songs were not seen as the deciding factor when people were asked directly, but the focus group interviews revealed that songs indeed had played a significant role in people's decision process.

Responses supported the theory that songs win a hearing of the message among non-believers. For example, one lady confirmed: "First I started listening to the Christian songs. They started to work in my heart, and then I believed in Jesus. The songs had, therefore, opened my heart and next I accepted the message."[16] It is significant that she indicates the songs had an ongoing influence in her life. She started listening to them. It was not a one-time occurrence, and she therefore had opportunity to continue to listen to the message of the songs. It appears that over a period of time a process of assimilation through repetition took place before she started to understand the implications of the message to "Come to Jesus."

Furthermore, the presentation of several songs may be the decisive factor in bringing about understanding that effects change. Events where singing takes place the whole night long, such as the Christmas festivals, can make a formidable impact on the participant. Another respondent attests to this: "One Christmas, I listened to all the songs and afterwards I understood and then I believed in Jesus."[17] It took more than one song to influence his thinking. He listened to the full repertoire presented and then it started to make sense to him. The influence of the songs, then, constituted an event that lasted over a long period of time. It took the whole night, with the presentation of several songs and their varying content. He was exposed to repetitive themes that led to a mounting understanding and triggered movement toward a decision.

Various Senufo believers attested to the fact that before they were believers, and also afterwards, songs influenced them to varying degrees. The effects mentioned range from songs that are like "sowing seed" to songs that "penetrate the person."[18] For others, the songs "give life like food."[19]

---

16. R. King, Focus Group Interviews, Foro, QII-2.
17. Ibid.
18. Ibid.
19. Ibid.

Decisions toward Spiritual Formation

Senufo believers spoke of songs working in four main areas of the Christian life, showing the wide range of ways songs can influence them as they seek to walk the "Jesus path." Songs help them (1) in their commitment to the Lord Jesus Christ, (2) to deal with their emotions, especially anger and distress, (3) to participate in church life/activities, and (4) to apply scripture to their lives. Let us look at an example of each of these areas, finding common traits in each situation.

COMMITMENT TO CHRIST

First, one of the common tendencies for Senufo believers, probably due to the dramatic change in life-style, is to feel pressured to turn back to their former way of life. One young person recounts how a song helped him deal with this problem. A friend explained that:

> When he had newly accepted the Lord, his mother was against his decision. There were many problems and difficulties. He didn't know what to do. He asked himself "Should I abandon the Lord? Should I do this or that? What should I do?" He was at a total loss in knowing what to do. In his confusion he went, then, to church. They sang a song that really comforted him and he continued with the Lord. He made a new decision to follow the Lord and in this way the song helped him a lot just like the Word of God.[20]

Notice that when the young person was in a predicament and did not know what he should do concerning his commitment to Christ, a song spoke directly to him. He accepted it as advice and decided to continue in his walk with the Lord.

CALMS EMOTIONS

Second, another common problem recognized among the Senufo believers is that of anger and handling one's emotions. Another believer relates:

> One day, one Sunday when he went to church, he was really mad and angry. He didn't know what he should do. He really didn't know. He was VERY mad but he went to church. After the service, a song really helped him like the Word of God. The song that says "Come Brothers, Come Brothers to Jesus Christ." That is the song that helped him a lot. He says that he was far away from Jesus Christ.[21]

---

20. R. King, Focus Group Interviews, Torhogo, QI-8.
21. Ibid.

Moving Further Along the Pathway of a Song

Notice again that it was a song that spoke to this person's need to deal with his emotions in the midst of turmoil. He was in a predicament, and the song that penetrated his world of concerns carried special significance concerning his emotions and relationship with Jesus Christ.

Participate in Church Life

Third, the church teaching that believers should give an offering to the church is difficult for people who are not in the habit of doing so. Again, it was a song that convinced a believer to give her offering:

> These songs help me a lot. They teach me about giving offerings, show me my sins, and show me my mistakes. There was a time when I did not give my offering with joy. I did not have any joy in my life. I was sick. One day, a singer sang about offerings and since that moment I started to give with joy. And now I have a great joy in my heart. The songs, therefore, help me as much as the Word of God.[22]

Again in this situation, a song spoke to the woman in the midst of her current dilemma. The song pointed out where she was making a mistake. The result was that she acted upon it and has developed a new habit of giving offerings.

Apply Scripture in Their Lives

Finally, songs provide an occasion whereby the singers/participants can learn to apply scripture to their lives. The song raises to their awareness the issues that need to be handled. Another Senufo believer explained:

> I [sing] a song that says "It is no longer I who live, but it is Jesus who lives [in me]." When I think of my former life and my life with Jesus [now], there is an enormous difference. Therefore, it is no longer I who live. When I have problems, I know that Jesus is my life and I entrust my problems to him. I'm no longer worried. He is my rock.[23]

Here the song, based on scripture (Gal 2:20), allowed the singer/participant to reflect on his present and former life. The song spoke to him in the midst of his own spiritual life and reflection on scripture. He evaluated his life and then drew conclusions that could help him as he encounters problems in the future.

---

22. R. King, Focus Group Interviews, Korhogo, QI-8.
23. R. King, Focus Group Interviews, Torhogo, QI-3.

The behavioral dimension (see Figure 24) is the point at which a period of evaluation takes place integrating together the various dynamics, both latent and current experiences, that have been activated through the song presentation. It is at this point that the two-sides of the cognitive dimension are brought together so that the message is evaluated in terms of the participant's real-life situation, both past and present. During this period of evaluation, the message of the song is applied to the participant's particular life story or present problem. The decision is then made by the participant as to whether to assimilate and follow through on the advice offered in the song.

Among Senufo believers songs play a vital role in their Christian life as they reconfirm the people's past experiences and pledges of allegiance to Christ. Songs function, then, as a means of building a foundation for creating understanding of Christian teaching. They also reinforce commitment to Christ and to the Christian community.

More specifically, though, the Senufo Christian songs are most influential in terms of effecting change when their texts speak directly to participants' felt needs or current predicaments and problems. All of this is carried out on the operational backdrop of the musical event that constantly keeps and provides for the interplay of these experiences, thoughts, beliefs, and values. As long as the music continues there is cognitive and affective interaction leading to possible changes in commitment and behavior. It is at this point that the three dimensions are weaving themselves together into a total experience.

Figure 24
The Behavioral Dimension

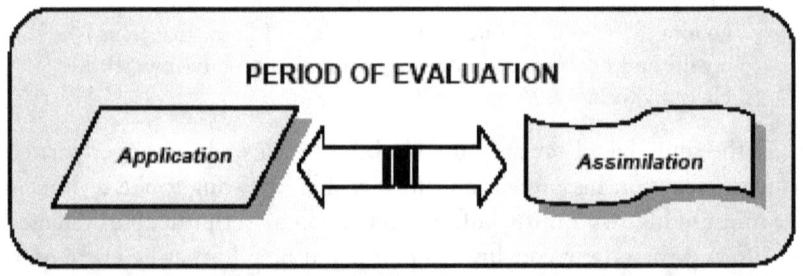

Key: The evaluation period moves from a time of application to assimilation with opportunity for repeatedly moving between the two areas.

Unique to the music event is that the communication process is not limited to a single presentation of a message. Rather, a song allows for repetition of the message multiple times within a particular music event. Furthermore, the song may continue on in its effects whenever participants may choose to once again sing a song to themselves or with a group. This is where the spiraling effect starts to take place and the song provides for further interaction and application in the life of the participants. In repeating a song, newer or more recent experiences are addressed and incorporated into the meanings derived from the song.

The song serves to update the receptors' understandings of a particular issue within their own context. It may be at this later point that the song suddenly strikes the right tone and pushes one to a new understanding and commitment. The pathway of the song returns to familiar terrain, but has also moved on to new territory, weaving its way into deeper levels of personal need.

Summary

In summary, then, we have seen that the pathway of a song meanders through the affective, cognitive and behavioral dimensions of the human personality. Rather than starting at the cognitive domain as in speech communication, its main entry point is at the affective level where values and attitudes are shaped and collected. No opening remarks are needed to catch the attention of the people. The music event is its own opening remark, immediately calling one into the particular subject matter at hand.

For Senufo believers the music event serves as a gateway to the wisdom that is proffered through song. They are both positive towards the music and open to its message. They do not view songs just as fillers, or as merely entertaining. Rather, they take them seriously as a spiritual encounter where God, through the song, advises them. Senufo non-believers, on the other hand, are immediately attracted to the musical style and are willing to participate in song production. However, they are initially perplexed by and antagonistic to its message.

As the song begins to follow its pathway (see Figure 25) it moves into the cognitive dimension, now communicating its message, now eliciting, and now playing upon the past and current experiences of the song participants' life history. A song simultaneously expresses one's beliefs, feelings, and totality of experience, while also influencing through instruction, helping balance emotions, and through its own approach to proclaiming the Word of God. As these two sides of the cognitive dimension interact within the totality of the music event, the behavioral dimension is approached, where a period of evaluation occurs by applying the message of the song to one's specific background and current situation. A decision is made to either assimilate or reject the teaching of the song in one's life. For the Senufo, songs are most effective and significant in effecting change in peoples' lives when they address current, particular problems or dilemmas. The pathway of a song winds through these domains with great liberty, often crisscrossing back and forth between the various domains in its persistent pursuit of persuasion.

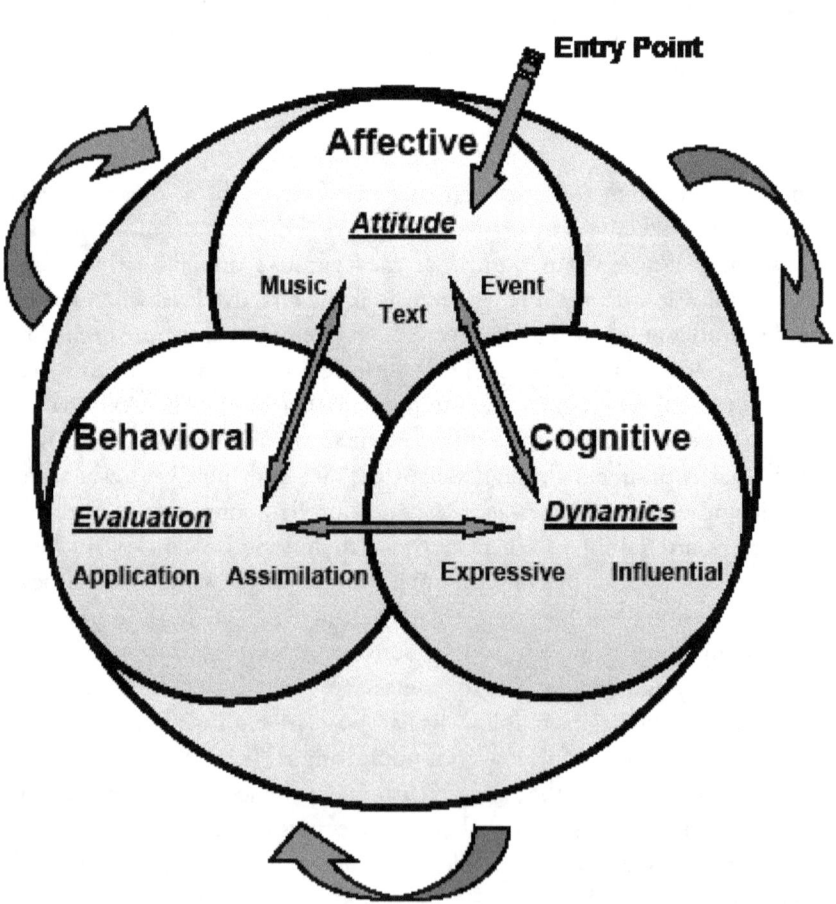

Figure 25
The Pathway of a Song

12

Reaching the Path's Destination

WE BEGAN OUR JOURNEY on the multiple paths of Christian music communication by reflecting on a current dilemma within missiology. This dilemma questions the relevance of contextualizing Christianity through the use of culturally appropriate songs. It raises questions of defining culturally appropriate songs and their role and influence in effective communication of the Christian message.

Therefore, I have addressed the question of whether the use of culturally appropriate songs makes a significant difference in effective communication of the Gospel. I have approached this question by creating a model for doing systematic research in Christian music communication. Approaches to ethnomusicological studies (both musicological and anthropological) and communication theory form its theoretical base. The design of the model (see Figure 26) allows us to deal with questions of "how and why" culturally appropriate music communicates with greater impact than inappropriate music that may have been imposed.

I have focused my attention within this case study of Christian music communication among the Senufo on the investigation of four areas in the research model: the historical development of Senufo Christian songs, musical aspects and structures contributing to the overall music communication process, song texts in relation to cognitive content, and the influence of songs in people's lives affectively, cognitively, and behaviorally. The study has been confined to a particular body of songs that has arisen within the Senufo Baptist churches of Côte d'Ivoire. They have drawn from their own particular cultural music system and created a song form that is culturally appropriate and relevant to Senufo music systems and Senufo society as a whole. These culturally appropriate songs are indigenous in style and easily received by Senufo society at large. What, then, are the major requirements in the development of culturally appropriate songs?

Requirements for Culturally Appropriate Song

There are many aspects that need to be taken into consideration when developing or evaluating the appropriateness of songs used within Christian music communication. In order to be most effective, a culturally appropriate song must find a "harmony" between each of these aspects. These aspects or areas of consideration are: (1) the way in which the songs are developed, (2) the musical sound structures and organization, (3) the content of the song texts, (4) the appropriateness of incorporating movement, (5) performance requirements, and (6) the influence and effect of songs in the lives of the participants.

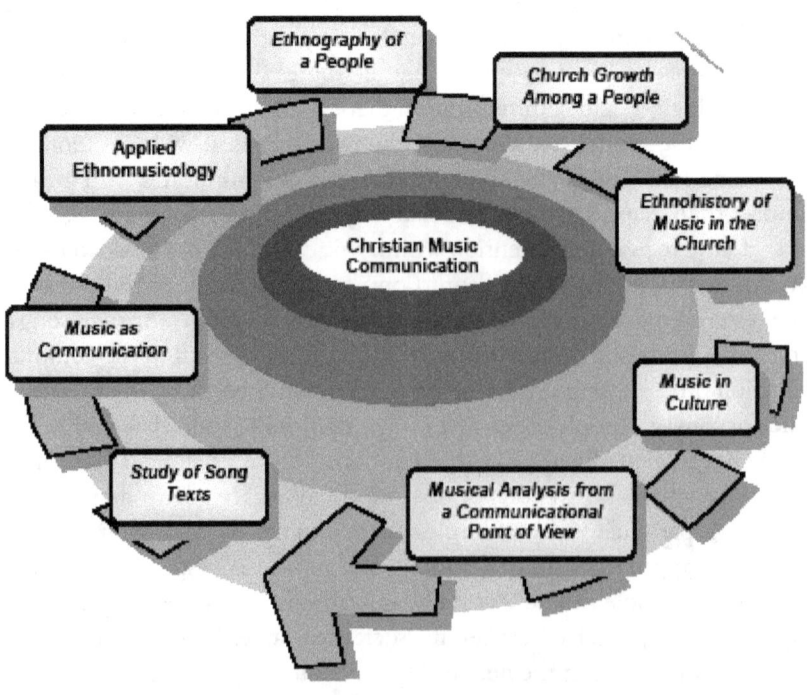

Figure 26
Model for Doing
Christian Music Communication Research

Key: The entry point would ideally be at the top of the model with an ethnography of the people. Investigations may start, however, in other areas of research.

The Development of Songs

The development of culturally appropriate songs relevant to the felt needs and spiritual concerns of the people ultimately relies on the encouragement of the national church. It appears to be best when songs develop from within the ranks of the church laity. Outsiders or missionaries may also play a role in encouraging the development of culturally appropriate songs, by modeling (1) interest in the music traditions through active research and participation in music events, and (2) willingness to attempt to create songs in the appropriate style alongside national believers. The creation of culturally appropriate songs must be viewed as a dynamic process that takes place over a period of time.

Musical Sound Structures and Organization

The musical structures that contribute to the creation of culturally appropriate songs need to work along with each element within the music channel towards a positive attitude to the musical sound itself. A new song form from within the musical traditions of the people should be developed in order to (1) avoid misleading associations with other song forms and (2) help create a sense of identity for the new believing community. There must be agreement between the language structures as they generate the melodic contours and rhythmic patterns. The instruments selected need to be able to support the overall musical framework, both melodically and rhythmically. Issues of previous (often negative) associations attached to instruments used need to be addressed by the believing community and may change over time.

Song Texts

Song texts may bring awarenessn to key cultural values and worldview perspectives. When a song is culturally appropriate it will naturally include these perspectives. The imagery of a text necessarily must draw from the cultural perspectives and cognitive concepts. Theological understandings, although not fully developed, and attempts to integrate the Christian message within a people's own cultural context, should also be present within the song texts.

Movement

The incorporation of movement as a communication channel must be considered in light of a particular society's concept of music. Movement or dance has its own symbolic code system and can be developed to enhance the music event overall, to lead the music event with respect to its communication value, or, as in the case of the Senufo, to serve as an integral part of the music event with respect to musical structures, spiritual transactions, and validation of faith.

Performance Requirements

The actual presentation of culturally appropriate songs within music events and worship services requires effective leadership skills. These skills include musical ability to deal with development of the text, appropriate vocal qualities, and the ability to lead in such a way that the group responds or becomes involved spontaneously. The leader also needs to possess an ability to evaluate the response to the song. A judgment and decision as to the length of the song then follows. These skills may develop over a period of time. A song leader should ideally have a high degree of personal credibility among the participants and a dynamically growing spiritual life.

Photo 15: Senufo believers sing their faith at a local parade

Influence and Effect of the Songs

Finally, culturally appropriate songs should be able to elicit meaningful responses to Christianity on the whole, to the musical style, and to the main messages of the songs. The ideal seeks to trigger positive attitudes toward songs that will translate as positive attitudes towards the message. For non-believers, the goal is to create a positive attitude towards Christianity. For believers, a positive attitude toward the teachings of the songs is the goal.

When culturally appropriate songs are pleasing and working within the cultural framework, they should generate a positive attitude toward an area of knowledge and belief coming from the "outside" (such as Christianity and its teachings). In this way, a highly valued, accepted, and trusted form from within a culture is effectively capitalizing on its own qualities for the introduction of a life-changing message. Thus, a culturally appropriate song should speak directly into the lives of a people in relation to their cultural background, their personal experience, and their present dilemmas.

Culturally appropriate songs should be dynamic expressions of Christian experience and vitality. Their impact should be to such a degree that the church is renewed and that non-believers are naturally attracted to the path of life offered in Jesus Christ.

Gleanings from the Senufo Case Study

The study of Senufo Christian songs yielded some basic discoveries about the use and influence of culturally appropriate songs for Christian communication. These discoveries and principles are foundational to pursuing effective Christian communication. They remain valid even though the contexts of music communication studies may vary in regards to specific cultures and the amount of contact with outside cultures.

Conclusion 1

The use of culturally appropriate songs does make a significant difference in the communication of the Gospel. The contrast in response to foreign hymns, where people slept during the singing in church, to the total involvement of the people during the singing of their own songs reveals a marked difference in reception. Once an appropriate song style was developed, the foreign hymns were dropped from regular usage. Only one hymn, based on a foreign tune textually comprehensible, is now used on a regular basis within the Senufo churches. Also, the fact that non-believers are now willing to come to evangelistic and worship services for the music (but still leave for the sermons) shows the relevance that the musical style has attained within the Senufo society as a whole. The musical structures, textual considerations, performance practices, and actual effects in the lives of the participants all underscore the fact that the main intention of the songs is to communicate.

Conclusion 2

Songs function as a primary means of proclamation and communication. The main intention of a song is communication, and for the Senufo believers the message of the song has the highest value to them. The text of a song, with its cognitive content, takes priority over the musical structures. Musical elements within the song structure are concerned with clearly presenting the song text. A new song form was developed by Senufo Christians to meet the requirements of communicating the Christian message. This song form allows for exegetical development of the text. The melody is generated by linguistic considerations in both melodic contour and rhythmic presentation of the text. Rhythmical clapping must be kept within the parameters of comprehension of the text and should not become overpowering in volume. Melodic instruments (the *jegele*) follow the linguistically determined melody and therefore also communicate the text.

Conclusion 3

Movement and clapping can serve as a visible and physical means of spiritual exchange with God. Dance and clapping is considered an integral part of the music event itself and cannot be divorced from it. They add up to more than mere physical involvement and participation: they are physical acts of worship for Senufo believers. They function as indicators of the measure of one's faith.

Conclusion 4

Song texts provide dynamic expressions of Christian experience. Christian teachings and problems in Christian living are integrated into the song texts as they are confront their worldview concerns and daily life problems. Thus, the song texts serve as a means of dialogue within the Christian community, of affirmation, and of guidance in responding to difficult problems, situations, and felt needs.

Conclusion 5

Song texts serve as theological indicators of a people's beliefs and understandings. From an emic perspective, theological beliefs and positions are revealed through song texts, and they also monitor the directions and gaps in spiritual growth and development at the popular level. This may be observed in the analysis of song texts that have developed over time.

Conclusion 6

Songs work simultaneously within both the affective and cognitive dimensions of the human personality. There is an interplay between the attitude one takes toward a song and the message it is communicating. If the attitude is negative toward the musical sound, the message is not heard. If the attitude is high toward both the musical sound and the song text, then there is also an openness to the message. If the attitude is high toward the musical sound but not the text, the musical sound continues to win access to the cognitive dimension and its message will eventually be heard.

Conclusion 7

Cognitively, culturally appropriate songs both (1) bring awareness of the past experiences and/or current life-situations of a song participant, creating relevance to a specific situation, and (2) influence and shape lifestyle and future decisions at a deep level. A song may not only reflect the needs and concerns of individuals or groups of people, but also advise, teach, admonish, and give direction.

For Senufo believers, songs functioned like the Word of God in their lives by (1) giving guidance, (2) preaching, and (3) bringing emotional balance back to them in the midst of difficult situations.

Conclusion 8

Culturally appropriate songs are influential in the decision-making process. They provide a period of expanded time where song participants have opportunity to evaluate what is suggested in a song. The song participants apply the message of the song to their own background and decide on the action or changes that might be required. Songs have the unique ability to present a message repeatedly and in many ways, within either a shorter or longer period of time. Multiple repetitions of a message are possible within a music event. A decision may not be made on the first presentation, but the repetition of the message over a longer period of time will lead to understanding and possible change.

From these statements, we arrive at the final conclusion: Senufo Christians have indeed developed culturally appropriate songs that suit the needs of the Evangelical Baptist church community. They have made a significant difference in the effective communication of the Gospel in the northern region of Côte d'Ivoire. This study, then, provides a number of implications for missiology.

Implications for Missiology

Missiology and the task of doing mission would benefit greatly if the development and study of Christian music communication were taken more seriously. The "pathways," or areas of study, involved in the development of culturally appropriate musics and music events for Christian witness and growth, offer contributions to each of the fields of study within missiology. Just as musics around the world interact within their diverse cultures, expressing and influencing the human sagas from which they originate, so Christian music communication interacting within the discipline of missiology may serve as a means to fruitful investigations and development of effective mission strategies.

Theology

First, Christian music communication offers missiology the opportunity to evaluate and chart the development of theological concepts within churches around the world. Based on the study of song texts in conjunction with the frequency of a song's usage, we may come to perceive a people's understanding, misunderstanding, and lack of understanding about God. From such a vantage point, we may then plan for further spiritual growth by drawing upon music's formative ability to shape a people's theology. While usually viewed as spiritual encounters with God, participation in and development of culturally appropriate musics and music events allows for theologizing and theological development at the grass-roots levels. This then leads to implications for church growth.

Church Growth

Church growth may benefit from studies in Christian music communication as it plays a role in fulfilling the Great Commission[1]. As we have

---
1. Matt 28:19–20.

noted from the Senufo church, the introduction and use of culturally appropriate songs leads to a more meaningful presentation of the Gospel message. There appears to be a correlation between numerical growth of the church and the use of culturally appropriate musics and music events, viewed and utilized as effective means of communicating the life-changing message of Jesus Christ.

Although we have not made a technical study of church growth in this investigation, we have recognized an apparent relationship between the positive way churches have grown in Côte d'Ivoire as more appropriate music was employed. Technical research in the precise relationships between this growth the use of culturally appropriate music would be helpful.

Positive exploits of Christian music communication, however, are not limited to numerical growth. Rather, the development and use of culturally appropriate songs engenders and fosters dynamic spiritual growth. This is accomplished when such songs, used appropriately, are viewed as working both in the affective and cognitive domains of the human personality, persuasively convincing and speaking to the inner recesses of a person. In order to know the appropriate usage of such songs, however, one must investigate the cultural patterns for music within a particular society. This leads to missiological studies in anthropology.

Anthropology

The interaction between music communication and anthropology is rich. Drawing mainly from the field of ethnomusicology, music communication offers anthropological studies in missiology an additional means for learning a society's cultural patterns, especially in the area of worldview. Pregnant with symbolic meaning, the study of traditional music events may lead to opportunities for translating the Christian message more meaningfully.

In societies, such as that of the Senufo, where multi-media events serve as the central part of aesthetic, emotional, and intellectual experience, people should not be cut off from their traditionally acknowledged avenues of communication. Rather, opportunities for transforming aspects of these events into meaningful and appropriate Christian experiences need to be studied.

Additionally, music communication provides the field of missiological anthropology concrete ways of working "with" culture on God's behalf, rather than against or in ignorance of it. In opposition to early missionary approaches, where there was a lack of respect for a society's traditions, the development of appropriate musics carrying the Christian Gospel works in conjunction with a society's cultural patterns. It does not compromise the Gospel; rather, Christian music communication in its application respects the dignity of a people created in the image of God.

Ethnohistory

Furthermore, Christian music communication provides missiology opportunities for studying church history via the development or lack of development of culturally appropriate musics within the church. At the same time as the beginnings of a people movement took place among the Senufo, there was an outbreak of new song. The parallels with and influences on such groundswells of renewal, in relation to a developing church music, provide a rich source of learning from historical dynamics.

Christian Music Communication

Finally, music should not be viewed merely as an alternative mode of communication but rather as an integral part of the Christian communication process. Research in Christian music communication offers a dynamic approach to completing the missional task. The development of culturally appropriate music and music events contributes powerfully to processes in which spiritual formation and evangelism are natural outgrowths. Thus, implementation of such development becomes imperative for the task of missions.

Further investigations of Christian music communication, as it is occurring in both rural and urban areas, on the continent of Africa, and around the world are needed. Its study will yield broad generalizations and communication strategies that will inform and under gird the Church's work of world mission. The Church needs to grab hold of the communicative benefits and advantages of using culturally appropriate music as it seeks to expand the Kingdom of God.

The Final Goal

Thus, in conclusion, the many paths in Christian music communication have an important role to play in fulfilling the Great Commission.[2] Ultimately, we must look to God's goal for us as human beings as it relates to music. Through the use of culturally appropriate songs and music events,

---

2. Ibid.

Reaching the Path's Destination

then, our goal is caught up with an image presented to us by the prophet Isaiah. In Isaiah 2:2–3 (NIV), he pictures worship in the Kingdom of God during the last days as going to the "mountain of the Lord's temple," where this mountain

> . . . will be raised above the hills, and all nations will stream to it. Many peoples will come and say, "Come, let us go up to the mountain of the LORD, to the house of the God of Jacob. He will teach us his ways, so that we may walk in his paths."[3]

May we develop pathways in Christian music communication that lead all peoples to walk in his paths.

---

3. Isa 2:2–3 (NIV).

Appendix A

Song Texts

THE FOLLOWING SONG TEXTS are representative of the 172 song texts collected. Due to the large corpus of texts available for analysis and the limitations of this dissertation, I have selected only a representative sixteen texts. The texts were first transcribed into Senufo from tape recordings and then were translated into French. Besides the English translations that are presented here, both the Senufo and French versions are available from me on request. Since I discussed the song texts based on three periods of collection in Chapters 8 and 9, I have divided the songs presented here according to these periods: (1) songs collected before the 1986 workshop, (2) the Current Senufo Repertoire—the most popular songs currently sung from both before and after the workshops, and (3) the most popular songs from the 1987 workshop.

Songs Before the 1986 Workshop

Song 1: Bariga Saʔa Wolo Kafɔw Zyezu (Thank You Very Much Jesus)

Thematic Statement:
    Thank you very much, Lord Jesus.
    You have chased away and lifted from us the wicked Satan.
    Thank you very much, Lord Jesus.

Response: Thank you very much Lord Jesus.

Development/Exegesis:
 (1) Oh, the work of our choice that you have pulled up and thrown away.
 (2) The work of the *marabout* that you have chased away and lifted from us.
 (3) The fetishes made of beef tails that you have pulled up and thrown away.

Appendix A

(4) The evil fetishes that you have pulled up and thrown away.

(5) The bad lies that you have chased away and freed us from.

(6) The wicked stealing that you have chased far from us.

(7) The kola nut sacrifices that you have lifted from us.

(8) Our own ways (paths) that you have lifted from us.

(9) The judgment that you have chased away and freed us from.

Thematic Statement:
    Thank you very much, Lord Jesus.
    You have chased away and lifted from us the wicked Satan.
    Thank you very much, Lord Jesus.

Song 2: People (Christians), Kneel Down to Worship Jesus

Thematic Statement:
    People (Christians), let us kneel down to worship Jesus.
    Because at the end of the world, Jesus will come back.
    People (Christians), let us kneel down to worship Jesus.

Response: People (Christians), let us kneel down to worship Jesus.

Development/Exegesis:

(1) Jesus, who takes away the *yawiiye*, said that he will put an end to the works of the demon (Satan).

(2) Jesus, who takes away the work of the *marabouts*, said that he will put an end to the work of the *marabout*.

(3) Jesus, who takes away the *yawiiye*, said that he will put an end to the works of the demon (Satan).

(4) Jesus, who takes away the troubles (of the heart) said that he will put an end to all these troubles.

(5) Jesus, who takes away awful stealing, said that he will put an end to the work of thieves.

(6) Jesus, who takes away the traditional initiations (*cologo*), said that he will put an end to that.

(7) Jesus, who takes away the vain discussions, said that he will put an end to vain discussions.

(8) Jesus, who takes away adultery of women, said that he will put an end to that.

Thematic Statement:
>People (Christians), let us kneel down to worship Jesus.
>Because at the end of the world, Jesus will come back.
>People (Christians), let us kneel down to worship Jesus.

Song 3: Every Moment the Hand of Jesus Is on You and Thus All His Blessing (Lalá)

Thematic Statement:
>Every moment the hand of Jesus is on you and thus all his blessing.
>If we have ever clearly explained our sins,
>Every moment the hand of Jesus is on you and thus all his blessing.

Response: Every moment, the hand of Jesus is on you and thus all his blessing.

Development/Exegesis:

(1) If we have clearly explained our wicked stealing.

(2) If we explain our fetishes made of ox tails to Jesus.

(3) People, stop speaking bad things and pray to Jesus.

(4) People, stop doubting and pray to Jesus.

(5) Let's leave these spiritual discussions in order to pray to Jesus.

Thematic Statement:
>Every moment the hand of Jesus is on you and thus all his blessing.
>If we have ever clearly explained our sins,
>Every moment the hand of Jesus is on you and thus all his blessing.

Song 4: It Is No Longer I Who Live, but the Lord Jesus Who Is Alive in Me (based on Galatians 2:20)

Thematic Statement:
>It is no longer I who live but Jesus who is alive in me.
>The life that I have, I have it by the Lord.
>It is no longer I who live but Jesus who is alive in me.

Response: It is no longer I who live but Jesus who is alive in me.

Appendix A

Development/Exegesis:

(1) The life that I have, I have it, thanks to Jesus Christ.

(2) The *sandoyo* that I've left, I have left them, thanks to Jesus Christ.

(3) The sins that I have left, I have left them, thanks to Jesus Christ.

(4) The worship with chickens that I have left, I have left, thanks to Jesus Christ.

(5) The adultery (with men) that I had, I have left, thanks to Jesus Christ.

(6) The lying that I've left, I have left, thanks to Jesus Christ.

Thematic Statement:
> It is no longer I who live but Jesus who is alive in me.
> The life that I have, I have it by the Lord.
> It is no longer I who live but Jesus who is alive in me.

Current Senufo Repertoire

Song 5: In My Father's House

Thematic Statement:
> There are many dwelling places in my Father's house.
> If it were not so, I would have plainly told you.
> But I am going there to prepare one for you.
> When I finish, I will come and take you.
> You will live in the dwelling place of my father.

Response: You will live in the dwelling place of my father.

Development:

(1) Abandon lying, Jesus is calling you.

(2) Abandon doubts, Jesus is calling you.

(3) Abandon sadness, Jesus is calling you.

(4) Abandon the *lɔsunnyi*, Jesus is calling you.

(5) Abandon the *coto-beeri*, Jesus is calling you.

(6) Abandon the *fani-wiiw*, Jesus is calling you.

(7) My fathers, Jesus is calling you.

(8) My mothers, Jesus is calling you.

(9) My brothers, Jesus is calling you.

(10) Abandon sadness, Jesus is calling you.

(11) Get up and walk, Jesus is calling you. Come!

Thematic Statement:
> There are many dwelling places in my Father's house.
> If it were not so, I would have plainly told you.
> But I am going there to prepare one for you.
> When I finish, I will come and take you.
> You will live in the dwelling place of my father.

Song 6: Alleluia, Alleluia, Thank You Jesus (Aleluya, Aleluya Zyezu Bariga)

Thematic Statement:
> Alleluia! Alleluia! Thank you, Jesus!
> Response: Alleluia! Alleluia! Thank you, Jesus!

Development/Exegesis:

(1) God, master of blessing and power, you are holy and good.

(2) God, master of blessing and power, you are perfect.

(3) Father *baba*, you are really holy, holy, holy.[1]

(4) Father *baba*, you are good, good. You are perfect.

(5) There was something like a grand body of water (a sea) before your throne.

(6) Father *baba*, you are really holy and just.

(7) There was something like a grand body of water (a sea) before your throne.

(8) Father *baba*, you are really holy and just.

(9) There was something in heaven. It was holy and perfect.

(10) Father *baba*, you are holy, holy, holy.

(11) And there was something in heaven like a lion.

(12) And there was something in heaven like a human being.

---

1. The word "holy" for the Senufo includes the ideas of perfection, of being without fault, and of being just.

Appendix A

(13) Father *baba*, you are really holy, holy, holy.

(14) There was something in heaven like a calf.

(15) And there was something in heaven that had many wings on it.

(16) Father *baba*, you are holy, holy, holy.

(17) Father *baba*, you are there, are you going there?

(18) You who have been since a long time, are you going there?

(19) Father *baba*, really, you are holy, holy, holy.

Thematic Statement:
Alleluia! Alleluia! Thank you, Jesus!

Song 7: Jesus Said, "I Am Going and I Will Come Again"

Thematic Statement:
Jesus said, "I am going and I will come again."
If you accept the word that I preach to you, you will be saved.
Jesus said, "I am going and I will come again."

Response: Jesus said, "I am going and I will come again."

Development/Exegesis:

(1) Alleluia! If we accept the words that he preached to us, we will be saved.

(2) Thank you. If we accept the teaching that he brought us, we will be saved.

(3) Eeh, if we accept his word, we will be saved.

(4) Eeh, abandon Satan. Come, you who will be with him!

(5) People, abandon the devil. We will go with Jesus when he comes.

(6) People, abandon lies. Come! We will go with Jesus when he comes.

(7) Awoo, abandon the *yawiiris*. Come! We will go with Jesus when he comes.

(8) Awoo, abandon adultery. Come! We will go with Jesus when he comes.

(9) Awoo, abandon your doubts. Come! We will go with Jesus when he comes.

(10) My father, abandon the fetishes. Come! We will go with Jesus when he comes.

(11) Look people! When Jesus comes, it is the believers who will go with him.

(12) Listen people! Believe on him! When he comes we will go with him.

Thematic Statement:
>Jesus said, "I am going and I will come again."
>If you accept the word that I preach to you, you will be saved.
>Jesus said, "I am going and I will come again."

Song 8: The Lord Is My Guide[2] (based on Psalm 23:1–3)

Thematic Statement:
>The father, Jehovah, is my guide. He is the one who takes care of me.
>David said it in the Psalms, people.
>He is the one who is my guide. He is the one who educates me.

Response: The father is my guide. He is the one who takes care of me.

Development/Exegesis:

(1) Eeh people! He leads me into beautiful pastures.

(2) Eeh people! Father (*baba*) guides me where there is clear water.

(3) Eeh people! Father (*baba*) gives me food.

(4) Eeh people! It is the father (*baba*) who guides me. He is the one who takes care of me.

(5) Eeh people! The father (*baba*) guides me where there is good pasture.

(6) Eeh people! It is Jesus who has taken me. It is the father (*baba*) who takes care of me.

(7) Eeh Christian! When you are sick, our father (*baba*) watches over you.

(8) Eeh Christian! When there is famine, Jesus watches over you.

---

2. *Nyaʔanfɔlɔ* refers to the Lord as being one's protector and provider, while *gboo* refers to the Lord as the one who carries the growing infant on their back until he/she is grown enough to walk. This implies a very intimate relationship. In this way, then, the Lord is a "guide."

Appendix A

(9) Eeh Christian! On your way to the fields, our father (*baba*) watches over you.

(10) Eeh Christian! When you're at home, our father (*baba*) watches over you

(11) Eeh Christian! When you are in difficult situations, our father (*baba*) sees you.

(12) Eeh Christian! When you have joy, our father (*baba*) watches over you.

(13) He gives me to eat in the presence of my enemies.

(14) Father (*baba*) lives in me because of his name.

(15) Christian, when you are in trouble, father (*baba*) watches over you.

(16) Christian, when there is no water, Jesus watches over you.

(17) Christian, when there is war, Jesus watches over you.

(18) Do not be afraid! Jehovah sees us.

(19) It is Jehovah, the author of peace, who watches over me.

Thematic Statement:
> The father, Jehovah, is my guide. He is the one who takes care of me.
> David said it in the Psalms, people.
> He is the one who is my guide. He is the one who educates me.

Popular Songs from the 1987 Workshop

Song 9: Grab Hold of Faith (Faith Is like an Egg, based on Hebrews 11:5)

Thematic Statement:
> People, grab hold of faith!
> Faith is like an egg. If it escapes and falls, it breaks.
> People, grab hold of faith!

Response: People, grab hold of faith!

Development/Exegesis:

(1) Faith is like an egg. If it escapes and falls, it breaks.

(2) It is because of faith that God raised up Enoch.

(3) It is by faith that Peter walked on the water.

(4) You cannot please God without faith.

(5) No one can please God without faith.

(6) There are the things of the world that you are looking at. And if faith escapes and falls ...

(7) There is the money of the world that you are looking at. And if faith escapes and falls ...

(8) It is the bad behavior (of a person) that you are looking at. And if faith escapes and falls ...

(9) There are the good-looking men of the world that you are looking at. And if faith escapes and falls ...

(10) There are the beautiful women of the world that you are looking at. And if faith escapes and falls ...

Thematic Statement:
    People, grab hold of faith!
    Faith is like an egg. If it escapes and falls, it breaks.
    People, grab hold of faith!

Song 10: Let Us Rejoice about Our Freedom (based on John 8:31–32)

Thematic Statement:
    Let us rejoice about our freedom.
    Jesus has chosen us and has given us freedom.
    Let us rejoice about our freedom.

Response: Let us rejoice about our freedom.

Development/Exegesis:

(1) Thank you our Lord Jesus. You are the one who has given us freedom.

(2) Jesus has chosen us and has given us freedom.

(3) The Jews have believed on our Lord Jesus.

(4) The Lord said, "People, if you believe ...

(5) my words that you hear. If you walk according to them.

(6) My words that I tell you, if you accept to practice them,

(7) You will really be my disciples."

(8) If you listen to the word of Jesus, people, and you walk according to it,

(9) Jesus said that you will be his disciple, people.

(10) The father (*baba*) has chosen us and has given us freedom.

(11) You who accepts to walk according to the word of our father.

(12) You who accepts to walk according to the word of Jesus.

(13) Jesus said, "I like that, I will give you freedom."

(14) The father has given us joy by granting us freedom.

(15) We were suffering in the hands of the *sando?o*.

(16) Jesus has chosen us and has given us freedom.

(17) We were suffering from the insomnia of Satan.

(18) Jesus has saved us from Satan and has given us liberty.

(19) We were suffering from the fetishes.

(20) Jesus has chosen us and has given us rest.

(21) Our Lord Jesus says, "Those who hear my word . . .

(22) . . . And accept to do what I say,

(23) The father (*baba*) said, 'They will be my disciples.

(24) If the father (*baba*) gives you freedom, you are a free person.

(25) If the son gives you freedom, you are a free person.

(26) We were suffering another time in the hands of the spirits.

(27) Satan made us suffer, he makes us suffer.

Thematic Statement:
    Let us rejoice about our freedom.
    Jesus has chosen us and has given us freedom.
    Let us rejoice about our freedom.

Song 11: I Will Tell Our Lord Jesus (Prayer for My Family)

Thematic Statement:
    People, that is why I will tell our Lord Jesus.
    We have come to Christ and those of our house have remained

nonbelievers.
People, that is why I will tell our Lord Jesus.

Response: People, that is why I will tell our Lord Jesus.

Development/Exegesis:

(1) We have come to Jesus and our elders have remained nonbelievers.
(2) We have come to the father and our elders have remained nonbelievers.
(3) We have come to the father and our juniors (youth) have remained nonbelievers.
(4) We have come to the father and our brothers and sisters have remained nonbelievers.
(5) Àbāa father, author of patience, call our relatives.
(6) Àbāa father, author of true love, call our brothers and sisters.
(7) Àbāa father, author of pardon, call our juniors (youth).
(8) Àbāa father, you who have mercy, call our relatives.
(9) When I think about how they will be burned (in the fire).
(10) When I think about how they will be in that place.
(11) We have come to Christ and the "*sando?o*" has stopped our relatives.
(12) We have come to Christ and the fetishes have stopped our relatives.
(13) We have come to Christ and the sacrifices have stopped our relatives.
(14) Jesus, author of blessing, call them for us.
(15) You have great power, retrieve them for us.
(16) You have great power, call our fathers for us.
(17) Even if someone is wicked, the Savior Jesus calls him/her.
(18) Even if someone is guilty (stained), the Lord Jesus can help him/her.

Thematic Statement:
People, that is why I will tell our Lord Jesus.
We have come to Christ and those of our house have remained

Appendix A

nonbelievers.
People, that is why I will tell our Lord Jesus.

Song 12: People, run! Run! For we are in a race!

Thematic Statement:
> People, Run! Run! For we are in a race!
> You will be joyful when Jesus comes because of the race that you are running.
> People, Run! Run! For we are in a race!

Response: People, Run! Run! For we are in a race!

Development/Exegesis:

(1) Paul told us that we are running a race.

(2) If you look around while running this race, you will depart from it.

(3) The meaning of the race is that you should walk together with Jesus.

(4) The meaning of the race is that you eat together with Jesus.

(5) The meaning of the race is that you work together with Jesus.

(6) You will be with Jesus when he comes because of the race that you are running.

(7) If someone suffers while running the race, he/she will have benefits.

(8) If you stop to drink while running the race, you will depart from it.

(9) If you stop to eat while running the race, you will depart from it.

(10) You will be joyful when Jesus comes because of the race that you are running.

Thematic Statement:
> People, Run! Run! For we are in a race!
> You will be joyful when Jesus comes because of the race that you are running.
> People, Run! Run! For we are in a race!

Song 13: There Is Everything with the Father

Thematic Statement:
>People, there is everything with the father (*baba*).
>It is enough to accept him and your part is reserved.

Response: If only you accept him, your part is reserved.

Development/Exegesis:

(1) People, there is patience with the father.

(2) People, there is eternal life with the father.

(3) People, there is genuine rest with the father.

(4) People, peace belongs to Jesus.

(5) People, self-control belongs to Jesus.

(6) The new Jerusalem belongs to Jesus.

(7) Eternal life is from Jesus.

(8) Tomorrow's new earth belongs to Jesus.

(9) Heaven belongs to Jesus.

(10) My habits belong to Jesus.

(11) You have your part there, you have your part,

(12) In the eternal life of our father.

(13) You have your part there in our father's village of peace.

(14) You have your part there in our father's place of patience.

(15) You have your part there in the place of eternal life.

(16) You have your part there in our father's village of peace.

(17) Your part is in tomorrow's village of peace.

(18) Your part is in the good place above.

(19) Your part is in the village of eternal life.

(20) Your part is in the new Jerusalem.

(21) Your part is in our father's village of patience.

(22) Your part is in our father's village of love.

(23) Your part is in the village without sickness.

Appendix A

(24) Your part is in the village without death.

(25) Your part is in the village without famine.

(26) Your part is in the village without sadness.

Thematic Statement:
>People, there is everything with the father (*baba*).
>It is enough to accept him and your part is reserved.

Song 14: Philip, When You See Jesus, It Is God Who You See (based on John 14:8)

Thematic Statement:
>Philip, when you see Jesus, it is God who you see.
>It is really God who you see.

Response: Oh, Philip!

Development/Exegesis:

(1) Philip asked Jesus,

(2) "Show us your father."

(3) Philip asked the father,

(4) "Show us your father."

(5) Jesus said, "Oh, Philip!

(6) Since I've been among you,

(7) You still don't recognize my father?

(8) When you see Jesus, it is indeed God who you see.

(9) When you see me, it is indeed God who you see.

(10) It is the God of peace who you see.

(11) It is indeed that God of love who you see.

(12) Yes, believe in me, believe in God!

(13) Leave those vain discussions and believe in me.

(14) When you see Jesus, it is indeed God who you see.

(15) It is the God who gives faith who you see."

(16) People, it is indeed God, the one who gives blessing, who you see.

(17) Eeh, people! It is indeed God, the one who gives peace, who you see.

(18) Eeh, people! It is indeed God, the one who gives life, who you see.

(19) Eeh, people! Jesus accepted to come into the world.

(20) The Lord, the father has come into the world.

(21) Eeh, people! Nothing but to show us the father!

(22) . . . to show us the God of faith.

(23) Eeh! . . . to show us the father, the God of blessing.

(24) Eeh! . . . to show us the author of eternal life.

(25) Eeh! It is indeed God, the creator of the heavens, who you have seen.

(26) It is the God of worship who you have seen.

(27) Christian, give your heart to our father, God.

(28) It is God, the one who gives patience, who you have seen.

(29) Christian, give your thoughts to our father, Jesus.

(30) It is God, author of the world, who you have seen.

(31) Christian, it is the God of power who you have seen.

(32) God has helped Jesus to do what he has done.

Thematic Statement:

Philip, when you see Jesus, it is God who you see. It is really God who you see.

Song 15: If A Spirit Leaves a Person, It Does Not Leave for Good (based on Matthew 12:43)

Thematic Statement:
    Grab hold of Jesus! We should not loosen our grip.
    Jesus said, "If a spirit leaves a person, it does not leave for good."
    Grab hold of Jesus! We should not loosen our grip.

Response: Grab hold of Jesus! We should not loosen our grip.

Appendix A

Development/Exegesis:

(1) Our Jesus said, "If a spirit leaves, it does not leave for good.

(2) When a spirit leaves the house where it is staying, people,

(3) It will walk in dry places.

(4) If it wanders in vain and finds no good place of habitation,

(5) Alas! It will say, "I will return to the house where I was before."

(6) And when it arrives and finds the place empty and well swept,

(7) The house, being well swept and filled with good things,

(8) I will go searching for its companions, people.

(9) It returns looking for seven other spirits beside itself.

(10) Eeh! Those that are worse than himself.

(11) They enter . . . and live in the house.

(12) And the things of the person become worse and worse.

(13) People, these actions become worse than before!

(14) Christian, you who already believe in Jesus Christ!

(15) If you have only one spirit and Jesus chased it away from you,

(16) And you leave the Jesus road saying that it is too difficult,

(17) People, and if you renounce Jesus and the bad one is informed,

(18) He'll search for several things that are worse than before.

(19) The spirits that are much worse than himself.

(20) People, then he'll pour out worse sufferings on your family.

(21) Alas, you will not have peace in this world. And in addition to this, you will pass through fire.

(22) You will not have happiness in this world nor in the world of Jesus.

(23) Christian, you who already believe in our father,

(24) Even when difficult suffering confronts you, the father (*baba*) sees them.

(25) Even when Satan comes to tempt you,

(26) Know that the power of Jesus is superior to that of Satan.

(27) Jesus allows you to suffer in order to test your faith.

(28) Jesus can abandon you to Satan in order to test your faith.

(29) Christian, when the bad one (Satan) comes with terrible suffering in order to test you,

(30) If he comes with difficult trials in order to test your faith,

(31) Even, if he comes to you with great anguish, people,

(32) If Satan comes with numerous things in order to tempt you,

(33) Look to the word of Jesus and do not renounce the father.

Thematic Statement:
    Grab hold of Jesus! We should not loosen our grip.
    Jesus said, "If a spirit leaves a person, it does not leave for good."
    Grab hold of Jesus! We should not loosen our grip.

Song 16: The Lord Jesus Has Great Power (based on Matthew 15:29–31)

Thematic Statement:
    The Lord Jesus has great power.
    He performed many miracles when he came.
    The Lord Jesus has great power.

Response: The Lord Jesus has great power.

Development/Exegesis:

(1) He performed many miracles when he came.

(2) One day, Jesus went to the Sea of Galilee.

(3) People . . . and he climbed up the mountain and sat down.

(4) They brought him many sick people.

(5) Even the paralytics and people possessed by spirits came to Jesus.

(6) They brought him the deaf and the dumb.

(7) They even brought him people with broken bones.

(8) Many people went there with these patients.

(9) And the Lord Jehovah healed all of them and they returned home.

(10) And the dumb spoke, the paralytics walked.

(11) And the people who had broken bones were all healed!

(12) Even those who were spirit-possessed were healed.

Appendix A

(13) Jesus healed many sick people in the world.

(14) It is in Matthew chapter 5 (*sic*) that this word is written.

(15) You must look at verse 29.

(16) Jesus healed many sick people in the world.

(17) Jesus even resurrected many of the dead and they lived.

(18) Even Lazarus was dead and he was raised up.

(19) And Lazarus was in the tomb four days,

(20) And Jesus went and placed himself close to the tomb.

(21) And people! And he prayed to his father, his father, *baba*!

(22) Look! Lazarus was resurrected and came out from among the dead.

(23) Thank you. He performed many miracles for people in the world.

(24) If you believe in Jesus about your sickness,

(25) Jesus will heal your sickness and save you from the second death.

(26) One day the disciples climbed aboard a large boat.

(27) Then Jesus entered the water and started to walk on it.

(28) When they saw Jesus, they were afraid.

(29) They thought he could be a spirit.

(30) The Lord Jesus said to them, "But it is me."

(31) Peter said to him, "My Lord, if it is really you, Jesus,

(32) Tell me so that I might also walk to meet you."

(33) He said to him, "Get out and come, Peter. It is I."

(34) He got out and started to walk on the sea.

(35) When he had some doubts, he failed and started to drown.

(36) Jesus said to him, "Man, your faith is small."

(37) Christian, you who believe in our father,

(38) You must not doubt your faith.

(39) The moment when you have doubts,

(40) The demon (evil one, Satan) will begin to seize you.

Thematic Statement:
    The Lord Jesus has great power.

He performed many miracles when he came.
The Lord Jesus has great power.

Appendix B

Senufo Song Survey—1987

THE FOLLOWING INTERVIEW SCHEDULE is a back translation from the Senufo language of what was actually asked during each individual interview conducted as part of the 1987 Senufo Song Survey. The interview schedule was originally written by myself in English. As I worked with both a national and a missionary translator, the schedule was changed in the translation process in order to communicate more effectively with the respondents. Thus, this schedule is more directly reflective of the Senufo language and thought patterns than the original schedule written in English. The Senufo version of the schedule is available on request.

The Interview Schedule

Greetings! They call me *Yɛlífiige*. Those songs that we sang in this church, they please me very much. But it would please me to know some more about their affair. Those songs that help you yourselves most in walking in the Jesus' road, it would please me to know about those ones. Therefore, if you are agreed, I want you to give me the responses to these questions.

Section I: Demographic Information

(1) What do they call you? (name)

(2) Which kind of words do you speak? (dialect)

(3) What is the name of your village?

(4) Age: Young people: ___ male ___ female

Old ones: ___ male ___ female

Middle ones (35–50): ___ male ___ female

(5) What kind of work do you do in the church?
___ make us new songs? ___ lead songs? ___ pastor?
___ deacon? ___ member?

(6) How many years have you finished in the faith?
___ 0–5 years ___ 6–15 years ___ more than 15 years

Section II: About Songs in General

(7) Show to me those songs that please you the most (if not enough response: Isn't there another one that also pleases you to add to those?). Three songs requested.

(8) Would you agree to sing them for me in order for me to hear them? (If not, then say: I beg you, if you can't sing them, that you would say their kind—say how they go to me.)

(9) Before you believed in Jesus

  (a) Did you sing the songs of others?

  (b) Did you sing (compose) your own songs?

(10) What kind of songs do unbelievers sing? Show three of them to me.

(11) Which of these do not go toward the work of the *Poro* or the *Sandogo*?

Section III: Newly Created Songs and Their Influence

Now I am going to open the machine in order that it can sing some songs for you to hear.

Song 1: Aleluya, Aleluya Zyezu Bariga

(12) Have you ever heard this song?

(13) Are you able to sing it? Possible responses:

___ embarrassed ___ doesn't know anything ___ knows a little
___ knows all of it ___ knows all except a little bit

If no response: Would you tell me how it goes?

(14) What are the words of the song saying? (meaning)

(15) Is the person singing when the machine is playing? (observation)

Appendix B

(16) How many times did the person listen to the song before its meaning could be told?

(17) Does this song please you?

(18) ___ no ___ a little (*cɛɛri*) ___ a lot (*gbanaʔama*)

(19) Is there something in the song that makes it that you do not want to sing it?

(20) If they were able to add two things to this song in order to make it more sweet, in your opinion, what two things should they add here? (things=musical instruments)

___ to clap the hands ___ to play the *kanrigi*
___ to play the *jegele* (*balafons*)
___ to play the "caliw" (shaker) ___ something else

(21) If it isn't in the church, do you sing this song other places? If so, where do you sing it? When?

(22) This song was a new song last year. I will show some other songs to you. Those that you have already heard, show these to me (list of twenty-five songs).

(23) Do you know other villages in which they sing these new songs that were made last year? If so, which are these villages?

The machine will play/sing another song.

Song 2: The Song from Hebrews

(24) Have you ever heard this song?

(25) Would you like to be receiving the song? Sing along with it? Sing the responses?

(26) What are the words of the song saying? (meaning)

(27) How many times did the person listen to the song before its meaning could be told?

(28) Are you able to know to be singing this song? (contains the idea of studying the song until you can sing it)

(29) Does this song please you? What is in the song that makes it pleasing to you?

(30) Is there something in the song that makes it that you do not want to sing it?

Senufo Song Survey—1987

(31) If you were able to add two things to this song in order to make it more sweet, in your opinion, what two things would you add here?
___ to clap the hands ___ to play the *kanrigi*
___ to play the *jegele* (*balafons*)
___ to play the *caliw* (shaker) ___ something else

Another new song is here which God gave us this year. Would it please you to learn it? I will let the machine sing it. If you want to respond to it, it is okay.

Song 3: The Lord Is My Guide (Psalm 23:1–3)

(32) Is the person singing while the machine is playing? (observation)

(33) What is the meaning of the song?

(34) How many times did the person listen to the song before able to tell its meaning?

(35) Are you able to know to be singing this song?

(36) Does this song please you? What is in the song that makes it pleasing to you?

(37) Is there something in the song that makes it that you do not want to sing it?

(38) If you wanted to tell the affair of this song to one of your friends, how would you speak to him?

(39) Would you like to say something to us the way the believers' songs helped you yourself in walking the Jesus road?

(40) Here is my last question: Would you like to say anything about the songs that are sung in the church?

(41) The songs that they sing in the church, were they the reason that you believed on Jesus?

(42) What is it in them that drew you and you believed in Jesus?

(43) Do you read?

(44) Do you write?

Appendix B

Data from the Survey

The full compilation of the 120 tables collected and compiled are available for perusal from the author on request.

Appendix C

Focus Group Question Guide and Interview Samples

THIS APPENDIX IS MADE up of the question guide, the song text, and sample responses from the Focus Group Interviews that were conducted in eleven villages in January 1988.

Focus Group Question Guide

(1) Introduction of all the participants.

(2) Prayer.

(3) Explanation of our goals:

    (a) To learn from the participants how to understand the songs better and also how to improve the songs

    (b) All answers are correct; there are no wrong answers.

    (c) We will be recording the interview session so that we will not forget what we have said.

Section I: Believers' Thoughts about the Songs

First, play the selected song, "I pray to you, our father, Jesus," on the tape recorder. Then ask the following questions.

(1) What is this song saying?

(2) Does this song touch your life? Why? How?

(3) Are there other songs that touch your life?

(4) Which songs touch (are meaningful in) your life? Do you have a specific story to show how the song has helped you?

(5) Do you know the song, *Kagbaana ga wire n too yɛ lɛ waa na, Zyezu a bgan li laʔaʔ*?

Appendix C

(6) Do you have a story to show how this song has helped you? A story about yourself or about someone else?

(7) Are there still other stories that have helped you in your Christian life? Which ones are they? Do you have any stories about them?

(8) Last year, the people told us, "The songs help us like the Word of God." Do you agree with this? What does this mean for you? How have the Christian songs helped you like the Word of God?

Section II: Non-believers' Thoughts about the Christian Songs

(1) Do the non-believers (pagans) like the Christian songs? How do the non-believers receive the Christian songs?

(2) Have the songs led any of the non-believers to Jesus Christ? Give some specific examples and stories.

(3) Are there any non-believers who sing the Christian songs? Give some specific examples and stories.

Section III: About the New Songs—The "Ideal" Song

(1) How do you like the new songs?

(2) What is it in the new songs that pleases you? (If necessary, read a list of the new songs to trigger their thinking.)

(3) Do you prefer songs that are long or short (in reference to length)? When?

(4) Do you prefer songs where the responses are long? Or do you prefer songs where the responses are short?

Example: Short—"Aleluya, Aleluya, Zyezu Bariga" Long—"Bibile abgan syɔɔn tama, Bibile abgan" "syɔɔn tama n lá bibilew pan dulunyaw ni, Bibile a bgan syɔɔn."

(5) Do you prefer songs where the lead singer says a lot of things? Or do you prefer songs where the lead singer has fewer things to say?

(6) Do you prefer songs with real strong rhythms? When?

(7) Do you clap your hands when we sing? If yes, when do you clap your hands?

(8) Do you prefer songs where we dance? When?

Focus Group Question Guide and Interview Samples

(9) What musical instruments do you like to have played along with the songs?

(10) What sort of song texts (themes) do you prefer?

    (a) Those that talk about God?

    (b) Those that talk about the love of God?

    (c) Those that talk about Satan?

    (d) Those that talk about the power of God?

    (e) Those that talk about the Christian life?

    (f) Those that praise God?

    (g) Any other topics?

(11) Good, that is the end. We have discussed many things. Is there anything else you would like to add to our discussion about the Christian songs?

Song Text Used for the Focus Group Interviews

Song: I Pray To You, Our Father, Jesus

Thematic Statement:
>I pray to you, our father, Jesus. I pray to you. Thank you.
>Because it was you who died, we have been delivered from the sufferings brought by Satan.
>I pray to you, our father, Jesus. I pray to you. Thank you.

Response: . . . our father, Jesus, I pray to you. Thank you.

Development/Exegesis:

(1) Look! It was he who died and we have been delivered from the suffering brought by the "*Yawiri.*" I pray to you *yoo* . . .

(2) Eeh, look! It was he who died and we have been delivered from the suffering brought by the funerals. I pray to you *yoo* . . .

(3) Eeh, father (*baba*)! It was he who died and we have been delivered from the suffering brought by the "*Yawiri.*" I pray to you *yoo* . . .

(4) Eeh, look! It was he who died and we have been delivered from the suffering brought by the funerals. I pray to you *yoo* . . .

Appendix C

(5) Eeh, look! It was he who died and we have been delivered from the suffering brought by the "*nanbwɔɔyi.*" I pray to you *yoo* . . .

(6) Eeh, look! It was he who died and we have been delivered from the suffering brought by adultery. Jesus, I pray to you *yoo* . . .

(7) Eeh, look! It was he who died and we have been delivered from the suffering brought by jealousy. Jesus, I pray to you *yoo* . . .

(8) Eeh, look! It was he who died and we have been delivered from the suffering brought by the fetishes. Jesus, I pray to you *yoo* . . .

(9) Eeh, father (*baba*)! It was he who died and we have been delivered from the suffering brought by the *nanbwɔɔyi*, the fetishes. Jesus, I pray to you *yoo* . . .

(10) Eeh, look! It was he who died and we have been delivered from the suffering brought by all kinds of evil. Jesus, I pray to you *yoo* . . .

(11) Eeh, father (*baba*)! It was he who died and we have been delivered from the suffering brought by the *yawiiri*. Jesus, I pray to you *yoo* . . .

(12) Eeh, father, (*baba*)! It was he who died and we have been delivered from the suffering brought by the *yawiiri*. Jesus, I pray to you *yoo* . . .

(13) Eeh! It was he who died and we have been delivered from the suffering brought by adultery. Jesus, I pray to you *yoo* . . .

(14) Eeh! It was he who died and we have been delivered from the suffering brought by the *yawiiri*. I pray to you *yoo* . . .

Thematic Statement:
   I pray to you, our father, Jesus. I pray to you. Thank you.
   Because it was you who died, we have been delivered from the sufferings brought by Satan.
   I pray to you, our father, Jesus. I pray to you. Thank you.

Focus Group Interview Samples

The following responses provide a sampling of the data that was obtained from the eleven Focus Group interview sessions. Due to the large body of information that was obtained, it is not feasible to include the whole corpus that is made up of 105 pages of transcribed responses. Further access to this body of information is available from me, the author, upon request.

Focus Group Question Guide and Interview Samples

In each case, the interview question is first stated and then followed by two samples for each question.

Section I: Believers' Thoughts about the Songs

First, play the selected song, "I pray to you, our father, Jesus," on the tape recorder. Then ask the following questions:

Question 1. What is this song saying?

Question 2. Does this song "touch" your life? Why? How?

Sample 1: Respondent 7 from the village of Fɔrɔ

> This song has many stories. When I grew up, my mother was a sorceress since my childhood. She was among the leaders of the sorceresses. She often stayed away from us for months. We did not know. She really suffered a lot during this time. Then later, one of my brothers became sorcerer and also one of my own children. I, too, was supposed to become a sorceress (*sandoyi*). It was after that that my mother became initiated into sorcery. I was in another village raising my twins. There was a child of the wife of my uncle who disappeared and was dead. However, the child was not sick. The uncle's son-in-law also died without being sick. If someone tells you, "Have a headache" then death will follow two days later. Said to my mother, "You've been initiated into the *sando?o* (sorcery society), you are a sorceress." She said to me, "You did not stay with your first husband, and the second one gave you *bafon* (a piece of land) that you are cultivating." I immediately asked her, "Is that why you have been initiated into the sorcery society?" She responded, "Yes, it is worth it."
>
> I was afraid since I had five children. How was I to protect them so that the sorcery did not kill them? I was really afraid. I worshipped all sorts of fetishes so that they would protect me and my children. And God helped me (Satan saved [spared] me too), my children were saved.
>
> My grandfather is dead and my mother is dead, too. God did something so that I would know that the sorcerers suffer. My mother died on a Monday. We said that the next Monday should pass before her funeral. The cadaver started to rot. It smelled. So we buried her anyway on Tuesday. The son of the sorceress who took over the reins of my mother, the one that we say saves was cut off. Those who dug up the grave refused to bury the body. That really hurt me. I said to

myself, "Since my mother stayed up late in order to have me and I have continued with her in suffering, how can that be?" She was a sorceress. Maybe the sorcerers will meet and kill my children saying that my mother was also a sorceress. I went to see Nangaluru, your man here (the interview leader), who is also the younger brother of my husband. I said to him, "If someone accepts Jesus into her life, are the sorcerers still able to do anything to her?" He told me, "The sorcerers will no longer have any power over that person. If you believe, they cannot do anything to your children." Thus, I collected all four of the *sandoyi* (a type of fetish) in a sack and I was in Zonifla (a village) with my husband who took me to Gorisiba where I believed in Jesus. We burned the fetishes.

But the song that is singing (playing) now, often when I am cultivating, I sing it when I remember. I put down my hoe in order to clap my hand and I sing it. After that, I can continue my work. My children and I have been saved from the sorcerers in the name of Jesus. It is a great joy for me. I thank the Lord for this song since I was saved from the sorcerers and the *sandoyi* (fetishes).

Sample 2: Respondent 8 from the village of Sɛʔɛlɛ

For me, my child was sick. He had suffered a lot and had been in many places [looking for help]. I searched for all sorts of leaves. We did a lot but he was not healed. I submitted to all sorts of suffering. He still was not healed. I worshipped the fetishes. I practiced sorcery. When we heard the Good News, they told us to take him to the village of Goitafla (a village in the region of Bouafle). I was really upset the day he left. I said to myself that my child would die there and that I would never see him again. And when I laid down, I did not know what would happen. So I sat up suddenly and said, "He left here sick. If he dies there, I will never see him again because they will bury him there." What was I supposed to do with this word? I said, "God, if you don't come to help me, I just can't (survive). Save me." That is what I said and I went to sleep.

Several days later I heard that my child sent me greetings. I said they were lying. Then my child arrived one day. My heart was troubled that day of his arrival just the same as the day that he left. I could no longer recognize him. In the same way that I viewed him from head to feet, I said to myself, "But this is not him!" I asked him, "So, what did they give you to drink?" "Nothing at all," he

Focus Group Question Guide and Interview Samples

answered. "Only prayer." I didn't have anything else to say. I knew that without God, man is insane. Leaves, sacrifices of beef, fetishes—if these things could have healed, my son would have been healed. Everything that my son could not do (when he was sick), he is able to do today. Glory belongs to our God. That is what I have to say.

Question 3: Are there other songs that touch your life?

Question 4: Which songs touch (are meaningful in) your life? Do you have a specific story to show how the song has helped you?

Sample 1: Respondent 4 from the village of Fɔrɔ

I like a lot of the songs but I just recently accepted Jesus. Even while I was still working for Satan, I had a desire to sing (the Christian songs).

Interviewer: Did you sing these songs while you were still a pagan?

Yes, but when I accepted him (Jesus) in my life, I could no longer sing. But I prayed that he would help me to remember everything and be able to also sing. Everyday I think about the songs. Because if someone suffers and he comes to Jesus, he will have rest. Now that is the truth! That is what I have to say.

Sample 2: Respondent 2 from the village of Dɛssingbɔ

Yes, the song that really pleases me is, "That is Why I Came to Jesus." (She sings the song.) This song pleases me a lot because when I was sick, I believed on Jesus and he saved me from the sickness. This pleases me very much. That is why I am happy. If I had not received Jesus, I would not have rest in my life. That is what the song says for me.

Question 5: Do you know the song, "Kagbaana ga wire n too vele waa na, Zyezu a bgan li laʔa?"

Question 6: Do you have a story to show how this song has helped you? A story about yourself or about someone else?

Question 7: Are there still other stories that have helped you in your Christian life? Which ones are they? Do you have any stories about them?

Appendix C

Sample 1: Respondent 2, a young person from Korhogo

> Myself, I had some problems when I was still a pagan. I was sick. They gave me lots of treatment in the hospital, but I was not healed. I was in the village for treatment but it was in vain. I believed in Jesus and I was healed in less than a month.

Sample 2: Respondent 3 from the village of Coonyɛʔɛn

> I was sick, but I was not yet a Christian. I went to the traditional healer. There they told me, "You must go find a sheep. You must find a kid. You must find a chicken." We offered all of this. Later, though, they said, "You must find a person who can (help). A real person. If not, then things are very serious. You must find a person who can help you." I thought and I thought. And I found that Jesus Christ could help me when I heard the song that says, "Jesus Christ helps in moments of temptations, in times of difficulty, and when you have problems." I came to the Lord Jesus Christ. When I was at the mission's dispensary in Torhogo, Joyce [the nurse] told me that my illness was really serious and that I should go to Korhogo for treatment. Actually, I am healed and in good health now. I know that I am healed, thanks to Jesus Christ.

Question 8: Last year, the people told us that "the songs help us like the Word of God." Do you agree with this? What does this mean for you? How have the Christian songs helped you like the Word of God?

Sample 1: Respondent 6, a young person from Dɛssignbɔ
> For me it was when we went to a Christmas *fête* (celebration). There was a singer there by the name of Nɔnyimɛ. She sang a song that really pleased me, "Christmas is a great joy since she has had a great joy. Christmas is the greatest joy." She cited many things and that Jesus has saved us. She said that the death of Jesus has saved us. If it had been the pastor who had preached this, I would say that the Word of God had helped me. But it is a song. Therefore, the songs help like the Word of God.

Sample 2: Respondent 6 from the village of Coonyɛʔɛn

> Yes, I agree. Because the words of the songs that we sing often say something and they offer us counsel like the Word of God.

Focus Group Question Guide and Interview Samples

Section II: Non-believers' Thoughts about the Christian Songs

Question 1: Do the non-believers ("pagans") like the Christian songs? How do the non-believers receive the Christian songs?

Sample 1: Respondent 7 from the village of Fɔrɔ

> When I go (to work in) the fields, if there are people working there, they like it when I sing the Christian songs.

Sample 2: Respondent 4 from the village of Sɛʔɛlɛ

> You are right; they know everything about us but they do not want to believe. When we were "pagan," we liked the Christian songs but not believing.

Question 2: Have the songs led any of the non-believers to Jesus Christ? Give some specific examples and stories.

Sample 1: Respondent 1 from the village of Coonyɛʔɛn

> Yes, the songs have led people to Jesus because there was our brother who lived in Basscott. While he was there, he heard the message on the radio—the songs. And above all else, it was the songs that helped him very much. He accepted the Lord Jesus Christ. He testified that these songs have life—like food. These songs pleased him very much and are the reason for his coming to the Lord Jesus.

Sample 2: Respondent 2 from the village of Dɛssignbɔ

> Yes, the "pagans" accept Jesus because of the songs. A tour first Christmas celebration when I was at the river with my little brother, I told him about our Christmas celebration. He said to me, "It is too far away. It should come quickly (be much sooner)." (The brother was still a "pagan" at that time.) The day came and he worked with us the whole time. He even stayed up all night and he also danced with us. I think that it is because of that Christmas celebration that my brother accepted the Lord.
>
> Interviewer: Does that mean that he accepted Jesus right after the Christmas celebration?
>
> Yes. He told me, "The songs at Christmas worked in my heart and I was wanting that we would be initiated in the *poro* when the time came. After that I will accept Jesus." I responded to him saying,

APPENDIX C

> "If you want to wait for that time before believing, they will say that you are afraid of the cost." He understood me and accepted Jesus. Today, he is still a Christian.

Question 3: Are there any non-believers who sing the Christian songs? Give some specific examples and stories.

Sample 1: Respondent 6 from the village of Fɔrɔ

> Yes, they really sing them. Certain of them have cassettes of our songs. Even when the young pagans get together, they sing our songs and clap their hands. They sing them and finally they say, "The Christian songs are really good, but if we believe, we are persecuted by the family."

Sample 2: Respondent 1 from the village of Dɛssignbɔ

> They sing them everywhere we celebrate Christmas or where we carry the Good News. The songs are sung there. They say that they like our song, but they can't see Jesus with their eyes.

Section III: About the New Song—The "Ideal" Song

Question 1. How do you like the new songs?

Question 2. What is it in the new songs that pleases you? (If necessary, read a list of the new songs to trigger their thinking.)

Sample 1: Respondent 6 from the village of Fɔrɔ

> Yes, we like them. Since we are Christians, we are trying to learn all of them.

Sample 2: Respondent 7 from the village of Fɔrɔ

> Yes, we like them because of their meaning. There are those songs that when we sing them we are filled with a great joy. They strengthen us in the faith. These songs help us like the Word of God. We wish to hear them all the time.

Question 3: Do you prefer songs that are long or short (in reference to length)? When?

Sample 1: Respondent 3, a young person from Korhogo

Focus Group Question Guide and Interview Samples

For me, there is not a long song. If one likes the song, even if it is long, yon don't know it. There is a song that says, "Quit Satan . . ." It is long but it pleases me. If we had not quit the path of Satan, certain ones of us would be dead. But it pleases me.

Sample 2: Respondent 4 from the village of Sɛʔɛlɛ

My friend, if you had not spoken like that for me, (I would have said that) I think the short songs are the best ones. They also help the people. There is a song that says, "That is why I came to Jesus." It is a short song, but we like to sing it all the time.

Question 4: Do you prefer songs where the responses are long? Or do you prefer songs where the responses are short?

Example: Short—"Aleluya, Aleluya, Zyezu Bariga." Long—"Bibile abgan syɔɔn tama, Bibile abgan" "syɔɔn tama n láa bibilew pan dulunyaw ni, Bibile a bgan syɔɔn."

Sample 1: Respondent 1, a young person from Korhogo

I like the short responses. I like them because if people do not know the songs, they cannot sing them with enthusiasm and they cannot sing them for a long time.

Sample 2: Respondent 8 from the village of Coonyɛʔɛn

If the singer can sing the song, even if the response is long or short, there is no preference. I like them all!

Question 5: Do you prefer songs where the lead singer says a lot of things? Or do you prefer songs where the lead singer has fewer things to say? (Apparently, this question was systematically left out, perhaps due to a sense of redundancy.)

Question 6: Do you prefer songs with real strong rhythms? When?

Sample 1: Respondent 1 from the village of Fɔrɔ

As I have always said, if everyone knows the song, we can sing it very strongly (with strong rhythms and fast). It will not upset anything. But if we do not know it (the song), then it is difficult.

Sample 2: Respondent 7 from the village of Fɔrɔ

Appendix C

> Yes, I like them. There are many types of songs. There are those songs that require a strong rhythm. On the other hand, there are those songs with slow rhythms. If we sing a song that requires a strong rhythm with a slow rhythm, then laziness sets in and bores everyone. Then we do not praise the Lord with enthusiasm. Also, on the contrary, we lose our breath. Therefore, each song merits its own manner of singing. What I prefer the most is that I do not want the rhythm to be either too slow or too hot (fast, strong). Yes, when it is medium. I do not like songs with slow rhythm, I do like songs with strong rhythms. That is what I think.

Question 7: Do you clap your hands when we sing? If yes, when do you clap your hands?

Sample 1: Respondent 6 from the village of Sɛʔɛlɛ

> If you see that I am clapping my hands, it is because my children were dying. When I had a child, they threw a wicked eye on him and he died. I came to the Lord Jesus. The others also followed me. I saw that those who believe continue in the faith and praise the Lord. It is this joy that pushes me to clap my hands when we sing.

Sample 2: Respondent 2 from the village of Coonyɛʔɛn

> Yes, he agrees that we clap our hands. For him, to clap his hands signifies joy. When we clap our hands, we are also encouraging the (lead) singer. The singer sings with enthusiasm and this praises our God.

Question 8: Do you prefer songs where we dance? When?

Sample 1: Respondent 7 from the village of Fɔrɔ

> Yes, it pleases me. I can dance everywhere. Dance and dance—in two ways. We can sit for dancing—in the church I just simply move my feet for dancing. We can dance outside. We can dance everywhere. That is what I think.

Sample 2: Respondent 8 from the village of Fɔrɔ

> Yes, when I sing, I also want to dance. Dancing and clapping the hands are the same, they are joy. We should praise the Lord with all our instruments and our thoughts.

Focus Group Question Guide and Interview Samples

Question 9: What musical instruments do you like to have played along with the songs?

Sample 1: Respondent 1 from the village of Fɔrɔ

> We can use the *kanrigi*, the *balafon* and also the *caliw*. I think we can use all the instruments. And when the people want to record the songs, we need to play them less so that they are able to record them without a problem. We understand that in the Bible, David praised his God with the guitar. Therefore, we should use all the instruments that we have. If someone buys a pot for praising the Lord, that is good. On the other hand, someone may buy a pot to worship the devil. Therefore, I think that it depends on the use of the instrument, or the master that the instrument serves. It is the same thing with the *kanrigi*. The "pagans" buy them for praising Satan, but the Christians also use them. I think that we can praise God with all the instruments that we have. That is what I think. We offer everything to God in order to praise him—the clapping of hands, the trumpets, the drums. Everything should praise the Lord—our words, our bodies. Everything that we have should praise God.

Sample 2: Respondent 1 from the village of Coonyɛʔɛn

> He agrees that we praise the Lord with all the musical instruments that we can make—the *jegele* (*balafon*), the *kanrig*, the *wologe* (an instrument made of iron by the blacksmiths). He agrees that we praise the Lord with everything that we can make—the drums—everything that we have. Because the Bible says that David worshipped God, praised God with the guitar and everything that was available to him. We should praise our God our Lord with everything at our disposal. This (means) our body—our spirit. He thinks that we can praise the Lord with everything.

Appendix C

Question 10: What sort of song texts (themes) do you prefer?

(1) Those that talk about God?

(2) Those that talk about the love of God?

(3) Those that talk about Satan?

(4) Those that talk about the power of God?

(5) Those that talk about the Christian life?

(6) Those that praise God?

(7) Any other topics?

Sample 1: Respondent 2, a young person from Korhogo

> I want that we praise God and not insult Satan. If these songs touch the "pagans," they will become discouraged. If we praise God and we sing the songs that speak about our love among Christians, that is good.

Sample 2: Respondent 1-8 from the village of Torhogo

> They really like the songs that talk about Satan and insult him. This is because they were in [the hands of] Satan and they really suffered. Therefore, they like insulting him so that he'll know they have abandoned him.

Question 11: Good, that is the end. We have discussed many things. Is there anything else you would like to add to our discussion about the Christian songs? (Nothing else was added.)

Appendix D

Storytelling Song: The Man from Torogo

ONE OF THE STORYTELLING songs that is currently having great impact within the Senufo Baptist churches is the one I've entitled "The Man From Torogo." Torogo is a Senufo village south of Korhogo town. It is the story of an evil spirit's destructive power over one Senufo man and his coming to the realization that Jesus has even more power than that evil spirit.

I described the dynamics of this song's performance in the third vignette found in Chapter 6, Musical Paths to Christian Music Communication. In this Appendix, I am giving two different presentations of the same story: (1) the story as told by Kafana, the man from Torogo, and (2) the actual song text as sung by Nɔnyimɔ, the singer who is well-known for her expertise in performing this song. These two presentations serve as a small study in the way in which one story has been transformed into a song for Christian communication.

An Official Mission Field Report

The following is a version of the story as related to missionaries following the conversion of Kafana, the man from Torhogo. This is the French spelling for the Senufo village of Torogo. It is presented here in its entirety as it is on record in the Wheaton CBFMS headquarters and dated November 1973. As Helen Skinner, the transcriber notes in her closing comments, "The full impact of some of these experiences is lessened when it is translated. Some places may sound stilted or awkward as a result. Also, it was difficult for Kafana to remember everything in the order it happened over five years, and all that happened is not included here. He is trying with the Lord's help, to forget it all." Although the report is written in the third person, it follows very closely the order and the way that Kafana told his story. Therefore, I have not changed the report except for a few editorial corrections to help the reader understand the text more clearly. The report now follows:

Appendix D

Kafana, a man of close to 40 years of age, lives in the village of Torogo. For five years, he was controlled by an evil spirit. The following is a transcription of his testimony which he gave on tapes following his conversion on Sunday, September 23, 1973.

Kafana was working his fields and became ill. Sores appeared on his body. His children became sick too, so he went to the sorcerer who divined for him. He was told he must stop working. This was to be a taboo for him. The sorcerer said that the *nikahau*, a powerful evil spirit, was wanting Kafana to work for him. The first thing he was to do was build a mud house about as tall as he is which would be the place where this evil spirit would communicate with him. This type of house is not covered with grass but has tree poles laid criss-cross across the top and then layers of mud are spread on top of the poles with an outlet on the side for rain to run off. This type of house is used for storage but seldom used for living quarters because it is too hot and closed in. Long ago they were used as dwellings.

Kafana agreed to do this and when the house was finished, the evil spirit began to communicate with him. How did he do this? The mud house which Kafana built was in his own courtyard across from his own house. When he heard the voice, he would close his eyes and listen. Then he would see the spirit over by the little mud house. He says it was a person, not black or white but a light-skinned person. He would speak to him just as a person speaks. On one occasion he saw him with a woman and another black person talking together in front of the mud house. At that time, he couldn't hear what they were saying but watched everything they did.

When the spirit came and talked with him, Kafana described it as "like seeing a movie." The spirit himself would come and go, as well as the things he was showing to Kafana or talking to him about. This included such objects as leaves for medicine or fetishes or other spirits. They would pass in front of his eyes and then fade into darkness. Because the spirit could produce things like this, Kafana was convinced that he was powerful and real. When the spirit finished talking to Kafana, he would fade away.

In the beginning, the spirit told Kafana that he was going to have to suffer much but that after it was all over, he would be rich and have rest. Kafana said he was willing to go through with the suffering. In order to further deceive Kafana, the spirit began by telling him that he would give Kafana the knowledge of native medicine and he would be able to heal people. He showed him the leaves which were good to cook and use as medicine. He told him he would be able to heal many people. Kafana

Storytelling Song: The Man from Torogo

actually did heal many. By deceiving him like this, the spirit exerted his power over Kafana. Actually, he didn't want Kafana to be wise to anything. Kafana agreed to all the deception that followed. He thought that after it was all over he would be wise and know all the truth.

The spirit told Kafana that he would have to take on all the spirit's taboos. He told him to sacrifice a tame rabbit and he would give him his work. Kafana bought and killed the rabbit. Then the spirit talked to him, naming certain people in the village, and said Kafana should tell them to sacrifice and this spirit would help them. Kafana was to go to these people and tell them this. They wouldn't come to him. When the Senufo people go to a sorcerer, they pay the sorcerer with money or animals but Kafana got nothing for doing this. If he began to question what the spirit told him, the spirit would get angry with him and he would have to take on another taboo or make an animal sacrifice. Kafana always complied. He knew when the spirit was angry with him because he would see an airplane and hear the sound of guns going off. When he was angry, the spirit wouldn't appear to Kafana for a time.

After a while, the spirit told Kafana that he could wear nothing but rags. Kafana thought that would be the end, but the spirit told him to kill a goat and then showed him more leaves in the bush that could cure sicknesses. Because of that Kafana was convinced of the power of the spirit. But then he didn't come to Kafana for a while and Kafana didn't know how he could continue working medicine if the spirit didn't keep showing him how.

Then the sick (people) stopped coming to him. When he complained about it the spirit promised he would send them to him but he didn't. He wouldn't let Kafana go after the sick ones. When Kafana began questioning the spirit about it he got angry and then told Kafana that only God was more powerful than the spirit was. No one has power to rule the world but the spirit and God. But God is in heaven and the spirit on earth, so God gave all the affairs of earth into his hands. Everything on earth was made by the spirit. God gave him the mud to make people with and he made everyone in the world. God and the spirit don't see each other but everything they do, they tell each other about. The spirit is the master of the devils. The devils are his workers. He hides, but nothing is hidden from him. If Kafana thinks he is deceiving him, who does Kafana think will tell him the truth? The spirit, then, told Kafana he wouldn't deceive him. He would tell him the truth, but Kafana would have to suffer before he rewarded him.

He said Kafana would become famous. He would have no other work except healing people. All things that are hidden from the people—things they go to divine about with the sorcerers—the spirit would show all these things to Kafana and he could explain them to the people. However, he mustn't reveal to people how he knows these things. That way, they will listen to him.

Because Kafana had questioned him, the spirit said he had to kill another goat. He did and then the spirit returned and showed him some more about healing people. This again convinced Kafana that the spirit spoke the truth. Always when Kafana violated the spirit or his commands in any way, he had to sacrifice an animal. Other taboos were placed on him.

Another time the spirit came and told him to kill a chicken and cook it just as it was—feathers, insides, etc. Then he was to tie it and hang it from a tree. Then he sat and closed his eyes and saw all the animals he had killed or eaten and they were alive. The spirit said this was to show him the meaning of death. Then he explained that when a person dies the soul goes to be with God and this evil spirit, and is alive. The body is buried, but the soul is alive with God and the spirit, like a person. When a person dies this spirit takes the mud of his old body and puts it with some new mud and makes a person out of it and brings him into the world. He used the example of the pottery makers who crush and grind broken pieces of old pottery and then mix that powder with new clay to make their new pots. So the person who dies isn't lost. All the dead appeared to Kafana to be going in a frame something like the rim of a bike wheel. This symbolized making the cycle from death to life. Not all come back as people, however. Those who have committed many sins in this life can't come back. Therefore, the animals Kafana killed and ate, he would see alive like that. After that, whatever kind of chicken he saw, when he closed his eyes, that was the kind he should kill.

He, the spirit, told Kafana this to prove he can explain things hidden from people and would give Kafana his desires. Therefore, Kafana mustn't go to a sorcerer, he mustn't become a sorcerer himself, he mustn't tell others what he'd been told. If he listened to a sorcerer he would die. If one came to him, that one would die. Kafana's own child was a sorcerer, so he couldn't go near her.

Earlier, the spirit had told Kafana to become a sorcerer, which he did. But then the spirit saw that Kafana was getting a little wise to the ways of the spirit world and so he reversed himself and told Kafana he couldn't be a sorcerer anymore. He proceeded to tell Kafana that the sorcery system

Storytelling Song: The Man from Torogo

and the sacred forest system were taboo for him and Kafana had to take on the spirit's taboos. The reason for this was that the spirit didn't want Kafana to become wise to the way he was being deceived. So, because Kafana had become a sorcerer he had to make animal sacrifices and ask forgiveness for having violated one of the spirit's taboos. After that Kafana had nothing more to do with sorcery or the sacred forest system, both of which are basic to the culture of the Senufo.

One time Kafana did something that displeased the spirit. As a result the spirit said neither Kafana nor his wife could work. They couldn't gather wood for cooking. They were to do absolutely nothing. Kafana told his wife and she agreed to this because she believed that Kafana was doing this for her good. They didn't know what to do.

The spirit would show Kafana who was sick but he couldn't heal him. Kafana then saw that the spirit couldn't help him to heal people. He questioned all this because sometimes when his eyes were closed he expected to be shown the leaves that would help a certain sick person but it wasn't shown to him. Then he began to think that this was no way to get wisdom—to be led ahead and then left dangling.

Neither he nor his wife worked. They didn't eat because most foods were taboo for Kafana. Then the spirit told him he couldn't speak to his mother or older brother and told him if he really observed this taboo, things would really work out well for him. The reason for this taboo was that his mother and brother had both said they didn't understand this spirit's words to Kafana. How could any good come of it all when he told Kafana he couldn't eat? This angered the spirit and he told Kafana he couldn't listen to either his mother or brother because after Kafana got his wealth they would receive things from him but wouldn't credit the spirit. The spirit was always afraid that Kafana would get wise to what was happening to him if he listened to what people said.

When Kafana objected because his mother was the one who had borne him, the spirit became angry and said: "Your mother doesn't know me and doesn't know that I'm going to help you." So Kafana asked pardon of the spirit and quit speaking to his mother and brother. For eight months until Kafana accepted the Lord, he didn't speak to them. He accepted all this (by) saying a person can't over-rule the one who is ruling him. Kafana said he saw this spirit was a very important person, since he himself had said no one was over him but God. If Kafana disputed that, then he felt he was disputing God. So, he left it at that. He asked forgiveness of the spirit but didn't get it. People told him he should leave the spirit who was too hard on him, but he said they didn't understand. He couldn't

Appendix D

be forgiven unless the spirit wanted it that way. He believed that nothing could remove this spirit's power from him.

Another time, the spirit told him to sell his bike. But he said it wouldn't please the spirit for him to have the money from the sale. Where would he get another bike? The spirit said that soon someone would give him a car because he Kafana would do a real good deed for that person in the power of this spirit. So Kafana sold his bike and gave the money to his mother and wife so they could eat. When that was gone, there was no money for them to buy food. No one gave them food.

When Kafana sold the fruit from his mango trees he bought a shirt but wasn't allowed to wear it. So he gave it to his brother. He couldn't have a door on his house. He couldn't sleep on a mat—only on the mud floor. He couldn't chase anything out of the house that entered while he was sleeping. He couldn't kill or chase mosquitoes at night. He begged the spirit to remove the latter taboo from him because the mosquitoes were so bad, but the spirit did it only a few times. If he killed any insects in the house he wouldn't be able to sleep all night. When he couldn't sleep he would go out and sit by the spirit's mud house. Once he went for a whole week that way without sleeping. He tried to ask forgiveness of the spirit so some of these taboos would be removed. But he [the spirit] wouldn't give it. Kafana says the spirit probably suspected that Kafana knew he was being deceived.

From the beginning, the spirit had told Kafana he couldn't eat certain foods. The first was corn and then, as his relationship with the spirit progressed, he was forbidden to eat any food except two varieties of yams. He couldn't eat them the same day they were dug up. He couldn't eat with the one in the field who dug them up. He couldn't greet any field workers. For five years he could eat hardly anything but kept believing that nothing was too hard to bear if he would become rich and have rest after it was all over. This past year, he found it was almost impossible. He was concerned because his wife didn't have anything to eat. So, he finally sent her to live with her sister in her courtyard so she could give her food. The food taboos continued until the time came when, three months before his conversion, Kafana couldn't eat anything. He didn't have money to buy the two kinds of yams he was allowed to eat. Even if he asked anyone for them, they weren't always available.

During those three months, hunger would cause him to nearly faint. He would be walking along and suddenly black out, rub his face, and then come to, to find he didn't know where he was going. He would go to the bush to find some leaves that he knew weren't poisonous and would eat them raw, gaining a little strength. After eating leaves for a week, the spirit came and told him, he couldn't eat them anymore.

When he really got hungry, he would ask someone in the village for five or ten francs so he could buy some white peanuts—the only variety he was allowed to eat. Even if someone gave him the money, he sometimes couldn't find that variety. At one time, he went for a whole week without finding any. Then one day, he got some money from someone and bought some peanuts. The spirit told him that wouldn't do. The person from whom he got the money was the spirit's enemy. Kafana had to return the money and couldn't talk to that person again. Before long there wasn't anyone in the village he could get money from. At this point Kafana thought he was going to die.

When he was without food or money, he asked the spirit where he was supposed to get the money to buy animals for the sacrifices he always had to make. The spirit told him to borrow the money from the villagers and one day the spirit would give him all the money needed tore pay the debts. So he began to borrow money. But then the spirit decided he couldn't borrow anymore and couldn't speak anymore to those who loaned him money because they would say things to him that would anger the spirit. He told Kafana: "Everyone doesn't know that I will help you but I know it." So it came about that he couldn't ask anyone for anything.

Another taboo Kafana observed was that he couldn't drink water from wells, springs or streams. He had to go to a place outside the village near the sacred forest where there was a pool of water. It was between two steep banks and water was there all year round but was stagnant. The spirit said that was where he lived. For a whole year, Kafana drew and drank only that water. No woman would go there to draw water. Later the spirit said he would allow Kafana's wife to get the water. But he had to go with her and draw it because the place was so steep. Then she would carry it back to the village.

Kafana thought that when the fruit on the trees around the water hole got ripe he would eat that. But the spirit told him he couldn't do that—it was another of the spirit's taboos. He couldn't eat any fruit of any tree that had been planted.

Each time a new taboo was placed on him he accepted it thinking the more he obeyed the evil spirit, the sooner it would all be over. He felt he could bear it all if he knew that in the end he would be wealthy and have rest. When things got unbearable he felt he would be able to forget them when it was all over.

Appendix D

He was not permitted to eat out of any bowl, enamel pan or cooking pot. He was not permitted to step in water that had been spilled near a well. One night he dreamed that he had done that and they took him and threw him into the well and he couldn't get out.

When he spit on the ground, he couldn't cover the spittle with his hands or feet—that was the same as working in the fields which was a taboo for him.

If the members of the sacred forest were burying someone in the village and he heard the drumbeats, the *balafons* or dancing as he sat in his house, and would think about what they were doing, the spirit would come to him and ask why he was thinking about things that were taboo. Then he would have to ask forgiveness for that. Each time he asked forgiveness he had to make a sacrifice. He began to see that he wasn't getting any smarter. He began to realize that this road wasn't taking him to a good place. He knew now that this evil spirit was taking him to his death. But he didn't know God wasn't speaking with the spirit.

During the time when Kafana couldn't get food to eat a relative of his, named Sanga, who lives in the same village would give him some of the two kinds of inyams he could eat when they were available. Sanga is a Christian and when he first knew of what Kafana was going through he asked several believers to pray for him. For several months a small group of Christians which meets each week for prayer were praying for Kafana, not knowing who he was but that he was suffering in the hands of this evil spirit.

One day, Sanga told Kafana he didn't see that all this suffering was getting him anywhere. He should believe in Jesus. Kafana asked why he should believe in Jesus. Sanga told him because of his suffering. Kafana told him that the one, in whose hands he was, was more powerful than Jesus—why should he believe on Jesus? Sanga asked him how he knew that. Kafana said: "I don't know it through my own power. The one who is my master told me that. He said no one is over him but God. How, then, can I know someone else is between him and God? I can't believe on Jesus. If you had said God, I would have listened but when you say Jesus I can't believe that!" Sanga told him: "Because you don't know him you say that. When you hear us say Jesus, that's the same as God." Then Kafana told him he understood what Sanga was saying and said nothing more. He was thinking, God hasn't yet spoken to me. In his heart he wanted God to remove the spirit's power from him.

After this the spirit didn't appear to Kafana as before. Then, finally he did and told him to throw away everything he had accumulated while

Storytelling Song: The Man from Torogo

worshipping the fetishes, and all that the spirit had told him to work with—he must also destroy the altars he had built to the fetishes and the evil spirit. Kafana was afraid to do this for fear the spirit would change his mind and cause more suffering. But the spirit told him not to fear but to get rid of everything. Then Kafana knew that during this period God was fighting with the evil spirit and was doing something to subdue him. The spirit saw that a power greater than he was after him and he was losing his grip on Kafana.

The spirit came to Kafana and asked him why he had listened to Sanga. Was he going to go with the believers? Then Kafana was afraid and asked forgiveness of the spirit. For a long time, he didn't see him again. So he thought the spirit was angry with him for receiving things from Sanga. For a whole month he didn't see the spirit. He knew that someone was talking with the spirit. At the same time, he knew that God was showing Kafana himself that he should believe on Jesus.

On a Sunday, he went to find Sanga but he was out preaching in another village. Kafana waited all day for him, knowing that he couldn't wait another day to believe. When Sanga came back in the evening, Kafana told him he wanted to believe. Sanga said they should ask God to make the spirit make good his promises to Kafana right away, if he really was working with God. If he wouldn't do it, then God would remove the spirit from Kafana. Those words pleased Kafana. Then to test him, Sanga said they should wait a week to see if the spirit would do anything. But Kafana said, "No!" He couldn't wait—he wanted to believe right away. So he trusted the Lord Jesus as his Savior that night.

When Kafana finished recounting the above experiences he said: "I have no intention of turning away from the Lord out of fear of this evil spirit. I know that God's power is greater than that of the spirit—he himself told me that. I know now that because of what Jesus did for me, God's power is greater. I don't fear the evil spirit anymore." Kafana now says that he believes it was Satan himself who came to him during those five years.

Kafana is now working his fields which his brother had worked for him during those five years. He eats everything. We (the Skinners) asked one of the Christians how Kafana ever stayed alive and didn't look emaciated after all he went through. That person said, "The evil spirit kept him alive so he could use him." Kafana believes the Lord kept him alive, so he would be saved.

Believers who have heard Kafana's testimony say they have never heard of anyone under the influence of this evil spirit being so persecuted as he was. There are many Senufos under the power of this particular sprit

Appendix D

but they don't know of any who have actually seen the spirit or heard him speak to them. They work with the spirit through the medium of the sorcerers. But even the sorcerers don't see any devils. The fact that Kafana actually saw this devil and heard him speak to him made it so terrible.

The Story Told in Song

Thematic Statement:

> Jesus said to come, and he will lift your burdens.
> If Satan has burdened you too much,
> Come, father (*baba*) will lift your burdens.
>
> Jesus said to come and he will lift your burdens.
> If Satan gives you bad (heavy) burdens,
> Father says to come, he will lift your burdens.

Development/Exegesis:

(1) Brothers, if you are too burdened, it is still the burdens of Satan.

(2) Brothers, if the *sandogi* tires you, it's the burden of Satan. Come to Jesus.

(3) Brothers, if traveling on the path and the *foofiiyi* of Satan wears you out,

(4) Behold, if the demons are tiring you, Jesus says to come to him.

(5) Sacrifices fatigue you. They are definitely the work of Satan.

(6) Behold, if the fetishes are tiring you, Jesus says to come (to him), he'll save you.

(7) If the troubles of Satan are tiring you, come to Jesus.

(8) Behold, if the bad *foofiiyi* definitely are the burdens of Satan,

(9) Jesus says to come; he'll free you from all these bad (heavy) burdens.

(10) He'll free you from these burdens of Satan and give you his.

(11) Jesus says that his burdens are not heavy, and that his work is not difficult.

(12) Brothers, Satan made me tired. Satan makes us suffer.

(13) Brothers, I'm going to tell you a story of a brother.

Storytelling Song: The Man from Torogo

(14) Our brother Kafana, the one who grew up in Torogo. Do you know him?

(15) Do you know Kafana of Torogo, who Satan caused to suffer?

(16) Brothers, the devil made Kafana tired. He suffered allot.

(17) At night, when he laid down to sleep, he saw . . .

(18) Brothers, the demons were close to him with cars.

(19) When the wicked demons stopped the cars, it was as if he made the electricity to go on (the lights were turned on).

(20) And he said, "If you accept my work and work for me,

(21) If you put up with all sorts of bad things and do my work,

(22) The prohibitions that I say, if you accept them,

(23) Afterwards, I will give you wealth and lots of riches.

(24) If you see these beautiful cars and they run, can you refuse them?

(25) In this world, everyone wants riches.

(26) If you see a great treasure, can you refuse it?"

(27) That is why Kafana accepted the prohibitions of the devil. It was in order to have riches.

(28) The demon told Kafana not to eat rice.

(29) Brothers, look how many ways that rice is good for you and the demon prohibited him from eating it.

(30) After that, the demon told Kafana to not drink water that the people have drawn from the well.

(31) The water that is in the cesspool, he drank this water.

(32) After that, the demon told Kafana to not eat any of the food that his wife prepared for him.

(33) After that, the demon told Kafana not to talk with his mother anymore.

(34) After that, the demon told Kafana not to talk with his wife anymore.

(35) Brothers, a man and his wife, not talk anymore?

(36) Brothers, with whom are we supposed to talk in order to have joy?

Appendix D

(37) After that, the demon told Kafana to not drink anymore water at all.

(38) He should drink the liquid from grass.

(39) Brothers, does such liquid sufficiently satisfy your thirst?

(40) After that, the demon told Kafana to eat leaves.

(41) Kafana ate all this and ate leaves.

(42) Brothers, the demon told Kafana to give him chickens as sacrifices.

(43) "Kafana, if you kill the chicken, do not eat it."

(44) Kafana attached the chicken to a tree; it hung there.

(45) Brothers, the demon tired Kafana. He suffered a lot.

(46) Brothers, a man of this century, he ate leaves?

(47) Has the man become an antelope in order to graze on grass?

(48) Jesus has really saved Kafana from such enslavement.

(49) One day the devil told Kafana, "Nothing in this world has power over me."

(50) "Nothing in this world has power over me."

(51) "Only God, the eternal one on high, has power over me—only him."

(52) Brothers, you who worship Satan, he knows that God has power over him.

(53) That is why Kafana thought of Jesus.

(54) However, he (Kafana) was waiting to speak about Jesus. He did not want to believe.

(55) Brothers, Jesus saved Kafana and delivered him from the demon.

(56) Jesus has power over the demon. He chased the demon far from Kafana.

(57) Jesus rescued Kafana from this slavery and gave him peace.

(58) Today, Kafana eats food, drinks water, and farms. Alleluia!

(59) You, who do not yet believe, and hear the word of Jesus,

(60) You say to us. "But do I suffer like Kafana?"

(61) You say, "The devil does not give me the same kind of burden as Kafana."

(62) Do you know that tomorrow there is an eternal suffering?

(63) For the eternal fire is much worse than that of Kafana.

(64) Think about heaven. Don't stop to look at the world.

(65) Jesus has come in order to give us eternal life.

(66) First of all, he has given us "rest" of the heart.

(67) Jesus has delivered us from the *sandogi* and chased the evil demon far from us.

(68) Jesus has saved us from the ruses of Satan and has given us rest.

(69) Brothers, the words at this cross-road: Jesus has saved us from all of this.

(70) Jesus has saved us from the initiation to the *sandogi*.

(71) Brothers, you who have a heavy burden, come to Jesus.

(72) You, who Satan is making suffer a lot, come to Jesus.

(73) You, who the devil is making tired, won't you believe?

Thematic Restatement:

> Brothers, Jesus said to come, and he will lift your burdens.
> If the burden of Satan is tiring you,
> If the *sandogi* of Satan is tiring you,
> If the *foofiiyi* of Satan is tiring you
> Father (*baba*) says to come, he will lift your burdens.

Appendix E

Senufo Song Transcriptions

THE FOLLOWING FOUR SONG transcriptions are representative of the general forms that Senufo Christian songs take in performance. Since the song form is so fluid, each transcription serves only as a type of guide to how the song may be performed. In other words, a lead singer may choose to sing the song differently on two occasions where the original melodic shape will remain the same, yet specific pitches may vary by moving to a neighboring note on the pentatonic scale. Likewise, rhythmic variation may occur within a basic rhythm pattern. Thus, the songs are rich with variations built around a foundational framework. These song transcriptions seek to picture the songs' basic frameworks.

Senufo Song Transcriptions

Song Transcription #2
EVERY MOMENT, THE HAND OF JESUS IS ON YOU AND THUS ALL HIS BLESSING (Lala O Lala)

and so on until it returns to the thematic statement.

APPENDIX E

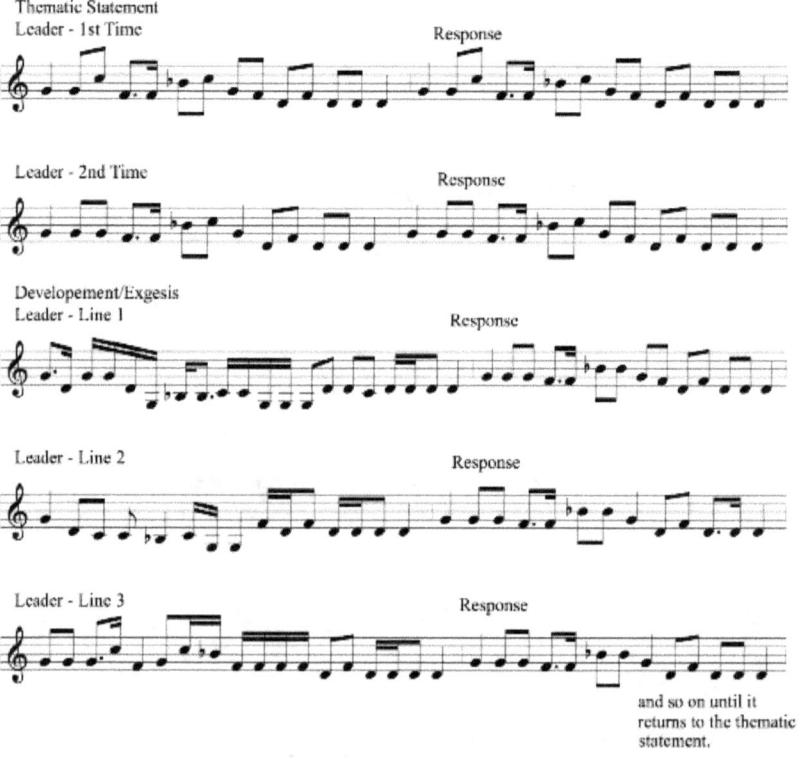

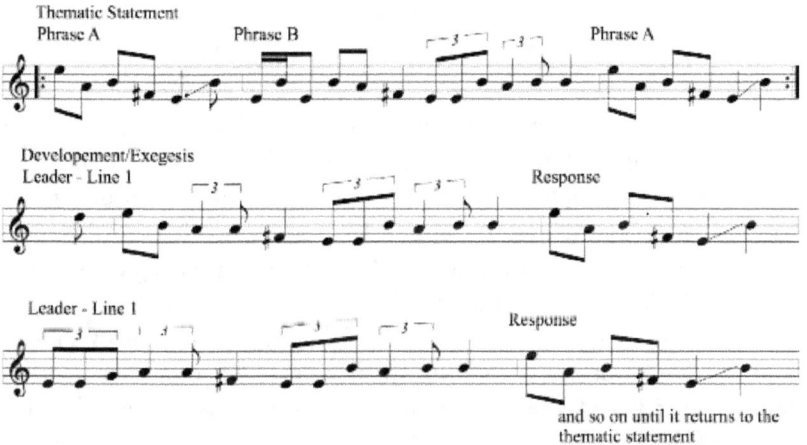

APPENDIX F

A Model for Initiating Grass-Roots Theologizing

THIS APPENDIX DEALS WITH cognitive processes that are inherent in the development of new songs. In chapters 8 and 9 I have discussed song texts as they reveal a people's worldview and their developing theology from the perspective of the overall picture within Senufo society. At this point, I want to look at a number of specific Senufo Christian song texts according to their thematic content. I am doing this with a view to discover and elucidate the ways in which the creation of Christian songs allows for the integration of worldview and Christianity. It is my contention that this integration takes place in the composition process as Senufo Christians encounter the Biblical message and its transforming principles. From this investigation, then, I am suggesting a model for initiating grass-roots theologizing.

Foundations for the Model

In his distinguished work, "Theological Foundations of African and Western Worldviews and Their Relationships to Christian Theologizing: An Akamba Case Study," Kaleli asserts that theological reflection at the "grass-roots" level is imperative for the African Church today.[1] This stands in contrast to the mere continuing of the traditional polemic training of the West that dominates current theological training. Both approaches to theologizing are valid within Africa, depending on the context and setting. "Giraffe" theologies, according to Kaleli, are intended for the African academic theologians, while "sheep" theologies introduce the concept of a pastoral dimension in theologizing that serves to nourish the fold. Furthermore, Kaleli wisely proclaims that ". . . if a theology is to serve the people and validate their faith, it is time African Christian theologians refocus their attention more on the task of shepherding the flock of God."[2]

---

1. Kaleli, 8.
2. Ibid.

I am in wholehearted agreement with Kaleli's contention. Moreover, it is my conviction that creating Christian songs, especially those based on Biblical texts, provides a means of working toward such theologizing. I would add, however, that "sheep" theologies would best be created by the "sheep" themselves. Such theologizing should not be done exclusively by African Christian theologians, who most likely would experience great difficulty in shaking off their well-trained aptitudes toward "giraffe" theologizing.

A model for initiating grass-roots or "sheep" theologizing assumes, then, the "priesthood of believers" (1 Pet 2:9), where each Christian believer is deemed capable of studying the Scriptures and applying them to their particular life situation and context. In the creation of songs based on Scripture, the Christian composer must have both the musical skills, the ability to interact with the Scriptures within their cultural and historical context, and a sensitivity to the leading of the Holy Spirit.

Such a model provides us with the opportunity to engage in the process of developing scriptural interpretations.[3] In this process, the Biblical message encounters culture-specific life situations and worldview assumptions. The Senufo Christian songs serve as an example of this where scriptural encounter and integration move toward a more understandable presentation of the Biblical message. Admittedly, this process will result in only partial theological understandings flawed by human sinfulness. However, they most certainly will touch deeper nerves of understanding. The ultimate goal of such a model, then, consists of clearer communication of God, His nature, and His redemptive work among human beings. At the same time, complementary goals seek to feed the "sheep," to make the Gospel clear within a specific culture, and to stimulate spiritual growth.

Senufo Christian Song Texts as Examples

How, then, do the Senufo Christian song texts serve as examples of such a model? Let us now examine six of these, taken from the Most Popular Songs of 1987 collection (see Appendix A), that are currently shaping popular theological concepts. They fall into three thematic categories: (1) concepts about God, (2) the Christian life, and (3) power.

---

3. Kraft, *Christianity in Culture*, 389.

More about God

We begin with two songs that give us a greater understanding about God from the Senufo perspective. They are among the most frequently sung and highly regarded of the song collection. In his version of the 23rd Psalm, the composer Sɛnyɛnɛgatɛnɛ transforms the Hebrew concept of shepherd to be more appropriate to his own worldview (see Appendix A, Song 8). For him, the Lord is his *nanʔanfɔlɔ*, the one who protects and provides food for his animals. He is totally responsible for their care. At the same time, Sɛnyɛnɛgatɛnɛ also calls out that the Lord is his *gboo*. Literally, this is the person who carries the growing infant on her back. The *gboo* cares for the child, is interested in all that concerns the child, and also raises or educates the child. An intimate bond and relationship develops as a result of their long hours together. This, then, becomes a lovely picture of the intimate relationship that can mature between the believer and God, in addition to God's role of protection and provider.

A further interpretation concerning God the Father and his activity in people's lives follows. The composer is declaring to both the non-believer and the believer that the father (*baba*) leads them into green pastures and beside the still waters, a basic reciting of the Biblical text. However, the composer then moves into specific applications for the Christian. This includes a further clarification that Jesus is the one who is the guide (*nanʔanfɔlɔ* and *gboo*).

How, then, does Jesus caringly interact with The Senufo believer in relation to their basic, everyday concerns? He does so by always seeing and watching over them during the Christian's sickness, during famine, on the pathway to the fields, in their homes, when there is difficulty, and when there is joy. Also, when they are troubled, when there is no water, and when there is war, one does not have to fear because the Lord, who is the author of peace, is watching and caring for them. In fact, there is the implication that God is always with them. In this way, then, important theological concepts and promises are definitely brought within their specific cultural context. They are expressed at a "grass-roots" level.

Another theological picture of God is presented to us in our second song, "Philip, When You See Jesus, It's God Who You See!," based on John 14:8 (see Appendix A, Song 14). Basically, the song tells the story of Philip asking Jesus to show him and the other disciples Jesus' Father. The opening statement of the song is the response that Jesus made, "Philip, when you've seen Jesus, you've seen God." For the Senufo, the thought that one may come into direct contact with God is one of amazement. Since the concept of *Kolocɔlɔɔ,* the benign god-woman from a far country, is so firmly entrenched in their worldview, excitement seeps out as they realize that they can have a direct relationship with a God who is not so distant after all.

As the text keeps reasserting that one can see and thus find God, he is attributed as being the God of peace, who appears cool on the outside, and the God of patience, who is also cool on the inside. These two descriptions of peace and patience are Senufo thought-patterns about such characteristics. In addition, God is described as the God of love, the God who gives blessing, and the God who gives us our temporal life and also eternal life. God is also acknowledged as the creator of the heavens and the earth and as the God of power. Thus, in the creation of this one song based on one verse of scripture, we come to see many aspects and theological concepts about God. Each one would serve as a basis for further theological development.

The Christian Life

Besides developing theological concepts about God in the composition of Christian songs, aspects of the Christian life may also surface in this "grass-roots" theologizing process. For example, from a song based on Hebrews 11:5 we learn that faith is "like an egg and if it escapes to fall," it breaks. Based on a proverb found within Senufo society, this expression is then amplified for the Christian in an effort to admonish the Christian to hold on to the faith.

The symbolism of the egg points to the interpretation that one must pay careful attention to an egg due to its fragility. Thus, one grabs hold of an egg carefully, does not leave it outside, and treats it with proper care and respect. Likewise, in order to treat faith properly, we are told that one should not look to the things of the world, nor its money, nor bad conduct, nor handsome men or beautiful women. The reference to bad conduct in the Senufo context speaks of the activities of a disobedient child, of living one's life as one pleases without regard for the rest of society, the lack of respect for others, of stubbornness towards others, of theft, and of beating others.[4] These things cause one to turn around (*sin ba too*) and come the wrong direction, triggering a fall or a "breaking" of faith.

Furthermore, the song text teaches us that faith is the way and the requirement to please God. Using Enoch as the song's example, the singers learn that Enoch pleased God so much that he was taken directly to heaven. Peter's faith, another example, allowed him to initially walk on

---

4. R. King, Field Notes and Texts, Korhogo Region, Ouattara.

the water. These two men, then, become models in life for encouraging perseverance in faith, a common problem among Senufo believers.

Another analogy made to the Christian life is that of a race. Based on Hebrews 12:1 (see Appendix A, Song 12), the song stipulates "People, Run! Run! For we are in a Race!" The race is then expressed in everyday activities that require one to "walk together with God" and to "work with God" by doing all things in his presence. Rather than dwelling on the "speed" of the race, the composer focuses on the ways in which to go about running the race.

The focus thus becomes one of relationship with God during this race. For example, the song text further explains the race where one must "eat with God," an indication that a person must be in communion with him and on good relations. In Senufo society, people do not eat together unless they are on good terms with each other. Parents do not allow their children to eat in the courtyards of those with whom they have poor relations. On the other hand, children may be required to eat in the courtyard of their parents' good friends.

Again, as is typical in almost every song, warning is given to not commit certain acts. People must not stop to rest, drink, or eat, for fear that they will disqualify themselves from the race. However, not all is discouraging or negative, since the hope and goal of remaining in the race is the prize of joy that will be given when Jesus comes again.

Power

Moving further in our themes reflecting grass-roots theologizing, we examine two songs that take up a dominant Senufo worldview value, power. Both songs are based on texts in the Gospel of Matthew that reveal and speak of the power of God. The first song, based on Matthew 12:43, tells the story of the spirit who departs from a person but returns to find its former residence empty and invites seven other spirits to join him. The story speaks to a very definite reality of life for the Senufo. who are constantly being controlled by the *madebele* (bush spirits). They recognize the influence and power of spirits, referred to in the song as *madebele*, in their lives.

However, the grass-roots theologizing advances when the composer, Jɛniba, gives the interpretation and application. She warns that if one leaves the "Jesus road," claiming that it is too difficult, and if the "bad one," meaning Satan, learns of it, the situation will be worse than before becoming a Christian. Satan will search out more *madebele* who possess heightened evil power. Nothing but sufferings for the family will be the result. These sufferings will include the lack of peace in this world, testing by passing through fire, and the absence of happiness in this world or in Jesus. Encouragement and hope is offered to the believing Senufo by reminding that the power of Jesus is superior to the power of Satan. Thus, one should not be discouraged when encountered by trials and sufferings. The sufferings of believers may be viewed as tests of faith. The admonition, at this point, implores believers not to turn their backs on their Father (*baba*) by continuing to look to his Word.

Thus, this song speaks to Senufo believers at a deep, crucial level by dealing with the common Senufo temptations to leave the "Jesus road" brought about by the *madebele* (bush spirits). This is serious business for the Senufo Christians. Still a relatively small group within their society, they have experienced great persecution by the *Poro* society that regulates traditional life and customs. Great consolation is found in the fact that the power of Jesus is greater than that of the *madebele* and Satan.

Due to the reality of their world, Senufo Christians cannot afford to be "powerless" Christians who do not know how to draw on the power of God. This song, then, initiates a beginning Senufo theological conception about the power of God.

Another issue within the realm of spiritual power that speaks to basic Senufo needs and worldview is that of healing. In the song entitled "The Lord Jesus has Great Power," based on Matthew 15:29–31 (see Appendix A, Song 16), the composer relates how Jesus healed many sick people including paralytics, the deaf and dumb, and even those with fractured bones. In addition to this, Jesus also raised people, such as Lazarus, from the dead. For the Senufo, each of these examples verifies the power of God. Thus, Jesus is credited with great power because of his ability to heal all sorts of medical problems and raise people from the dead.

The advice of the song, then, is that if you place your trust in Jesus, he will not only save you but that he will also heal your infirmities. The role of healing as a means of power encounter is highly significant among the Senufo in a valid presentation of the Christian Gospel. The national church has stipulated that if the mission were ever to uproot its medical work among them, then mission presence would no longer be desired.

Thus, these two songs provide a beginning look at theological concepts of power in relation to spirits and healing. They serve as significant indicators of an area that calls for careful development within the national church. They are dealing with crucial grass-roots theological perceptions.

Summary

In summary, then, we may postulate that grass-roots theologizing, utilizing the composition of songs based on Scripture, affords a Christian community a necessary opportunity to interact with God's Word within their own frame of reference, especially at the worldview level. From these six song texts, we may observe that believing composers will choose to emphasize different points found within a scripture verse than what an outsider might. They will also clothe the text with appropriate analogies for their own context. Using concrete terms, such as "Faith is like an Egg," rather than abstract ideas, they will focus on those parts of Scripture that are more significant and meaningful to them. Theological issues, such as power, that may lie dormant among Christian communicators from outside a people's cultural context, are allowed to surface and develop. Finally, the composers' conclusions and advice found within the songs will most often be more culturally appropriate and specific to their particular context. They will come to different conclusions than expected by outsiders. This is due to the fact that their conclusions will be generated by their differing worldview assumptions.[5]

Ultimately, theological correctives may be desired. However, these should be allowed to take place within the context of the national church. Just as the western church has had freedom to develop and dispute her own theological positions, a national church should have the same opportunity. Thus, in this way, the composing of culturally appropriate songs may serve as a forum for initiating grass-roots theologizing as a developing church seeks to grow into maturity and search out its own relevant "sheep" theologies.

---

5. C. Kraft, *Christianity in Culture*, 57.

Glossary

THIS GLOSSARY CONSISTS MAINLY of Senufo (Senari) vocabulary of the Cebaara dialect. It consists of key terms that have been employed throughout the text. Thus, the glossary does not include all the linguistic data necessary for Senufo language analysis. The official Senufo orthography has changed in the last five years. Words may, therefore, be spelled two different ways. Wherever possible, I have attempted to use the current official orthography. However, differences in orthography may be observed when quoting other sources. The "ty," for example, carries a sound of "ch" as in the word cheat and has been changed to "c". Therefore, *kolotyolo* becomes *kolocɔlɔɔ*.

Specialized French terms that have been used in the main corpus of the text are also included.

bā/baba—Means both father/daddy and son. The father calls the son *Aba* or *Baba* and vice versa. Includes the intimate relationship of father and son.
cangā—means one day. A term used for starting a story equivalent to the English Once upon a time . . .
charlanter—to consult the spirits concerning the future and to discover what one must do in one's life.
coló—one of the initiations into the *Poro* society most often done among the young
cologi—the secret society known as the Poro where the elders have the ultimate authority and direct all activities. The *colobele* (initiates) must obey all the instructions that are given them. They must follow out the orders. Such compelling allegiance is the main reason behind the Senufo Christians' claim that the *cologi* is a type of bondage.
cotó-beeri/cotó-beeyi—of the initiations into the *Poro*.
dé—term used as a reinforcement for what follows in the text.
dibiw—a fetish that allows people to become invisible to other people. When a bad thing happens, such as a fierce animal attacks a person, a

dibiw will make that person invisible so that the attacking animal will no longer see his victim. It is considered a very powerful fetish. Senufo Christians consider such fetishes to be satanic in origin and therefore do not use them.

fani-wiiw—a specific type of fetish. *Fani* is a piece of traditionally woven cloth by the village specialists.

fe—family totems based on philosophical values and represented by animal names. For example, *Soro* means leopard.

feuilles—(Fr.) leaves that function as a traditional medicine. They are broken up, placed in a cooking pot, and boiled with water. One then washes with the resulting potion as a ritual means of washing away a disease. They are used as a traditional means of healing.

fɔrɔ—literally means tired but also includes suffering.

feticheur—(Fr.) one who practices divination.

fijembele—artisans. For example, weavers.

funyingi—having inside peace, literally cool insides.

gbóo—to care for (*s'occuper de*), raise, educate, literally to carry on the back like a mother does a child who cares for it from infancy.

Goïtaflaa—village situated in the Bouafle area where the Christian Pastor Samuel effectively prays for healing of the sick, the paralyzed, and the insane.

kabganna—a test or temptation that causes a difficult time such as sickness, death, poverty, anxiety, distress, or theft. It is considered a time when one has need of help and/or assistance. Example: Adam had a *kabganna* when he ate the fruit in the garden of Eden.

kaceleeo—the protective, nurturing aspect of the Senufo bipartite deity.

kafɔw—the owner, used to indicate master, Lord, for Senufo Christians.

kakpolayo—refers to awesome and great things that happen. Senufo Christians have taken over this term and built into it the meaning of miracle.

kolocɔlɔɔ—one of two principal Senufo deities, the creator God; non-visible and wholly good in nature (Glaze 1981:257). A term already within the culture but now used by Christians to refer to God the Father. *Kolo* means from a far distant country. *Cɔlɔɔ* relates to woman. Thus, a literal translation would be God-woman from a far county.

kanrigia—Senufo musical instrument made of a metal open cylinder. Played with a metal baton by running it against the teeth like edge of the cylinder.

katiolo—Senufo settlements that include both the predominant farmer group and artisan groups.

kpɔʔɔ rɔ—to worship

kpɔʔɔ rɔfɔdelèbélè—the true owners of worship.

kúségi tɛɛcɛngɛ—paradise for those who do good. A concept inherent in Senufo thought.

kuufuloria—part of the funeral ceremony where Senufo Christians do not participate.

kuugi—funerals, death.

kuufulori—a part of the funeral ceremony where a Christian is not allowed to participate due to its association with spirits.

kulɛ leri—a traditional funeral event that occurs after the actual burial of the corpse. It is said that one must do funerals or else the dead one will not be accepted/ received by the ancestors in the land of the dead.

likembe—otherwise known as *mbira* or sansa. A musical instrument, idiophone, played by pushing down with the thumbs on metal keys mounted on a wooden box or plank.

lɔɔsunyii—bodies of water believed to contain protective spirits and worshipped by non-Christian Senufo people. *Lɔɔsunyii* are inherited and the worshippers are always considered about their relationship with the *lɔɔsunyii*, asking themselves if they have been well received by it.

madebele—". . . bush spirits; quasi-human spirits believed to inhabit the forest, fields, and waterways surrounding the Senufo village; maleficent and unpredictable beings who demand constant propitiation; they work harm but are not considered wholly evil, as are the deebelel."[1]

marabout—an Islamic holy man who practices divination.

moa sasɔgi—Senufo equivalent to hell for those people who did poorly in this life.

Naakwɔɔcaa—currently a very famous fetish in the Korhogo area located at the village of Fanakaʔa.

Poro—". . . an initiation society that is universal for Senufo males. The authority structure of a village is composed of the leadership of its several *Poro* societies, each having its own sacred grove and age sets of initiates. *Poro* societies function as systems of government, education, and economic controls and as channels for the worship of bush spirits, lineal ancestors, and Ancient Mother"[2]

Sando—a person who practices divination with statues of cowry shells a traditional type of money. This person tells the future, and discovers

---

1. Glaze, *Art and Death*, 258.
2. Ibid., 259.

if an enemy is casting a spell (*jeter un mauvais sort*) on someone. May also be hired to cast a spell on someone else.

Sando ʔo/sandogo—". . . women's divination society constituting the core female leadership in the village; Sandogo elders work closely with male authorities in the *Poro* society.[3]

Sandobeyi—a traditional custom where one consults and talks with the evil spirits. It is the spirits who give/ordain one's ministry/life work.

Senabele/Senambele—people, generic term in the Senufo language for farmers of the several Central Senari dialect groups.[4]

Senyambele—brothers

Taamadelegi—true friendship that Christians have incorporated to indicate true love.

tagafɔlɔ—believers, owners of belief. Senufo Christians refer to themselves as *tagafɔlɔ*.

wobeewi—literally the evil one, used to refer to Satan.

yaabeemi—any extreme sickness.

yasunyi—either made of earth, carved out of wood, or made of stone and traditionally worshipped by the Senufo.

yawiire—a protective fetish used to counteract trouble and murder and usually worn on the body. Most often these are charms attached near the kidneys or worn around the hand, around the neck, on the ankles, or on a finger. They may also be found in the home and are thought of as a protector, companion, and savior.

yɛnyingi—an outward peace shown to others.

yirigafɔlɔ—the idol that a person worships in the belief that this is his/her creator. The Senufo believe that every living being has a creator and thus, one makes an image of this creator, called the *yirigafɔlɔ*.

yɔɔ/nyɔɔ—a poetic device use to call for one's attention and indicates that something important follows; used as a connector at the end of sentences or sung phrases.

---

3. Ibid.
4. Ibid.

Bibliography

Axtell, James. "Ethnohistory: An Historian's Viewpoint." *Ethnohistory* 26 (1979) 1–13.
Barnlund, Dean C. *Interpersonal Communication: Survey and Studies*. Boston: Houghton Mifflin, 1968.
———. "A Transactional Model of Communication." *Foundations of Communication Theory*, edited by Kenneth K. Sereno and C. David Mortenson, 83–102. New York: Harper and Row, 1970.
Bebey, Francis. *African Music: A People's Art*. Translated by Josephine Bennett. Westport: Lawrence Hill, 1975.
Bellman, Beryl Larry. *The Language of Secrecy: Symbols and Metaphors in Poro Ritual*. New Brunswick, NJ: Rutgers University Press, 1983.
Berlo, David K. *The Process of Communication: An Introduction to Theory and Practice*. San Francisco: Rinehart Press, 1960.
Blacking, John. *Venda Children's Songs: A Study in Ethnomusicological Analysis*. Johannesburg: Witwatersrand University Press, 1967.
———. *How Musical is Man?* London: Faber and Faber, 1973.
———. *A Common Sense View of All Music: Reflections on Percy Grainger's Contribution to Ethnomusicology Music Education*. Cambridge: Cambridge University Press, 1987.
Brandel, Rose. *The Music of Central Africa: An Ethnomusicological Study*. The Hague: Martinus Nijhoff, 1973.
Bright, William. "Language and Music: Areas of Cooperation." *Ethnomusicology* 7:26–32, 1963.
Butt-Thompson, Frederick William. *West African Secret Societies, Their Organizations, Officials, and Teaching*. Westport, CT: Negro University Press, 1970.
Campbell, Warren, and Jack Heller. "An Orientation for Considering Models of Musical Behavior." *Handbook of Music Psychology*, edited by Donald A. Hodges, 29–36. Lawrence, KS: National Association for Music Therapy, 1980.
Carrington, John F. "African Music in Christian Worship." *International Review of Missions* 37 (1948) 198–205.
Chenoweth, Vida. *Melodic Perception and Analysis: A Manual on Ethnic Melody*. Ukarumpa, Papua New Guinea: Summer Institute of Linguistics, 1972.
———. "Spare Them Western Music!" *Evangelical Missions Quarterly* 20, no. 1 (1984) 30–35.
———. and Darlene Bee. "On Ethnic Music." *Practical Anthropology* 15 (1968) 205–212.
Chernoff, John Miller. *African Rhythm and African Sensibility: Aesthetics and Social Action in African Musical Idioms*. Chicago: University of Chicago Press, 1979.
Conservative Baptist Foreign Mission Society. *Ivory Coast Report: OD-IVORY 239*. Wheaton, IL: CBFMS, 1986.
Coulibaly, Dusu. Interviewed by Roberta R. King. Tape recording. Korhogo, Côte d'Ivoire, 1988.
Coulibaly, Sinal. *Le Paysan Senoufo*. Abidjan: Les Nouvelles Editions Africaines, 1978.

Bibliography

Craigie, Peter C. *Psalms 1–50*. Word Biblical Commentary 19. Waco: Word, 1983.
Eid, Jakline. *Paroles de Devin: La fonte a la cire perdue chez les Senoufo de Côte d'Ivoire*. Paris: Musee National des Arts Africains et Oceaniens, 1988.
Ellis, Alexander. "On the Musical Scales of Various Nations." *Journal of the Society of Arts* 23 (1885) 485–527.
Engel, James F. *Contemporary Christian Communication: Its Theory and Practice*. Nashville: Thomas Nelson, 1979.
Ekwueme, Lazarus Nnanyelu. "African Music in Christian Liturgy: The Igbo Experiment." *African Music Society Journal* 5 (1973) 12–33.
Erlmann, Veit. "Trance and Music in the Hausa Booriie Spirit Possession Cult in Nigeria." *Ethnomusicology* 26 (1982) 49–58.
Feld, Steven. "Linguistics and Ethnomusicology." *Ethnomusicology* 18:2 (1974) 197–218.
Finnegan, Ruth. *Oral Literature in Africa*. Nairobi, Kenya: Oxford University Press, 1970.
Friesen, Albert W. D. "A Methodology in the Development of Indigenous Hymnody." MA thesis, Mennonite Brethren Biblical Seminary, 1981.
Gibbs, J. L. "Poro Values and Courtroom Procedures in a Kpelle Chiefdom." *Journal of Anthropological Research* 42 (1986) 279–88. Originally published in *Southern Journal of Anthropology* (1962).
Glaze, Anita J. *Art and Death in a Senufo Village*. Bloomington, IN: Indiana University Press, 1981.
———. "Abstract." In *Path and Circle: Senufo Art*. Unpublished preliminary draft for proposal to the National Endowment for the Humanities. New York: The Center for African Art, 1988.
———. "The Religious and Metaphysical Foundation for the Arts." In *Art de Côte d'Ivoire*, edited by Jean-Paul Barbier. Geneva: Barbier-Muller Museum, 1988.
Goodeau, Eugene. "Toward an Indigenous Hymnody." MA thesis, Harding Graduate School of Religion, 1980.
Gottschalk, B. *Madebele: Buschgeister im Land der Senufo*. Meersbusch: B. Gottschalk, 1988.
Griffin, Emory A. *The Mind Changers: The Art of Christian Persuasion*. Wheaton, IL: Tyndale House, 1982.
Gudykunst, William B. and Young Yun Kim, editors. *Methods for Intercultural Communication Research*. International and Intercultural Communication Annual. Beverly Hills: Sage, 1984.
Hall, Edward T. *Beyond Culture*. Garden City, NY: Doubleday, 1977.
Hanna, Judith Lynne. "African Dance: the Continuity of Change." In *Yearbook of the International Folk Music Council*, 165–74. Urbana, IL: University of Illinois Press,1973.
———. *To Dance is Human: A Theory of Nonverbal Communication*. Austin, TX: University of Texas Press, 1979. Reprint, Chicago: University of Chicago Press, 1987.
Harley, George Way. *Notes on the Poro in Liberia*. Cambridge, MA: The Museum, 1941.
Harrison, Frank. "Universals in Music: Towards a Methodology of Comparative Research." In *The World of Music*. n.p., 1977.
Herndon, Marcia, and Norma McLeod. *Music as Culture*. Darby, PA: Norwood Editions, 1980.
Hiebert, Paul G. "Culture and Cross-Cultural Differences." In *Crucial Dimensions in World Evangelization*, edited by Arthur F. Glasser et al., 45–60. Pasadena, CA: William Carey Library, 1976.
———. *Anthropological Insights for Missionaries*. Grand Rapids, MI: Baker, 1985.

Bibliography

Holas, B. *L'Art Sacre Senoufo: ses differentes expressions ans a vie social.* Abidjan: Les Nouvelles Editions Africaines, 1985.

Hood, Mantle. "Ethnomusicology." *Harvard Dictionary of Music*, pp. 298–300. Willi Apel, ed. Cambridge: Harvard University Press, 1969.

———. *The Ethnomusicologist.* New York: McGraw-Hill, 1971.

———. "Universal Attributes of Music." *The World of Music* 19 (1977) 65.

Hustad, Donald P. *Jubilate! Church Music in the Evangelical Tradition.* Carol Stream, IL: Hope, 1981.

Jessup, Lynne. *The Mandinka Balafon: An Introduction with Notation for Teaching.* La Mesa, CA: Xylo, 1983.

Jones, A. M. *Studies in African Music.* London: Oxford University Press, 1959.

Jorgensen, Knud. "Role and Function of the Media in the Mssion of the Church." PhD diss., Fuller Theological Seminary, School of World Mission, 1981.

Kaleli, Jones Maweu. "Theoretical Foundations of African and Western Worldviews and Their Relationship to Christian Theologizing: An Akamba Case Study." PhD diss., Fuller Theological Seminary, 1985.

Kearney, Michael. *World View.* Novato, CA: Chandler and Sharp, 1984.

Keil, Charles. *Tiv Song: The Sociology of Art in a Classless Society.* Chicago: University of Chicago Press, 1979.

Keletigui, Jean-Marie. *Le Senoufo Face au Cosmos.* Abidjan: Les Nouvelles Editions Africaines, 1978.

Key, Mary. "Hymn Writing with Indigenous Tunes." *Practical Anthropology* 9 (1962) 257–62.

Kientz, Albert. *Dieu et les Genies: Recits Etiologiques Senoufo.* Paris: Societe d'Etudes Linguistiques et Anthropologiques de France, 1979.

Kilson, Marion. *Kpele Lala: Ga Religious Songs and Symbols.* Cambridge: Harvard University Press, 1971.

King, Louis L. "Indigenous Hymnody of the Ivory Coast." *Practical Anthropololgy* 9 (1962) 268–70.

King, Roberta R. Senufo Field Notes and Texts. Research Project in the Korhogo region of Côte d'Ivoire, 1985.

———. Senufo Field Notes and Texts. Research Project in the Korhogo region of Côte d'Ivoire, 1986.

———. Senufo Song Survey. Research Project in the Korhogo Region of Côte d'Ivoire, 1987.

———. Senufo Field Notes and Texts. Research Project in the Korhogo Region of Côte d'Ivoire, 1987.

———. Senufo Field Notes and Texts. Research Project in the Korhogo Region of Côte d'Ivoire, 1988.

———. Focus Group Interview Transcriptions: the Village of Foro. Research Project in the Korhogo Region of Côte d'Ivoire, 1988.

———. Focus Group Interview Transcriptions: Korhogo. Research Project in the Korhogo Region of Côte d'Ivoire, 1988.

———. Focus Group Interview Transcriptions: the Village of Coonyɛʔɛn. Research Project in the Korhogo Region of Côte d'Ivoire, 1988.

———. Focus Group Interview Transcriptions: the Village of Dessingbo. Research Project in the Korhogo Region of Côte d'Ivoire, 1988.

———. Focus Group Interview Transcriptions: the Village of Sɛʔɛlɛ. Research Project in the Korhogo Region of Côte d'Ivoire, 1988.

Bibliography

———. Focus Group Interview Transcriptions: the Village of Torhogo. Research Project in the Korhogo Region of Côte d'Ivoire, 1988.

Klem, Herbert V. *Oral Communication of the Scripture: Insights from African Oral Art*. Pasadena: William Carey Library, 1982.

Knight, Roderic. "The Style of Mandinka Music: A Study in Extracting Theory from Practice." In *Selected Reports in Ethnomusicology: Studies in African Music* 5:3–65. UCLA, Program in Ethnomusicology, Department of Music, 1984.

Knops, P. s.m.a. *Les Anciens Senufo: 1923–1935*. Berg en Dal, Nederland: Africa Museum, 1980.

Kraft, Charles H. *Christianity in Culture*. Maryknoll: Orbis, 1979.

———. *Communication Theory for Christian Witness*. Nashville: Abingdon, 1983.

———. and Tom N. Wisley eds. *Readings in Dynamic Indigeneity*. Pasadena: William Carey Library, 1979.

Kraft, Marguerite. *Worldview and the Communication of the Gospel: A Nigerian Case Study*. Pasadena: William Carey Library, 1978.

Krieg, Karl H. and Wulf Lohse. "Kunst und Religion bei den Gbato-Senufo." In *Elfenbeinkueste*. Hamburg: Hamburgisches Museum für Volkerkunde, 1981.

Locke, David. "Principles of Offbeat Timing and Cross-Rhythm in Southern Ewe Dance." *Ethnomusicology* 26 (1982) 217–46.

———. *Drum Gahu: A Systematic Method for an African Percussion Piece*. Crown Point, IN: White Cliffs Media, 1987.

Lomax, Alan. *Cantometrics: An Approach to the Anthropology of Music*. Berkeley: University of California Extension Media Center, 1976.

Luykx, Boniface. "Christian Worship and the African Soul." *African Ecclesiatical Review* 7 (1965) 133–43.

Mapoma, Isaac Mwesa. "The Use of Folk Music among some Bemba Church Congregations in Zambia." Yearbook of the International Folk Music Council 1 (1960) 72–88.

Martin, Marie-Louise. "The Mai Chaza Church in Rhodesia," *African Initiatives in Religion*, edited by David B. Barrett, 109–21. Nairobi: East African, 1971.

Mbiti, John. "The Ways and Means of Communicating the Gospel." *Christianity in Tropical Africa*. Oxford: Oxford University Press, 1968.

McCroskey, James C. *An Introduction to Rhetorical Communication*, 2nd ed. Englewood Cliffs, NJ: Prentice-Hall, 1972.

McLaughlin, Terrence. *Music and Communication*. New York: St. Martin's, 1970.

Mensah, A. A. "The Akan Church Lyric." *International Review of Missions* 49 (1960) 183–88.

Meki Nzewi. "Traditional Strategies for Mass Communication: the Centrality of Igbo Music." In *Selected Reports in Ethnomusicology: Studies in African Music* 5:319–38. UCLA, Program in Ethnomusicology, Department of Music, 1984.

Merriam, Alan. "African Music." *Continuity and Change in African Culture*. W. R. Bascom and M. J. Herskovits. pp. 49–86. Evanston, IL: University of Illinois Press. 1958.

———.1963 "The Purposes of Ethnomusicology: An Anthropological View." *Ethnomusicology* 7:206–213.

———. "The Anthropology of Music". Evanston:Northwestern University Press. 1964.

Meyer, L. *Emotion and Meaning in Music*. Chicago: University of Chicago Press, 1956.

Mills, Elizabeth. *Senufo Phonology, Discourse to Syllable (A Prosodic Approach)*. Arlington, TX: The Summer Institute of Linguistics and the University of Texas, 1984.

Mills, Richard and Elizabeth. Tape-recorded and transcribed interview by Roberta R. King. Abidjan, Côte d'Ivoire, 1985.

Monts, L. P. "Conflict, Accommodation, and Transformation: The Effect of Islam on Music of the Vai Secret Socities." *Cahiers d'Etudes Africaines* XXIV (1984) 321–42.

Nettl, Bruno. *Theory and Method in Ethnomusicology.* New York: Free, 1964.

———. "Ethnomusicology: Definitions, Directions, and Problems." In *Musics of Many Cultures*, 1–9. Berkeley: University of California Press, 1980.

———. *The Study of Ethnomusicology: Twenty-Nine Issues and Concepts.* Urbana, IL: University of Illinois Press, 1983.

Nida, Eugene A. *Customs and Cultures.* New York: Harper, 1954. Reprint, William Carey Library, 1975.

———. *Message and Mission.* New York: Harper and Row, 1960. Reprint, William Carey Library, 1975.

Nketia, J. H. Kwabena. *Funeral Dirges of the Akan.* Exeter: James Townsend and Sons, 1955.

———. "The Contribution of African Culture to Christian Worship." *International Review of Missions* 47 (1958) 265–78.

———. *African Music in Ghana.* Chicago: Northwestern University Press, 1963.

———. *Folk Songs of Ghana.* London: Oxford University Press, 1963.

———. *The Music of Africa.* London: Victor Gollancz, 1975.

———. "Interaction Through Music: the Dynamics of Music-Making in African Societies." In *International Social Science Journal*, vol. 34, no. 4 (1982) 639–56.

———. "The Juncture of the Social and the Musical: the Methodology of Cultural Analysis." Unpublished paper presented at UCLA, 1982.

Olson, Howard S. *African Music in Christian Worship.* Edited by David B. Barrett. Nairobi, Kenya: East African, 1971.

Ouattara, Dossongmon. Tape-recorded and transcribed interview by Roberta R. King. Korhogo, Côte d'Ivoire, 1987.

Republique de Côte d'Ivoire. "Recensement General de la Population d'Avril 1975: La Population de la Cote d'Ivoire." Abidjan: Ministere du Plan et de l'Industrie, Direction de la Statistique, 1981.

Riccitelli, James M. "Developing Non-Western Hymnody." *Practical Anthropology* 9 (1962) 241–56.

Richter, Dolores. "Further Considerations of Caste is West Africa: The Senufo." *Africa* 50 (1980) 37–53.

Rogers, E. M., and Floyd Shoemaker. *The Communication of Innovations: A Cross-Cultural Approach.* 2nd ed. New York: Free, 1971.

Samovar, L. A., and R. E. Porter. *Intercultural Communication: A Reader.* Belmont, CA: Wadsworth, 1972.

Sapir, Edward. "The Status of Linguistics as a Science." *Language* 5 (1949) 209.

Sindzingre, N. "Healing is as Healing Does: Pragmatic Resolution of Misfortune among the Senufo, Ivory Coast." *History and Anthropology* 2 (1985) 33–57.

Scott, Joyce. Personal correspondence. Nairobi, Kenya, 1988.

Seeger, Charles. "Music as a Tradition of Communication, Discipline, and Play." *Ethnomusicology*, vol. 6, no. 3 (1962) 156–63.

Skinner, Merrill. Tape-recorded and transcribed interview by Roberta R. King. Korhogo, Côte d'Ivoire, 1986.

Smith, Donald K. *Make Haste Slowly: Developing Effective Cross-Cultural Communication.* Portland, OR: Institute for International Christian Communication, 1984.

Soro, Nambe. Tape-recorded and transcribed interview by Roberta R. King. Ferkessedougou, Côte d'Iovire, 1988.

Bibliography

Spradley, James P. *The Ethnographic Interview*. New York: Holt, Rinehart and Winston, 1979.

———. *Participant Observation*. New York: Holt, Rinehart and Winston, 1980.

Starosta, William J. "Qualitative Content Analysis: A Burkeian Perspective." In *Methods for Intercultural Communication Research*, edited by William B. Gudykunst and Young Yun Kim, 185–94. Beverly Hills: Sage, 1984.

Stone, Ruth M. *Let the Inside Be Sweet: The Interpretation of Music Event among the Kpelle of Liberia*. Bloomington, IN: Indiana University Press, 1982.

———. *Dried Millet Breaking: Time, Words, and Song in the Woi Epic of the Kpelle*. Bloomington, IN: Indiana University Press, 1988.

Temu, A. J. *British Protestant Missions*. London: Longman, 1972.

Tippett, Alan R. "Hymns as a Theological Index." In *Solomon Islands Christianity*, 286–96. South Pasadena: William Carey Library, 1967.

Tuo, Donyime. Tape-recorded and transcribed interview by Roberta R. King. Korhogo, Côte d'Ivoire. 1985.

Turner, H. W. *Religious Innovation in Africa: Collected Essays on New Religious Movements*. Boston: G. K. Halland, 1979.

Turner, Victor W. and Edward M. Brunner, eds. *The Anthropology of Experience*. Urbana, IL: University of Illinois Press, 1986.

van den Berg, Harold and Dorothy van den Berg. Tape-recorded and transcribed interview by Roberta R. King. Torhogo, Côte d'Ivoire, 1986.

Vine, W. E. *An Expository Dictionary of New Testament Words*. Nashville, TN: Thomas Nelson, 1952.

Von Allmen, Daniel. "The Birth of Theology." In *Readings in Dynamic Indigeneity*, edited by Charles H. Kraft and Tom N. Wisley, 325–48. Pasadena: William Carey Library, 1979.

Warnock, Paul Willard. "Trends in African Church Music: A Historical Review." MA thesis, UCLA, 1983.

Welmers, William E. *African Language Structures*. Berkeley: University of California Press, 1973.

Weman, Henry. *African Music and the Church in Africa*. Uppsala: Uppsala Universitetsarsskrift, 1960.

———. "The New Praise in Ancient Tunes." In *The Church Crossing Frontiers*, 177–88. Gleerup: Vandenhoeck and Ruprecht, 1969.

Willetts, Karen Faye. "The Senoufo: The Tiembara of Korhogo." Unpublished manuscript. Advanced Ethnology: International Linguistics Center, 1979.

Wilson, Monica. *Communal Rituals of the Nyakusa*. Oxford: Oxford University Press, 1959.

Wimmer, Roger D., and Joseph R. Dominick. *Mass Media Research*. 2nd ed. Belmont, CA: Wadsworth, 1987.

Yin, Robert K. *Case Study Research: Design and Methods*. Beverly Hills: Sage, 1984.

Zemp, Hugo. "Ivory Coast." In *The New Grove Dictionary of Music and Musicians* 9, edited by Stanley Sadie, 431–34. London: Macmillan, 1980.

Zie. Tape-recorded interview by Roberta R. King. Korhogo: Côte d'Ivoire, 1980.

Discography

Augier, Pierre, Paul Dagri, and Adepo Yapo. 1982. *Côte d'Ivoire: Chants et Danses de Boundiali*. Agence de Cooperation Culturelle et Technique, CD ACCT 18211.

de Lannoy, Michel. 1984. *Côte d'Ivoire, Senoufo: Musiques des Funerailles Fodonon*. Le Collection Musee de l 'Homme. *Chant du Monde*. CD LDX 74 838.

Forster, Till. 1987. *Musik der Senufo/Elfenbeinkueste*. Germany, West Berlin: Musikethnologische Abteilung Museum für Volkerkunde Berlin Staatliche Museen Preussischer Kulturbesitz. Audiocassette.

Zemp, Hugo. n.d. *The Music of the Senufo*. Vol. 8 of *An Anthology of African Music*. Edited for the International Music Council by the International Institute for Comparative Music Studies and Documentation, Paul Collaer, general editor. UNESCO Collection. Barenreiter Musicaphon, CD BM30 L 2308.

Index of Song Titles

A Mighty Fortress is Our God, 3
Abandon Satan, the Devil, 156
Aleluya, Aleluya, Zyezu Bariga, 103–4, 107, 209, 225, 230, 239
Bariga Sa[glottal]a, 107, 156, 205
Come and Go with Me to My Father's House, 64
Come, Believe on Jesus Christ, 172
Come Brothers, Come Brothers to Jesus Christ, 188
Come, Come Brothers and Sisters. Come and Let Us Rejoice!, 172
Come Thou Fount of Every Blessing, 69
Come to Jesus, 153, 160
Every Day Satan is Walking Around and Fooling People, 70
Every Moment the Hand of Jesus is on You, 207
Grab Hold of Faith, 160, 212–13
Hallelujah Chorus, 66
Heaven Came Down and Glory Filled My Soul, 3
How Great Thou Art, 67
I Pray to You, Our Father Jesus, 178, 229, 231–33
I Will Tell Our Lord Jesus (Prayer for My Family), 214–16
If a Spirit Leaves a Person, 219–21
In My Father's House are Many Dwelling Places, 74, 130, 208–9
It is No Longer I Who Live, 189, 207–8
Jesus is Calling You, 96, 104, 130, 172, 208–9

Jesus Said, 'I am Going and I Will Come Again', 153, 210–11
Jesus is Fairer than Ten Thousand, 67
Let Us Rejoice About Our Freedom, 213–14
Man from Torhogo, 84, 86, 243
My Father has Everything, 155
My Friend, Jesus is Calling You, 96, 172
Offer Yourselves to Jesus, 156
One Door and Only One, 66, 73
People, Kneel Down to Worship Jesus, 206–7
People, Run! Run! For We are in a Race, 216, 264
Philip, When You See Jesus, 218–19, 262
Pressing on the Upward Road, 67
Satan Get Away From Us, 156
That is Why I Came to Jesus, 179, 235, 239
The Father, Jehovah is My Guide, 105, 211–12
The Lord Jesus Has Great Power, 221–23, 265
There is Everything with the Father, 217–18
What a Friend We Have in Jesus, 3

Index

Accompaniment, 71, 74–75, 93, 116, 127
Activities that Christians Abandon, 129–30, 132, 136
Affective dimension, 16–167, 176
Africa Inland Church, 4, 154
AIC School of Music, 4
Africa Inland Church School of Music, 154
Ancestors, 56–57, 117, 134, 269
Ancient Mother, 54, 57, 269
Anthropology, 43–46, 48, 128, 201
Art, 94
Artisan groups, 52, 268
Assemblies of God, 59
Association of Evangelical Baptist Churches of Côte d'Ivoire, 25, 61–62
Attitude, negative, 168, 173, 195, 199
Attitude, positive, 168, 170, 186, 195, 197

Balafon, 17, 67, 75, 85, 112–13, 115, 117, 172, 241
Baptist churches of Côte d'Ivoire, 16, 86, 193
Baptist churches in Zaire, 6
Baptists, 6, 8, 15–16, 19, 21, 25, 60–63, 83, 85–86, 193, 200, 243, 271
Barnlund, Dean C., 38
Bedel and Fer, 59
Behavioral dimension, 166, 186, 190, 192
Believers' attitudes, 169, 171

Believer's interaction with God, 150, 152–53
Believer's position before God, 150–52
Berlo, David K., 5, 35
Blacking, John, 29–31, 34, 91
Boloye, 55–56
Bright, William, 29
Brown, Richard H., 33
Burkina Faso, 22, 51, 59
Bush spirits, 57–58, 114, 117, 128, 133–34, 264–65, 269

Calabash shaker, 82, 112, 117
Caliw, 112, 117–18, 226–27, 241
Case study, 9, 13–15, 18, 23, 41, 44, 48–49, 81, 193, 197, 260
Call-and-response, 40, 71, 74, 93, 102–3, 111
Campus Crusade for Christ, 159
Catholics, 58–60, 62, 85
Cebaara, 52, 267
Channels, 5, 31, 37, 39, 41–42, 47, 86–87, 92, 100–102, 123, 269
Chenoweth, Vida, 8, 45
Children, 6, 57, 84, 91, 128, 151, 152, 158, 161, 174, 180, 233–34, 240, 244, 264, 271
Choirs, 6, 86
Christian and Missionary Alliance, 69
Christian formation, 26, 139
    identification, 86
    life-style, 16, 85
    music communication research, 23, 25–26, 194

Index

Christian worship patterns, 7
Christianity, paths of, 58
Christmas festivals, 2, 99, 187
Church Growth, 4, 8–10, 23, 25, 43–46, 48, 61–62, 194, 200–201
Church planting, 14
Circumcision, 5
Clapping, 71, 74, 82–84, 90, 93, 96, 98, 109–12, 167–68, 198, 240–41
Code, 10, 36, 47, 196
Cognitive, 8, 24, 42, 44, 124, 127, 165–66, 170, 176, 183–84, 190–93, 195, 198, 201, 260
Cognitive dimension, 166, 175–77, 180, 185–86, 190–91, 199
Commitment to Christ, 187–88, 190
Communication
    traditional, 81
    transaction models, 34, 38
Communication process,
    music, 23, 47, 86, 97, 101, 119, 165, 193
Communication theory, 18, 23, 34, 47, 97, 100, 193
Conservative Baptists, 8, 25, 58, 60, 63
Content analysis, 17–18, 24, 124–26
Contextual, contextualized, 6, 8–11, 76, 193
Contextualization, 6, 9–11, 76
    creative, 76
Conversion, 16, 61, 73, 174, 186–87, 243–44, 248
Cɔɔnye?en, 123
Côte d'Ivoire, 8, 15–17, 22, 24–25, 48, 51, 59, 61–62, 86, 124, 140, 193, 200–201
Coto-beeri, 130–31, 208, 267
Coulibaly, Dusu, 64–65, 72–74
Coulibaly, Sinai, 53
Craigie, Peter C, 138
Cross-cultural, 3–4, 44, 46, 139

Culturally appropriate, 4, 7, 9–11, 21, 26, 41, 45, 47–48, 137–39, 170, 193–97, 199–202, 266
Current Senufo repertoire, 19, 126, 130, 140–45, 147–53, 155, 158, 160, 205, 208
Customs, 5, 7, 46, 76, 131–33, 136–37, 265

Dance, 5, 29–32, 34, 39, 55–56, 73–74, 83, 94–96, 119, 167, 169, 172, 196
Daystar Communications, 4
Death, 72, 125, 129, 146–48, 154–55, 218, 222, 233, 236, 246, 250, 268–69
Decision, 16, 166, 180, 186–88, 190, 192, 196, 199
Deity, 54, 57, 157, 268
Digo, 7
Divination, 56–57, 133–34, 157, 268–70
Diviner/s, 57–58, 133–34
Drama, 31, 33, 46
Drum/s, 3, 46, 54, 74–75, 112–15, 241
Dynamically equivalent church, 10
Dynamically equivalent message, 47

Egg, 99, 212–213, 263, 266
Eid, Jakline, 53
Emic, 16, 19, 126, 174, 199
Emotions, 27, 166–67, 182, 188–89, 191
Engel, James F., 37, 165
Enoch, 147–48, 212, 163
Ethnography, 23, 25, 194
Ethnohistorical study, 23
Ethnohistory, 25, 43–44, 46, 48, 194, 202
Ethnomusicologist/s, 8, 10, 14, 16, 27–30, 34, 45, 97
Ethnomusicology, 4, 9, 11, 24, 26–31, 33, 45–46, 48, 124–25, 201

282

Index

Ethnomusicology (cont.),
    applied, 24–26, 194
Evangelism, 7, 26, 76, 94, 114, 182, 202
Evil, 134, 156, 206, 224, 232, 243–244, 246, 249–51, 255, 265, 269–70
Expressive, 27, 31–32, 185–86, 192

Family/ies, 53, 55, 58, 64, 99, 123, 129, 136–37, 174, 220, 238, 265, 268
Fani-wiiw, 130, 131–32, 208, 268
Fathers of the African Missions of Lyon, 59
Feedback, 34, 37–38, 40–41, 88, 98
Feld, Steven, 29
Ferkessedougou, 22, 61, 137, 172
Fêtes
    Youth, 16
Feticheur, 180, 268
Fetish/es, 60,–61, 73, 75, 97, 108, 115, 131–33, 156, 205–7, 211, 214–15, 232–35, 244, 251–52, 267–70
Fijembele, 52, 268
Flaca, 98–99
Folklore, 29, 128
Foreign tune/s, 5, 64, 197
Form and function, 9
Foro, 13, 96, 109, 115, 169, 170, 172, 178
Friesen, Albert W. D. 45
Funeral/s, 43, 52, 85, 107, 115, 117, 132–33, 135, 156, 172, 231, 233, 269

Ghana, 6, 51
Glaze, Anita J., 52–4, 56–57, 94, 113, 133–35, 140, 268–69
God,
    characteristics of, 143, 145–46

Gospel, 4, 7–8, 58, 60, 64, 70–76, 143, 174, 193, 197, 200–202, 261, 264–65
Gottschalk, B., 53
Grass-roots theologizing, 138, 162, 200, 260–61, 263–66
Growth of churches, 45–46

Hanna, Judith Lynne, 95
Harmony, 47, 92–93, 108, 169, 194
Heal, 61, 178, 222, 244–45, 247, 265
Healing, 61, 149, 180, 246, 265, 268
Heaven, 13, 65–66, 146–148, 154–55, 162, 209–10, 217, 245, 255, 263
Hiebert, Paul G., 44, 76, 128, 139
High-context, 180
Holas, B., 53
Holy Spirit, 70, 141, 162, 261
Hood, Mantle, 28–29
Hymn/s, 3–4, 6–8, 44–45, 63–73, 76, 116, 139, 168, 197

Illness, 64, 109, 137, 178, 236
Impact/s of music, 10, 32
Indigenous
    church, 10
    composers, 45
    hymnody, 45–48, 63
    hymns, 4, 45
    music, 5, 8–9
Influential dynamic, 185–86
Initiation, 5, 113, 131–32, 134, 255, 269
Initiator, 40–41, 88, 97, 154
Instrument, 28–29, 67, 75, 113–17, 241, 268–69
Instruction, 81, 183, 185–86, 191
Interactant, 40, 42, 88
Intercultural communication research, 125
International Institute for Christian Communications, 4

Index

Interpretation, 33, 38, 40, 42, 64, 99, 180, 262–64
Intonation, 69, 106
Islam/Islamic, 58, 133, 269
Ivory Coast, 45, 51, 60, 63, 70, 113

Jegele, 75, 103, 112–18, 198, 226–27, 241
    performance patterns, 116–17
Jehovah's Witnesses, 59
Jɛniba, 98–99, 264
Jesus, path of, 13, 58, 151
Jesus road, 16, 62, 109, 135, 158, 220, 224, 227, 264–65
Jorgensen, Knud, 34, 38–39

Kaceleeo, 54, 268
Kafana, 243–55
Kaleli, Jones Maweu, 260
Katiola, 22
Kazye, 13
Kagbanikaʔa, 70
Keletigui, Jean-Marie, 53
Kenya, 3–8, 154
Kientz, Albert, 53, 114
Kikuyu, 5
Kinesic, 10, 31, 41–42
King, Louis L., 45
King, Roberta R., 13, 15, 45, 82, 95–96, 109, 115, 123, 129, 136, 169–70, 173
Kingdom of God, 10, 202–3
Kissankaʔa, 115
Klem, Herbert V., 44
Knight, Roderic, 75, 89–90, 125
Knops, P., 53, 113
Kolocɔlɔɔ, 54, 60, 66, 112, 140–43, 263, 267–68
Koto, 28–29
Kpelle, 31
Kraft, Charles, 10, 35, 47, 76, 97, 100, 128, 139, 261, 266
Krieg, Karl H. and Wulf Lohse, 53
Kunst, Jaap, 28, 53

Language, 5, 16, 30–32, 41, 45–46, 51, 53, 65–66, 68–71, 89, 91–93, 95, 106–8, 115, 124, 128, 195, 224, 267, 270
Lead singer, 71, 82–83, 102–3, 105, 108, 111, 118, 168, 230, 239–40, 256
Leadership training, 26
Liberia, 31, 55
Life-style, 7, 16, 58, 85, 155, 188
Likembe, 67, 269
Linguistic channel, 40–42, 87–92, 97, 123
Linguistics, 29, 128
Literacy, 51, 139–40
Lɔɔsunyi, 130–31, 134, 269
Lyric theology, 24, 138–40, 171

Maasai, 154
Madebele, 54, 134, 264–65, 269
Mali, 22, 51, 58–59
Mandinka, 75, 89–90, 125
Mande-Jula, 58
Marabout, 58, 132–133, 205–206, 269
Martin, Marie-Louise, 76
McCroskey, James C., 37, 40
McLaughlin, Terence, 32
Meaning/s, 18, 33–34, 38–42, 65, 87–88, 94, 107, 125, 128, 140, 143, 170–71, 191, 201, 216, 225–27, 238, 246, 268
Media, 15, 34, 38–39, 201
Melody, 47, 90–93, 106–8, 116, 198
Merriam, Alan, 27–29, 31, 124, 128
Methodology/ies, 11, 13–18, 45
Mills, Elizabeth, 51, 106, 125
Mills, Richard, 68
Miracle/s, 149, 221–23, 268
Missiological literature, 8–9, 46
Missiological study, 5, 11
Missiological theory, 6, 9
Missiology, 11, 26, 42–47, 193, 200–202

284

Mission, 3, 5, 43, 48, 61, 63, 75, 200, 202, 265
Missions, 5, 10, 44, 48, 59, 202
Mission strategy, 61
Missionary/ies, 4–6, 11, 16, 28, 45–47, 59–60, 63–64, 67–70, 73–76, 95, 168, 195, 201, 224, 243
Missionary-attitudes, 5
Mombasa, 3
Most popular songs of 1987, 126–27, 140–45, 148–49, 151–53, 155–56, 158, 160, 205, 261
Movement, 31, 40–42, 47, 66–68, 70, 76, 83–84, 87–88, 94–97, 101–2, 106, 165, 187, 194–95, 198, 202
Music
    as an educational tool, 45
    as behavior, 31, 46, 48
    as communication, 23–25, 30–34, 194
    as sound, 45–46, 48
    behavior, 28, 30
    channel, 40, 87–89, 92–94, 97, 101–102, 119, 123, 195
    communication model, 24, 39
    communication process, 23, 47, 86, 97, 101, 119, 165, 193
    culture, 24, 30
    education, 2 event/s, 3
    function/s of, 27, 31–32
    in culture, 11, 25, 194
    workshop, 68–69, 76
Musical
    analysis, 24–25, 88, 92, 194
    behavior, 8
    language, 5
    preferences, 7
    sounds, 30–31, 66, 87
    structures, 30, 74–75, 77, 89, 91, 95–96, 195–96, 198

Musical (cont.),
    styles, 7, 10, 21, 63, 72, 74, 76, 168–73, 191, 197–98
    vignettes, 81, 85
Musicology, comparative, 29

Names of God, 140, 142
Nangaluru, 20, 234
Napieolodougou, 70, 75, 81
National
    Christians, 18, 67
    informants, 19
    church leaders, 11
    pastors, 16, 62, 69
Nawokaʔa, 68, 70
Nettl, Bruno, 28–30
New song workshop, 17–19, 98, 106, 126, 167, 171
Ngana Soro, 20, 104, 180
Nida, Eugene, 46
Nigeria, 44, 62
Nigerians, 62
Nketia, J. H. Kwabena, 10, 30, 32, 41, 92, 96, 109, 125
Noise, 37–38, 40, 109
Non-believers, 99, 162, 169, 171–74, 177, 187, 191, 197, 230, 237–38
Non-Christian musician, 68
Nɔnyimɔ, 84, 98–99, 236, 243
Nsenge, 31
Nyaʔnafolo, 168

Oral musical traditions, 45
Ouattara, Dossongmon, 58, 75, 85, 134, 263

Participant-observation, 16–17
Path of Jesus, 13, 58, 151
Pathway of a song, 165–67, 177, 191–92
People movement, 68, 70, 202
Peres Blancs (White Fathers), 59

Index

Performance, 3, 27, 30, 33, 81, 92–94, 97–98, 100, 102, 104, 114, 116–17, 119, 194, 196, 198, 243, 256
    patterns, 92–94, 117, 119
Performer/s, 34, 40–42, 87–88, 97, 100–102
Persecution, 55, 60, 73, 174, 265
Personal beliefs, 178, 180, 186
Personal problems, 131, 136–37
Poetry, 29, 31
Polyrhythms, 117
Poro, 54–57, 59, 85, 107, 113–15, 117, 129, 131–32, 134–35, 179
Portuguese, 3
Positive activities for Christians, 157, 159–60
Power, 6, 31, 54–55, 57, 61, 103, 133, 137, 144–46, 156, 159, 179, 209, 215, 219–23, 231, 234, 242–43, 245, 248, 250–51, 254, 261, 263–66
    encounter, 156, 265
Praise, 62, 66, 70, 81, 96, 108, 110–11, 115, 125, 156–57, 167, 169, 231, 240–42
Prayer/s, 54, 61, 65, 84–85, 133, 152–53, 156, 158, 214, 229, 235, 250
Preaching, 12, 47, 60, 63, 173, 182, 185, 199, 251
Problems, 5, 32, 45, 64–65, 69, 76, 110, 124–25, 131, 136–37, 154–55, 158, 172, 178, 180, 183, 188–90, 192, 198, 236, 265
Proverb, 99, 128, 263
Psalter, Hebrew, 138
Psalms, 105–6, 143, 168–69, 211, 227, 262

Qualitative analysis, 19
Quantitative analysis, 19
Question guide, 20–21, 229
Questionnaire, 18

Real-life
    context, 9, 14,
    situations, 177, 180, 185–186, 190
Receptor/s, 5, 10, 13, 23–24, 32, 35, 37–38, 40, 101, 165, 186, 191
Reformation, 3
Relationship
    with God, 5, 96, 110, 138, 150–51, 161, 264
    with Jesus Christ, 179, 189
    with the Lord, 99
    with others, 160–61
    with spirits, 132, 135
Research
    investigatory, 16–17
    qualitative, 19
Rhythm/s, 4–5, 47, 67, 69, 74, 90–93, 95, 97, 99, 106, 109, 117, 230, 239–40, 256
Richter, Dolores, 52
Riccitelli, James M., 45, 69
Ritual/s, 52, 54, 56–57, 85, 94, 133, 158, 268
Rogers, E. M., and Floyd Shoemaker, 34
Roman Catholics, 58–60, 62, 85
Roots, 21, 46
Rural, 6, 51, 202

Sacred, 5, 54, 66, 113, 269
Sacred forest, 54–55, 57, 59, 85, 247, 249–50, 269
Sacrifice/s, 54, 59–60, 74, 97, 108, 110, 114, 132–34, 136, 157–58, 206, 215, 235, 245–47, 249–50, 252, 254
Samovar, L. A., and R. E. Porter, 34
Sandogo, 56–57, 113, 133, 136, 225, 270
Sanga, 69–70, 250–51
Sapir, Edward, 128

Scripture, 16–17, 44, 72, 106, 143, 157, 185, 188–89, 261, 263, 266
Secular, 9, 86, 110, 128–29, 172
Secular musical forms, 9
Senabele, 51, 270
Senari, 51–52, 267, 270
Senegal, 8
Sheep, 236, 260–61, 266
Song Survey, 17–19, 22, 115, 126, 129, 170, 181–82, 187, 224–25, 227, 273
Senyenegatene, 99, 168
Sermon/s, 68, 73, 84, 86, 101, 173, 184–85, 198
Sickness, 154–55, 179, 217, 222, 235, 262, 268, 270
Singing
    congregational, 6
Sin/s, 16, 132, 136, 145, 150, 160, 189, 207–8, 246
Sinzanga, 57
Skinner, Helen, 243
Skinner, Rev. Merrill and Helen, 60, 70
Smith, Donald K., 4, 176
Sociologists, 33
Song/s
    culturally appropriate songs, 4, 7–11, 21, 26, 41, 47–48, 137, 139, 193, 195–97, 199–202, 266
    influence of, 174, 193
    lullabies, 85
    new, 6, 13–14, 16–18, 21, 68, 70, 72–74, 76, 94, 167–69, 171, 260
    non-Christian, 129
    pleasing nature of, 169
    wedding, 85
    work, 85
    worship songs, 85
Song form
    call-and-response, 40, 71, 74, 93, 102–3, 111

Song form (cont.),
    development/exegetical section, 74, 103, 198
    new, 102, 195, 198
Song leader, 71, 74, 84, 94, 97–99, 103–4, 108, 111, 196
    credibility, 97, 99–100, 196
    musical skills, 97, 100, 261
Song leader (cont.),
    spiritual development, 97, 99–100

Song text/s,
    non-Christian, 129
Songs before the 1986 workshop, 126, 140–143, 145, 148–50, 152–53, 155, 158, 160–61, 205
Sorcerer/s, 124, 233–34, 244–47, 252
Sorcery, 124, 132–34, 233–34, 246–47
Sound, 30–31, 66–67, 87
South Indian, 44
Spirits, 54, 57–58, 60, 114, 117, 128, 131–37, 157, 161, 214, 220–21, 244, 264–65, 267, 269–70
Spiritual formation, 16, 76, 186, 188, 202
Spiritual transaction, 96
Spradley, James P., 126
Stages of musical development, 63, 112
Starosta, William J., 125
Stone, Ruth, 28–29, 31, 33
Storytelling, 74, 243
Sufferings, 150, 178–79, 220, 231–32, 265
Symbolic interaction, 88
Symbolism, 41, 46, 94, 263

Tempo, 74, 92–94, 118–19
Texts,
    unacceptable, 172
Theatre, 29
Theological analysis, 139

Index

Theological analysis (cont.),
    gaps, 162
    themes, 153
    understandings 44, 124, 137–38, 140, 153, 161, 195, 261
Theology, 28, 44, 138–41, 200, 260, 276
    lyric, 44, 138–40
Tippett, Alan, 20, 44, 139
Tone languages, 65, 107
Tone qualities, 67, 92–93, 119
Torhogo, 60–61, 64, 72, 84, 86, 137, 178–79, 188–89, 236, 242–43
Tours, France, 25
Traditional African music, 47, 94, 117
Traditional customs 131–33, 136–37
Traditional initiations 132–34, 206
Translation 19–20, 64, 66, 70, 224, 268
Translator/s, 18–19, 45, 66, 127, 180, 224
Transmission, 32–33, 38, 40, 44
Triangulation, 15
Tuo, Donyime, 64
Tyetin, 178

University of Oregon, 4
Urban, 6, 202

van den Berg, Dorothy, 69
van den Berg, Rev. Harold, 60, 64–66, 68, 70, 72
Villages, 18–19, 70, 73, 226, 229
Von Hornbostel, 91

Wapieka?a, 70
Warnock, Paul Willard, 46
Wedding/s, 16, 85
Welch, Rev. and Mrs. Robert, 60
West Africa, 8, 45, 51–52, 55, 75
Western hymns, 6–8, 45, 67, 69, 126, 168
Westernization process, 7

Willetts, Karen Faye, 58
Wimmer, Roger D. and Joseph R. Dominik, 15
Women, 53, 55–57, 81–83, 95, 113, 119, 132–33, 167–68, 180, 207, 213, 263, 270
Women's conference, 81, 95, 167
Word of God, 5, 21, 170, 173, 177, 181–86, 188–89, 191, 199, 230, 236, 238
Workshop, 16–19, 68–69, 76, 126, 140–43, 145, 148–50, 152–53, 155, 158, 160–61, 167, 171, 205, 212
Worldview, 7, 19, 24, 46, 54–55, 58, 72, 123–25, 127–31, 133, 135–38, 144, 154–55, 162, 175, 195, 198, 201, 260–66
Worship,
    of the dead, 134
Worship service/s, 9, 16, 48, 64, 68, 72, 85–86, 104, 174, 196, 198
Worshippers, 76, 83–84, 86, 269

Youth, 6, 16, 20, 21, 51, 59, 119, 215

Zaire, 6
Zambia, 31
Zanaka?a, 15–16, 67, 71, 83, 127
Zie, 69, 171

www.ingramcontent.com/pod-product-compliance
Lightning Source LLC
Chambersburg PA
CBHW061431300426
44114CB00014B/1630